DATE DUE

The Study of Theology

The Study of Theology

GERHARD EBELING

Translated by Duane A. Priebe

FORTRESS PRESS   PHILADELPHIA

175429

Translated by Duane A. Priebe from the German *Studium der Theologie: Eine enzyklopädische Orientierung*, published by J. C. B. Mohr (Paul Siebeck), Tübingen, 1975.

Library of Congress Cataloging in Publication Data

Ebeling, Gerhard, 1912-
　The study of theology.
　Translation of Studium der Theologie.
　Bibliography: p.
　1. Theology. I. Title.
BR118.E2413　　　201'.1　　　78-5393
ISBN 0-8006-0529-2

7121D78　　　Printed in the United States of America　　　1-529

Contents

Translator's Preface

Attention should be called to one issue of translation. The German word *"Wissenschaft"* and its cognates have a range of meaning that includes both science, which is a common translation, and scholarship in general. In English the word "science" is so closely associated with the natural and social sciences that to translate *"Wissenschaft"* simply as "science" can be confusing at times. For that reason I have chosen to translate *"Wissenschaft"* both as "science" and as "scholarship," depending on the context. At times, of course, the meaning lies on the boundary between these two English words. Whenever the reader sees "science" or "scholarship," or their cognates, the other meaning should be kept in mind. Correspondingly, I have consistently translated *"Wissenschafts-theorie"* as "the theory of scholarship."

Ebeling's book was written for a German context. Little has been done to alter the character this gives to the discussion, although it will differ somewhat from the reader's context, especially in Chapter 7. Awareness of this difference fits in well with the purpose of the book to provide an impulse toward one's own thought. However, I deemed it necessary to completely rewrite the subsection "The Concept 'Humanities'" in Chapter 7 (pp. 89–90) to apply to the English usage, since little of Ebeling's discussion applies to "humanities" as the English equivalent of *"Geisteswissenschaften."* Also, some minor modifications were made in Chapter 8 in the subsection "Social Sciences" (pp. 96–97) to adjust it to the usage in English. The Bibliography has been modified for the English reader; hopefully that has not made what is included and excluded too arbitrary.

I would like to express my appreciation to my wife, Kathy, and to Martha Myers, Craig Nessan, and Greg Gaskamp for their help with the manuscript.

Foreword

Within the context of a basic course in theology during the summer semester, 1972, I attempted for the first time to develop an introduction to the principal disciplines of theology and to some of the adjacent non-theological disciplines. This took place in a brief process of reflection intended to stimulate and assist further reflection on the whole of theology. Two years later I approached the task anew before a broader audience, and almost completely rewrote the presentation for that purpose. In so doing I became more and more aware of how risky, if not audacious, such an undertaking is. However, this experience could not dissuade me from the opinion that the undertaking involved an instructive for every theologian, whatever his degree of maturity. The risk, which was even perceived as impossible, merely confirmed the necessity of such an accounting. Therefore, the intention was fused for myself to inform outsiders and beginners of this process of reflection, which is scarcely separable from the need of creating clarity for myself, and to prepare the way for it step-by-step. Thus this book is directed to everyone who is interested in general theological reflection.

To supplement what has been noted in the first chapter about the objective and procedure of these reflections, the reader is asked to take account of the formal principles of an experiment.

The accent lies not on sharing the specialized knowledge of the individual disciplines but on their connection with one another. Therefore one should follow the general course of reflection and not merely select particularly interesting themes. Nevertheless, in each case the discussion dwells on the individual areas. Thus it is directed primarily toward the different subjects and avoids a systematic procedure. This is both an expression of reserve and is beneficial to the breadth of the field of view.

As much as the question about the unity and wholeness of theology has provided the impulse for this discussion, this question still cannot be answered forceably and at the cost of impoverishment. Therefore, the presentation is at times only indirect, yet it still clearly reflects the fact that it is governed by a conception that is unified in itself. In any case, it involves not a recipe for dealing with theology but a direction for finding the correct inner style for that involvement. Therefore, the following line of thought moves along a course different from that of a curriculum reform, although consideration about that would have to follow a corresponding course of reflection.

The scope of the consideration of each discipline was limited by the time framework of a lecture period. In the text presented here in its final revision, that limitation has been overstepped only occasionally. Such an external standard was necessary so that the material would not get out of hand. How the brief space was to be used, which viewpoints deserve priority, and what must be omitted were in each case difficult decisions, which always left behind a feeling of dissatisfaction. The task could always have been approached differently. Among other things, intuition and accident played a role in the way it took place, although, I hope, not in contradiction to the basic intention and not to the injury of the whole. To lament the brief simple intimations, to miss what is lacking, to desire other accentuations, and if need be to contradict decidedly what is said are reactions of the reader that are constituent parts of the project itself. For the project fulfills its meaning only as an impulse to the reader's own reflection. The Bibliographic Appendix is intended to provide further encouragement to that. Out of necessity, only direct documentation could be included in the footnotes. The points at which I am indebted to others or owe a critical answer cannot be mentioned or developed here.

As a Postscript I have added remarks of Luther to the study of theology. The fact and the content of this citation should be understood by each reader as an expression that infinitely more is necessary for overcoming the crisis in orientation in which we find ourselves than an encyclopedic reflection.

I have received encouragement and help from various sides. My co-workers Walter Mostert and Volker Weymann repeatedly provided valuable help. To all who shared in the coming into being of this small book I say a hearty thanks.

Zürich
September 15, 1974

Gerhard Ebeling

1

Theology as a Whole

THE CRISIS IN ORIENTATION

The study of theology is beset by a crisis in orientation. Because our access to the unity and totality that constitutes the subject matter of theology is disrupted, the domain of its subject matter and tasks has broken apart and crumbled into a bewildering conglomeration of individual items. It is not immediately apparent how traditional theological materials are interconnected, or how these are connected in turn with nontheological fields of experience and knowledge. Expressed in the schema of text and context, both the text of theology, which is only present in infinitely many texts, and its relation to the context of theology, which is all the more vast, appear to be difficult to understand. The latter for its part hides the relation to the text of theology rather than making it apparent. However, both difficulties are focused in a single one. The text of theology as such can only be expressed through engagement with its context. The situation with respect to the inner unity and wholeness of theology and the way in which this is related to the totality of the experience of reality are not two distinct problems. That both form a single complex certainly reinforces the discouraging impression that finding one's way in the theological enterprise is a task like that of Sisyphus.

One cannot do justice to the present crisis in theological orientation if it is isolated. If something helpful is to be said to the crisis, one must be aware that the difficulties indicated did not originate from modern times. The crisis has become acute in repeatedly new impulses since the emergence of a changed horizon for Christian faith when it entered the modern situation. However, even before that threshold between epochs, involvement with the subject matter of theology was by no means unproblematic. One ought not to be deceived by the change of perspectives about the fact that theology has always been subject to extraordinary difficulties. To

1

be mindful of that relativizes the appraisal of the contemporary problem. That does not mean that it is thereby minimized. The more clearly the contexts within which it stands become visible, the more sharply its uniqueness emerges. An orientation should help us pay attention to that

Of course, in the following limited attempt to meet the crisis in orientation, the whole depth of its causes cannot and should not be made explicit themes any more than this historical dimension. Certainly one may not forget in a textbook on orientation that today people extensively can see their way clearly not only *in* theology but above all *with* theology. That calls for assistance that exceeds the limited possibilities of this project. It calls for a thorough discussion of the subject matter of theology and an elementary presentation of what it is that makes one a theologian and also allows one to stay with the subject matter of theology. However, all this will still be addressed when an aid to orientation of a more modest sort is offered. Initially we shall approach this task through considerations that reach further.

TENSIONS IN DEALING WITH THEOLOGY

Whoever deals with theology encounters difficulties of various sorts. They can be traced back to three relationships of tension. Each in its way makes theology a scholarly field laden with tensions. On the one side, it therefore becomes an exciting undertaking from which people can no longer escape, and, on the other, it becomes a contradictory subject which they cannot manage. Often enough both remain linked together: not being able to manage it and not being able to escape from it.

Study and Vocation: The Ecclesiastical Character of Theology

The step from study into vocation can also be difficult in other cases, and is often more like a leap that requires courage. Nevertheless, for the theologian complicating conditions are added that generate nervousness about the churchly practice that awaits. Perhaps a person fears not being equal to the task of publicly representing the subject matter of theology. Or one sees oneself exposed to a conflict of conscience in the case of becoming obligated to something one cannot support with full conviction. Or the role expectations with which congregations and church leaders constrict a person's freedom of movement create anxiety. Or before a person's eyes stands the specter of being overburdened by the work of a generalist, which does not allow time for theological reflection and places a person before tasks for which academic study appears to be more of a hindrance than a preparation.

The justification in such misgivings is, certainly, easily falsified by making global judgments. A person often possesses only a distorted picture of the pastor's vocation. Commonly, people are not clear about the fact that the contemporary ecclesiastical practice, in spite of its problems, offers room for freedom in a way offered by scarcely any other vocation—to the extent that someone as a free person makes use of it in a way that is prepared for conflict when necessary. If people avoid practical involvement, this deprives them of a source of experiences that can enliven a deadlocked study of theology and lead it into new paths.

Certainly a person must be warned against a flight into practice that seeks to outmaneuver and suppress theological reflection. The principal difficulty in remaining a theologian under the demands of the calling arises less from an external compulsion to submit to a routinized and functionary existence than from an insufficient readiness to persevere in continued study of theology. Yet what is called the study of theology in the technical sense is only the introduction to the continuous study of theology in a person's vocation. One does not do justice to that study by having a special theological hobby alongside one's vocation, but only with that inner liveliness that allows theology and the experience of life to interpenetrate each other. This also provides theologians in academic positions with the decisive reason for accepting theology as a calling in an appropriate way.

A higher evaluation of a scholarly career generally betrays a poor understanding of theology. The exercise of the theological vocation in which it develops its most comprehensive relation to life may not be placed in the shadow by the necessary special service of academic theology. In each form, however, the measure of a theologian's vocation is whether what so easily threatens to break apart comes into a unity: that which is the object of knowledge and understanding and that which is the subject of innermost persuasion and utmost living devotion. It belongs to the peculiar office of theological activity that the unity of study and vocation is in fact endangered. People and their lives can be shipwrecked on it. Nevertheless, those who are grasped by the subject matter of theology can bring their lives into service for it in an unusually rewarding way.

SUBJECT MATTER AND METHOD:
THE SCHOLARLY CHARACTER OF THEOLOGY

The tension between study and vocation permits the ecclesiastical viewpoint to come to the fore. To be sure, the problem of theology's scholarly character was already involved. It lies close at hand to focus the question directly on the relation between scholarly study and ecclesiastical vocation.

Yet the problem would be curtailed if a person were to see it as rooted merely in the exercise of theology in an ecclesiastical vocation rather than in the nature of theology itself. The decisive question is not how a person can do justice to scholarly theology in an ecclesiastical vocation, but whether and in what sense theology is a scholarly activity. The tension to be considered now adheres, therefore, to the study of theology as such. Scholarly techniques and the subject matter of theology appear to be incompatible, whether a person characterizes the latter by the catchword "ecclesiastical" or by the fact that it deals with God, revelation, and faith. At any rate, theology involves something that does not seem to be compatible with scholarship.

Highly contrasting attitudes join, therefore, in rejecting theology altogether, which, according to customary linguistic usage, is understood as theology practiced in a scholarly fashion. The one side asserts that a person destroys the truths of revelation if the judgment of reason and the methods of scholarly criticism are allowed. The other emphasizes that it contradicts the nature of scholarship to anticipate dogmatically the results and to guard against criticism. The former casts suspicion on the work of theology as unbelieving and as a danger for Christian existence. The other defames theology as a shady apologetic, which contradicts honest thought.

Between these extremes lies the broad field of debated theological self-understanding. The common presupposition is that theology involves a reflected account of the Christian faith. Opinions diverge widely as to how to do justice to this task. Nevertheless, an understanding of it may be attained along certain lines. One of these, for example, is the fact that the question about the scholarly character of theology is not to be decided in advance, but it must constantly be rethought in the actuality of theological work. All scholarly work reverts to the methodological problems, and these in turn can be discussed only on the basis of involvement with particular scholarly tasks. In theology, people should also agree that its scholarly character should not be granted from outside but must be explained by the nature of Christian faith itself. Put differently, it would be so explained if it were appropriate for Christian faith not to evade in a traditionalistic way giving an account of its own living actualization, but rather to give an account of itself in a way that is open to all sides and is simultaneously self-critical. That means giving an account of its basis, its content, and its consequences.

To do detailed theological work and also to repeatedly reflect on it in a fundamental way requires the patience to allow both to mature simultaneously. A person should never lose a sense for what lies closest at hand under the burden of unfulfillable demands and the pressure of unclarified questions. The suction toward what is endless, which belongs to the strength of scholarly methods, and the mass of scholarly overproduction, which can never be worked through, should never hinder a person from turning to limited tasks and concentrating on some particular things with inner peace and good conscience. To become absorbed in this way in theological work should also never mislead a person into becoming distant from life and from that which serves it.

UNITY AND MULTIPLICITY: THE HISTORICITY OF THEOLOGY

The publication dates of theology immediately produce a relationship of tension, in addition to the problems characterized by the catchwords "ecclesiastical character" and "scholarly character." The poles of unity and multiplicity point to the problem of historicity.

Theologies That Supercede One Another Historically

The problem manifests itself most tangibly in the historical sequence of theological sketches and diverse theological types. Already in the New Testament we meet the fact of historical layers of theology. What necessitates such a movement and change in theology? The idea of progress serves poorly as a key to the history of theology. Rather, the impression of decadence and falling short of unattainable theological examples is common. Nevertheless, these theologies cannot be conserved or repristinated. Even being oriented to them does not release one from one's own theological responsibility. In view of the situation and its historical change, this responsibility is to be accepted in each case in a new and creative way. This is probably represented in the most illuminating way by the model of preaching, which has to be accomplished independently again and again.

With that, one meets the problem of identity in change. The identity of Christian theology cannot be demonstrated apart from what is variable but is rather effective in what is changing itself. By what criteria then is one to judge the preservation and loss of identity? Is it perhaps the case that the greatest possible conservative shielding against the unrest of time is a sure symptom of the preservation of identity, and progressive engagement in the altering circumstances an unambiguous sign of the loss of identity? Or may one conversely accuse the concern for preservation automatically of betraying what is Christian and, in contrast, regard the progressive trend in itself as the demonstration of living Christianity? In contrast to demagogic slogans, the theological development of judgment has to maintain the differentiating viewpoint that the unity of the subject matter of theology constantly offers itself in multiplicity, and the multiplicity as such does not contradict the unity.

Theologies That Substantively Exclude Each Other

Certainly the matter cannot rest with that. Theological responsibility would be rendered irrelevant if a person were to adjudge all theological formulations to be equally justified in a boundlessly variable historical cosmos. There are obviously irreconcilable contradictions between theological conceptions that exist at the same time in history. We have come to mistrust earlier self-evident theological censures like "orthodoxy" or "heresy" for good reasons, although we are perhaps not sufficiently mistrustful with regard to making orthodox ridiculous and flirting with what is heretical. Here also a person ought not to disregard historical conditioning. Fundamental differences of a confessional sort, for example, are passed on with formative power as soon as they are established. Then they become transmitted in a rigid way if a person is no longer able to realize the process by which decisions were made that lead to such contrasts. All-inclusive condemnation or even damnation, especially as conventional prejudices, does not further substantive clarification. On the other hand, today we see the confessional distinctions, which were once held to be definitive, coming into so much movement that the decisive theological fronts appear to cut across them. Already one must warn against an ecumenical enthusiasm that could result in new confessional separations (possibly according to political credo). Confessional differences can be overcome only when justice has been done to the underlying statements of the problem itself by superior theological insight.

The same thing is true of contrasts between theological directions and schools. Here particular historical and individual limitations, preference for partial aspects of the subject, and substantive contrasts that are irreconcilable are involved. How these intermesh should be taken into account in theological conversations with hermeneutical care. Since theological differences rest upon different basic experiences, and since theological statements are closely connected with one another, a person easily tends to make the total judgment of complete agreement or none at all. Although theology finally involves a single matter, this is still many-membered and can be articulated in many voices, because it is capable of and requires inexhaustible unfolding. No stated theology is self-sufficient and capable by itself of saying everything necessary. Therefore, to be in unison is not an appropriate conception of the goal of theological agreement. The genuine contrasts are endured and maintained without distortion or without being rendered harmless only if a person has an appropriate concept of theological consensus and an honest longing for it.

Disciplines That Compete Methodologically

However, the tension between the unity and multiplicity of theology does not only arise from historical change and from the conflict about the right theology. In the study of theology a person is primarily confronted by the division into different disciplines. This division dominates the activity of teaching and research so strongly that the whole of theology is not explicitly encountered at all. No one seems to be responsible for theology as a whole, and people must see for themselves how what is scarcely capable of being reconciled can be reduced to a common denominator. Here the previously discussed relationships of tension come into play more intensely. However, they also thereby move under an aspect of the subject that needs separate discussion and reflection.

If a person proceeds from the five or six basic disciplines as they are found in the course offerings and in required examinations, the principle of division seems to be one that has to do with subject matter. Old Testament, New Testament, and church history follow one another chronologically as different historical complexes represented by particular literary documents—in the case of church history by entire libraries. Certainly interests and responsibilities overlap historical boundaries. Nevertheless, the disciplines named seen as a whole are apparently so clearly differentiated from one another in terms of the areas covered that they can be added on to one another without problem. In contrast, in systematic and practical theology one's view is turned toward the present. Certainly only a superficial conception can mislead one to the opinion that the chronological sequence of disciplines simply continues into one's own time in history, with the subject matter categorized according to the viewpoints of the faith as well as of general ethical and ecclesiastical behavior. As much as that may take account of the empirical situation, the normative aspect of theology comes into play in these disciplines in a different way than in the historical disciplines.

A person becomes more clearly aware of this tension if it is clear that the scheme of disciplines we are familiar with is relatively recent. Certainly—formulated in a summary fashion—Christian theology has recognized two procedures from the beginning: following exegetically the biblical text and a procedure oriented to particular issues. Of course, theologically it came to the same thing without competition: to a discussion tied to dogmatics whether it proceeded exegetically or systematically. Only in recent times was biblical work emancipated from dogmatics. Initially this took place under the banner of a biblical-theological critique of the dominating school-dogmatics and of particular church dogmas, and then under the banner of a historical-critical investigation of the biblical tradition. That led to a methodological dualism that seemed to coincide with the association and contrast of historical and systematic disciplines, but which in fact never really coincided. For the biblical-exegetical disciplines can become the champions of dogmatic thought, as well as the systematic disciplines can become the advocates of historical-critical thought. Not only is the relation between the disciplines methodologically more complex than its appearance, but under the apparently harmonious viewpoint of the material, competing claims can be generated—one thinks of the conflict over the status of theological disciplines. If one includes this fact, then a discomforting impression arises. The disciplines, which in themselves have their purpose in the division of labor and mutual supplementation, in fact work like a broken mirror in which the image of the whole of theology is broken up into many pieces. Therefore no image of the whole emerges.

ATTEMPT AT AN ENCYCLOPEDIC ORIENTATION
THE LIMITED GOAL SET

The following attempt to provide help in orientation is directed at the problem sketched last. It does not claim to be a fundamental theology. That would consist in a comprehensive reflection on the nature of theology, its subject matter and methods, its language and truth. Also, what is called "theological encyclopedia" is intended only in a narrowly limited sense. As distinct from a so-called formal encyclopedia, of which Schleiermacher's *Brief Outline of the Study of Theology* is the unequaled model, this discussion will do without an explicit scholarly methodological foundation and strongly systematic form. As distinct from a topical encyclopedia, it only involves impulses to reflection about the individual disciplines, without being able to offer a well-balanced introduction to method, the state of research, sources, and literature.

The disciplines will be presented individually one after another. Within such a limitation there lies, nevertheless, an extraordinarily ambitious task. The question of theological principles, which could be initially delineated, is certainly not approached directly, but it unavoidably accompanies the entire undertaking. Each discipline will be discussed for itself, but not in the mode of a self-presentation by a representative of that field.

Rather, it will be a continuous course of reflection dared by one and the same theologian who is an amateur in most disciplines by academic standards. Thereby a solidarity with those who suffer under the crisis of orientation is expressed—certainly, if one wishes, an egotistical solidarity, since the need of my own general theological orientation has motivated me to it. The task is also ambitious with respect to the fact that it is presented in a way that, to a certain degree, is extremely contradictory. In each case the structure requires attention to the individual disciplines. In contrast, the intention of the book constantly aims at the whole of theology. Whether this orientation can be maintained in the to and fro of the individual segments, and whether it leads to its goal, should be deliberately tested.

THE PROBLEM OF DIVISION INTO DISCIPLINES

In the following we will proceed from the fact of the different disciplines but will still constantly relativize that fact in view of the whole of theology. Hence, two more pointers should guide us in opening this subject matter.

The Foundation of the Disciplines

The sacrifice of a systematic deduction of the disciplines from the nature of theology should neither encourage thoughtless consolidation of what is customary today nor relativize that fundamental systematic reflection. To be sure, it is difficult to doubt the necessity of the classical basic disciplines. If one agrees with the understanding of theology as Christian theology, then it can scarcely be disputed that a place must be given in it to the study of the Old and New Testaments and church history, as well as to the questions of doctrine, ethics, and the church's mode of existence. To consciously and fundamentally exclude only a single one of these from one's educational canon is to disclaim being a theologian.

With that, certainly, little has been said in a positive way. For what appears to be simply one thing added to another is braced and overlaid with three distinctions in particular, which neither coincide with nor are numerically identical to particular disciplines. The schema of each basic discipline leaves open the question as to how the distinctions between the relation to history and present responsibility, between historical and systematic methods, as well as between faith and action, are related to that schema. Since theological disciplines are involved it is to be assumed that all these distinctions play a role in each of them, even if in very different constellations.

The Unity of the Disciplines

The connection with the other disciplines already intrudes in carrying out the work of the individual disciplines, even when there is a high degree of specialization. That makes a certain degree of general theological education necessary also for the specialists and summons them to inter-disciplinary cooperation. But the burning problems often lie in areas in which two or more disciplines overlap or for which none appears to be responsible. Beyond that, all the disciplines are held together by the hermeneutical process taking place in each of them and throughout all of them as a process of theological understanding. Therein lies a tension that cannot be resolved. Each discipline is only a part of the whole and requires a high degree of caution on the part of its practitioner with respect to the totality of theology in order more effectively to make a partial contribution to the whole through specialization. On the other side, insights into the whole are ignited in the area of work of each discipline. Only so are they understood as theological disciplines.

THE PROCEDURE

Selection and Sequence

Concentration on the basic theological disciplines should not devalue other theological fields that already exist or are newly constituted. The relation to the whole is intended to be underscored by mentioning them in the broader context, even though in a passing way. In contrast, such a concentration does not contradict the fact that a few nontheological fields or groups of sciences will be included in the considerations. These are intended to serve the relation between text and context mentioned in the beginning, and, thus, to sharpen our view for the whole of theology.

The chosen sequence also serves the concentric orientation about which more precise information will be given from case to case. For the preview it may suffice to indicate that theological and nontheological fields alternate according to a plan in which the principal movement from the New Testament, as the core of the whole, leads across areas that partly appear to be far removed from a comprehensive total reflection over theology. In detail, the sequence leads from the study of the New Testament and the Old Testament to the study of religion and philosophy, which is followed by church history as the most universal theological discipline. After that the broad field of the natural sciences and humanities, as well as the social sciences, is opened. With that the passage through the disciplines enters a final phase. As a reflection about the total theological responsibility, it begins with practical theology, and from there it moves further through dogmatics and ethics to fundamental theology. The sequence is fundamentally variable and makes no further claim than to allow something of the living movement of theological work to be perceptible.

Mode of Presentation

The presentation does not proceed according to the same schema each time. It must suit the various situations with respect to the problem, and this above all involves the relation of the respective disciplines to the whole of theology. As a result, however, certain questions repeat themselves in the theological fields: To what extent does the discipline represent a necessary aspect of theology? Why must it be treated as a necessary discipline? And what makes it a theological discipline? In general, the presentation lives from the courage for what is fragmentary and the freedom to accent things in one's own way. It intends to encourage independent thought and to provide aid toward a fruitful involvement with theology.

2

The Study of the
New Testament

THE BASIC SOURCE OF CHRISTIAN THEOLOGY

The pathway through the theological disciplines begins with the study of the New Testament. This clearly expresses the fact that "theology" means Christian theology. That may seem self-evident to us, since in our part of the world no alternative is present. In general there is possibly no complete equivalent to what is recognized as theology from the Christian perspective. The extent to which other religions have developed something comparable may remain open for now. If it were the case that Jewish, Islamic, Buddhist, or whatever other theologies were available for our choice alongside Christian theology—just as one apparently has to choose between evangelical and Catholic theology within Christianity—the same problem would still result. With what justification does a person become attached to a particular form of religious tradition? On what basis can a choice be made here at all? Theology in this sense obviously means not the description of a particular religion from the outside but the self-reflection of that religion on its own movement of thought proceeding from within. In order to accomplish this, it is necessary that theology be appropriately rooted in that tradition in a way that is not arbitrarily interchangeable.

However, we will now set aside the problems in the theory of scholarship that result for theology. Fundamental theology, which is responsible for that, stands intentionally at the end of the overview, not at the beginning. The discussion of questions of methods and principles requires that a person has already been involved in the topic and understands something of the subject matter. Therefore we begin with the basic source of Christian theology, the New Testament. Yet we do it in such a way that we are aware of what we are doing thereby. Starting with the

13

New Testament leaves no doubt about what we are doing. Although philosophical theology must be kept in mind throughout the discussion, in our plan we intend a theology that grows out of the living reality of religion. And although openness to the general field of religious studies must be preserved, theology, as distinct from the study of religion, is constituted by being centered in a particular religion—precisely, the Christian faith. Apart from that, theology would be literally without basis for us. If we were not touched by the Christian word, though even in a vague way, it also would not occur to us to ask about theology.

THE UNITY OF THE NEW TESTAMENT

The reference to the New Testament as the basic source of Christian theology is not so unproblematic as one might think. Why not the Bible instead? The canonical character of the whole is a common Christian conception. In view of the complicated process of the formation of the canon in early Christianity a person may, certainly, make the following modification: temporarily the Old Testament even had priority, although it also was temporarily threatened with complete elimination in favor of a collection of Christian literature by the Marcionites. Nevertheless, through these events of the second century a situation was conclusively established that was germinally present in the origins of Christianity. This is the tension between the old and the new, which was resolved in a way different from a merely chronological sequence from one to the other. On the contrary, this tension belongs to what is Christian in an enduring way.

If, nevertheless, the New Testament is initially treated separately, this results from a development within the history of scholarship which we shall discuss later. Yet that alone is not the source of its special place. In terms of language and content the books of the New Testament are so clearly distinguished from those of the Old Testament that in no case does a doubt arise about the assignment of a book to one or the other. There is also a clear distinction with regard to importance and historical impact. Both Jews and Christians share the one collection of writings, while the other belongs to Christians alone, unanimously and to all without exception. That does not render unnecessary the question of what constitutes the New Testament and what forms its unity. Does it not appear to be merely a torso if it is taken for itself, or internally contradictory if a person claims it as the basic source of Christian theology? Nevertheless, the question about its unity intrudes as soon as a person asks about its validity, its form, and its content.

THE PRIORITY OF THE NEW TESTAMENT

The reality of the New Testament as canon, its liturgical and theological use in the history of the church, and, to top it off, the emphasis with which the Reformation claimed Scripture as the sole theological principle of knowledge easily conceal the question of the appropriate canonical usage of the New Testament. This question has been brought to consciousness from two sides: from the alteration of the situation resulting from the emergence of the New Testament canon as well as with a view to an appropriate relationship with it.

From the beginning an essential aspect of Christian faith was the relationship to the tradition concentrated in the name of Jesus and explicated in homologous formulas as well as in narratives and sayings. The progressive process of interpretation, which had to take place through appropriation and transmission, was precipitated initially as a linguistic transformation or re-creation within the form of the tradition itself. This productive phase was brought to a definitive end through the idea of the canon. The appropriating reception of the tradition must now move along-side the fixed text of the tradition as explicit interpretation. A person can dare assert critically that the Spirit has been frozen to the letter only if one keeps in view the danger that the tradition would run wild into what is not the Spirit and if one considers the immeasurable benefit deriving from the fact that the origins of the Spirit have been preserved in letters and thus remain perceptible. Through canonization various separate strands of tradition, which were originally self-sufficient and were not oriented toward mutual supplementation, were accommodated to one another. One can scarcely overestimate the enrichment that the tradition thereby underwent. But one must also see that a harmonization emerges which can deflect a person's view from the essential in favor of a leveling out to the average.

Thus, the relationship with the New Testament canon summons us to make its canonical character precise. A formal conception of its authority lacking orientation can, certainly, be normed by a so-called "canon within the canon." That may be done through the rule of faith of the ancient church, which Tertullian explicitly declared to be the *gubernaculum interpretationis* (norm of interpretation).[1] Or it may be done through the doctrine of justification, which as the "material principle" is supposed to regulate the "formal principle" of the Reformation, which is thereby mis-

---

1. *De praescriptione haereticorum* 9, 3 *Corpus scriptorum ecclesiasticorum Latinorum* (Leipzig: Freytag, 1907), vol. 70, p. 13.

understood. However, it is questionable whether this does justice to the fact of the New Testament. How then can the New Testament be the standard for all theological disciplines, which is what "in compliance with Scripture" means, when contemporary dogmatic or ethical statements are involved? Is the study of the New Testament, or a more comprehensive biblical discipline, supposed to be in a position to exercise directly the functions of the whole theological task? If not directly, however, how then are the theological disciplines so to speak to bring in the discipline devoted to what is canonical?

THE POLAR STRUCTURE OF THE NEW TESTAMENT

The New Testament has unqualified priority for Christian theology because it transmits the authoritative tradition of what is Christian. Nevertheless, this transmission encounters difficulties connected with the form of the New Testament. In view of that it is not at all advisable to probe its content independently of its form. Rather, a person should be led to an appropriate grasp of the content through a deeper penetration into its form. Proceeding from the literary phenomenon of the New Testament, a person can make a series of observations leading to the definition of the contents and can make material connections apparent under the seemingly formal viewpoint of the polar structure of the New Testament.

Unity and Diversity

The New Testament is a body of writings whose canonicity, to be sure, raises the claim to unity. It is, however, put together out of very different sorts of literary material. These resist systematization and also contain conceptions that strongly diverge theologically. This induced Käsemann's provocative thesis that the New Testament canon as such establishes not the unity of the church but the multiplicity of confessions.[2] Certainly this judgment could be governed by a conception of unity that from the beginning must miss what binds the writings of the New Testament to a unity in spite of the indisputable multiplicity. Doubtless the New Testament is neither literarily, linguistically, nor theologically a unity. Historically, however, it bespeaks a close coherence defined by the development of an event that proceeds from Jesus Christ and remains connected with him. This coherence is marked not only by the appeal to his name but also by specific statements about him that proclaim his appearance as God's

---

2. Ernst Käsemann, "The Canon of the New Testament and the Unity of the Church," in *Essays on New Testament Themes*, trans. W. J. Montague, Studies in Biblical Theology 41 (London: SCM Press, 1964), pp. 95–107.

revelation and, indeed, as gospel. In such statements, phenomena like faith, Spirit, and church are causally related to him. If one speaks of a historical coherence, one must also simultaneously emphasize how fragmentary our insight into this genetic development is. Beyond that, it is inherent to this type of coherence that it takes its departure in a linguistically creative event in which the multiple voices of those who bear witness belong to the unity of that to which they witness.

Text and Event

That directs our attention to the following: the New Testament is a book whose center of gravity lies outside itself in an event to which being fixed in writing is coordinated in a subsidiary way. The decisive event from which all New Testament writings emerge and to which they are related is the coming of Jesus of Nazareth. In this event the turn from the Old to the New Testament takes place. Nevertheless, these writings do not report this event simply as a historical occurrence. Rather, they are diverse stations along the way and documents of a process of proclamation from which they have emerged and which they intend to influence further. The New Testament moves beyond itself as a book into an event whose various dimensions build a single coherent reality. It is a word event that has become a text, which in turn aims at the reemergence of a living word from the text. For that reason it is related to its own situation to such a high degree and is full of narratives, and it intends to enter into new situations and to produce again what is capable of being narrated.

Christ and the Body of Christ

A living process takes place throughout all the differences between New Testament authors and their themes. The basis for the life of this process is Jesus Christ, and its agent and manifestation is the church as the community of those who believe in Jesus Christ. Paul expressed the polarity that inheres in the unity of this living reality in a particularly pregnant way by designating the church as the body of Christ. By that he means a coherent reality for which Jesus Christ does not simply lie in the past but is present and is positively determinative. For its part, this coherent reality does not have a historically limited significance. It announces the fulfillment of history and is permeated by the certainty of continuing until the end of history. The polarity of Christ and the body of Christ is suggested in the old division of the canonical writings of the New Testament into the "Gospels" and the "Epistles." If this is not to be a matter of separation but is to be grasped as an expression of one living process to which testimony is borne therein, then one must allow oneself to be led more deeply into the facts of the New Testament through the viewpoint of polarity.

"Jesus" and "Christ"

The name Jesus Christ itself represents the basic polarity that constitutes the appearance of this person and is the substance of Christian proclamation to which we are to bear witness. Both the proper name of a historical person and the title of honor expressing his mission together name the event that allows Jesus Christ to be the basis of faith and the living Lord of his body. By virtue of this event he is present for his people and through his people for the world. Historically seen, this polar fact grasped in the name raises the question that is the key problem of the whole New Testament: how does the one who proclaimed, which is the way Jesus worked among his contemporaries, become the one proclaimed, who makes all people of all times his contemporaries. The witness of the New Testament presents this change as a turning point of unsurpassable radicality. The one whose earthly life was extinguished and completed in the death on the cross became recognized and believed as the one whom God raised from the dead and exalted to himself. As theological reflection on this message advanced—beginning already in primitive Christianity and coming to its dogmatic conclusion in the early church—the mystery of the sequence of death and life was elucidated and deepened through the mystery of the inseparable unity of God and humanity in *one* person. It gives food for thought that Jesus Christ can be expressed as the center of the New Testament only in such polarities as proclaimer and proclaimed, humiliated and exalted, crucified and resurrected, true God and true man. That is the case because his office and, therefore, his connection with the body of Christ is not to be separated from his person.

Perfectum praesens and praesens futurum

The viewpoint of polarity also determines the form taken by the theme of eschatology, which permeates the whole New Testament. The determining factor in this theme is not the customary temporal distinction between now and then, between the present and the future. Rather, the decisive distinction is between "now" and "not yet." In its strongest formulation, this is the distinction between a realized eschatology, which as Christology bursts the customary apocalyptic expectation, and a future eschatology. Both together are linked to the polarity of the present time of faith. The coming of Jesus, the occurrence of his resurrection, and the working of the Spirit point to the fulfillment of promise, the eschaton that has already come upon the scene, and the victory that has been definitively gained.

The promise of fulfillment, the awaiting of the eschaton amid the suffering of the present time, and the struggle involved in certainty about what still must become manifest are accented by the cross. These characterize the existence of the church in the world and correspond to the concentration of Christian existence on word and faith. Yet both these poles are so indissolubly related to one another that the orientation to the future takes effect precisely in the present time of the Spirit, and the reality of the resurrection life under the sign of the cross.

Law and Gospel

Even when a person finally considers more closely the reality of the church as it is seen and comes to view in the New Testament, one encounters the structure of polarity. These do not have the character of rigid duality, but they are the expression of an event that is directed toward reconciliation, whether it involves unity of Jew and Gentile or the justification of the sinner, the relation between assembling in a community and mission to the world. The Pauline distinction between letter and Spirit, law and gospel, provides an impulse for referring the multilayered character of these polarities to their general theological common denominator.

THE MATERIAL BASIS FOR THE STRUCTURE OF POLARITY

What does it matter that what binds the New Testament into a unity and, therefore, constitutes the subject matter of theology is presented in polarities? This question, together with the observation upon which it rests, requires a far-reaching investigation, which cannot be offered here. There is a double purpose in indicating it: to stimulate reflection about the unity of the New Testament as well as to illustrate the relativity of the boundaries of the discipline. The New Testament scholar widely perceives such a question, which is systematically oriented and presses into what is fundamental, to be something that exceeds his responsibility. On the other hand, it is not harmless to break off the intruding hermeneutical process prematurely, even though it apparently requires a person to ask questions that go beyond the narrowly understood boundaries of disciplines toward the whole of theology. The longer the question is endured, precisely under the control of technical knowledge of the New Testament, the more a purely speculative treatment of the problem is restrained.

It appears to me that the answer is to be sought in the following direction. The New Testament's polar structure apparently has to do with its comprehensive relation to life. If life itself is determined in a polar way—one thinks of birth and death, creating and receiving, subject and object, passivity and activity, the fulfillment and the failure of life, and the like—then when the question involves true life, attention must be directed to the polarities that are determinative and that set it right. This is to be done not in mere theoretical reflection but in a corresponding process of proclamation and life. That is the reason that the problem of the fundamental distinction is so important for theology. This fundamental distinction is most sharply polarized and, therefore, is in the most need of precision as the distinction between God and the world.

THE STUDY OF THE NEW TESTAMENT AS AN INDEPENDENT DISCIPLINE

Since this first discipline deals with the basic source of theology as a whole, the accent lies on observations about the facts of the New Testament. Thereby the existence of a special scholarly field devoted to the New Testament was already in view. Its nature and problematic, however, still remain largely in the background.

THE RISE OF THE HISTORICAL STUDY OF THE NEW TESTAMENT

The study of the New Testament became an independent field as a result of the historical-critical treatment of the New Testament. It is obvious that impulses toward historical explanation of individual matters had always been present. What was new was that simply everything, including and precisely statements of faith, was understood and investigated as being determined by time and environment. Therefore, the study of the New Testament constituted itself in emancipation from dogmatics. That meant emancipation from the basic injunctions and prohibitions derived as sacred hermeneutics from the dogmatic Scripture principle and its intensification to the doctrine of verbal inspiration, as well as emancipation from particular dogmatic conceptions and their claim to correspond to Scripture. Such a revolt of New Testament studies against the prevailing dogmatics could even appeal against it to its own theoretical Scripture principle with some justification, which it was now legitimate to establish and practice in freedom. What took place with antidogmatic passion was itself, certainly, in a varied way through many transformations, dogmatically interested and determined. That was true whether a person hoped for a timeless kernel beneath the historical shell or sought a modern adaptation of dogmatics by means of historical criticism. A prominent example was the attempt to eliminate the ecclesiastical Christology through a return to the historical Jesus. The fact that this emancipation from dogmatics resulted in a simultaneous release from the totality of a biblical-exegetical discipline probably had more incisive consequences for the study of the Old Testament. However, for the study of the New Testament the question of the primary context also became acute. This primary context was now shifted over into Judaism and Hellenism—not without mutual competition.

THE INFRASTRUCTURE OF THE STUDY OF THE NEW TESTAMENT

Such far-reaching specialization accompanied the independence of New Testament studies that only the specialist could be fully informed to some extent, and even the specialist could only be an expert in segments of the field. In the New Testament field, contact with nontheological branches of study is frequently much stronger than is the case in other theological disciplines. This included different areas of philology and historical studies, from linguistics to numismatics, from the techniques of textual and literary criticism to comparison in the history of religions. In the course of the history of research, various subdisciplines developed. They were modified from time to time, due partly to changes in methodology and partly to educational needs. Schematically one can distinguish five areas of work. (1) Textual criticism has to reconstruct the history of the text and the most authentic text possible from the manuscript tradition since we no longer possess the original. (2) There is the broad complex of New Testament introduction understood as a history of literature. This includes, among other things, literary criticism, which analyzes the text with regard to its origin if necessary by distinguishing sources, or form criticism, which illuminates the earlier process of oral tradition by means of the investigation of classes of material [*Gattungsforschung*] and therefore is primarily oriented to smaller units. The study of the history of redaction in turn directs its attention to the composition and total conception of books. (3) People investigate the historical context as the history of New Testament times, which, above all, takes into consideration the environment in the history of religions and seeks to reconstruct the history of primitive Christianity itself. (4) There is exegesis of particular texts and complexes of texts with a view to their relation to the situation, linguistic form, and content. (5) The interpretation of the interrelatedness of the parts in view of the whole New Testament is ordinarily designated "theology of the New Testament." For that purpose a systematic arrangement similar to dogmatics appears questionable. However, analyzing the material to develop a history of the theology of primitive Christianity also has its problems to the extent that the question of the unity of the New Testament thereby remains unconsidered. It would be decisive to attain an access to the whole that would be capable of rendering the historically differentiated character of the material fruitful for a substantively relevant synopsis.

THE ACHIEVEMENT AND LIMITATION OF HISTORICAL WORK ON THE NEW TESTAMENT

Because of this, New Testament scholarship finds itself in a peculiar situation. Its basis—a book of a few hundred pages and a fragmentary historical complex of about a hundred years—is extremely small, but it is a disproportionately differentiated field as a result of an immense history of activity and corresponding debate. The ground is furrowed in an incomparable way by investigation and constantly produces new hypotheses. At the same time, the efforts involved with it take place in such a central religious field of power that, in one way or another, people's engagement in it is tied to tendencies and is emotional in character. In view of this situation, the achievements and limitations of historical study will be sketched in a generally pointed way.

Definitively Soluble and Inexhaustible Tasks

The self-critical assessment of scholarly results is particularly pressing in the study of the New Testament, if also difficult. There are—to the extent a person can talk about it at all—tasks that can be definitively solved, perhaps in the area of textual criticism or of distinguishing sources. Yet these tasks are sparks compared with the broad field of provisional attempts at solutions that are subject to constant revision. Beyond that there are interpretive tasks that, as a consequence of changing perspectives and due to the inexhaustible character of the content, require ceaseless attempts at understanding. A person basically cannot expect that the task of exegesis can be solved once and for all.

Alienation

If in the investigation of the New Testament opinions are frequently diametrically opposed and are periodically subject to turbulent change, then traditional assessments are repeatedly brought into question: for example, in the question of authorship, the historicity of reports, the relation to the history of religions, and the like. The critical analysis of the transmitted schema of the Christ event itself as well as of the course of the history of primitive Christianity was particularly drastic. The alienating effect is ambivalent. It destroys prejudgments, but it also provides a surprisingly better understanding of the subject matter and compels some distance from customary forms of thought. Certainly, scholarly assessments that have already become traditional are equally not spared.

With the introduction of new questions from other areas—today perhaps sociological or linguistic methods—alienation is also produced vis-à-vis the familiar status of investigation. However, as is known, the implements of historical criticism also can be placed in the service of conservative interests. Precisely in the study of the New Testament one ought not underestimate the danger of a high-powered scholarly technique that has become sterile. There is a corresponding danger of resignation that no longer expects much from scholarly study of the text or from the text itself.

Mediation of Experience

The fruitfulness of the expenditure of scholarly energy in the study of the New Testament depends on whether the concern for historical concreteness presses through as much as possible to those living processes to which the text testifies and for which a person is indebted to it. To the degree to which that happens, it is unavoidable to bring in one's own experience and to critically place it at stake. That opens the expansion of one's own horizon, which is the essential benefit of all historical work. At the same time it initiates the concentration that New Testament scholarship requires if it is to do justice to its theological task.

THE STUDY OF THE NEW TESTAMENT AS A THEOLOGICAL DISCIPLINE

This aspect of the problem seems superfluous in view of the fact that the study of the New Testament deals with the basic source of Christian theology. Nevertheless, some aspects that we shall repeatedly encounter in a similar way must be mentioned here.

THE THEOLOGICAL OBJECT

It is self-evident that it is primarily the field covered by the subject matter that makes this discipline a theological one. The subject matter of theology is fused with that of the New Testament to such a degree that engagement with the New Testament necessarily drives one into theology. Certainly, the material as such does not guarantee its theological treatment. A person can approach it with other interests, such as an interest in the history of late Hellenistic religions. Nevertheless, this collection of texts is stamped by the designation "New Testament," by its delimitation as canon, and by its relevance to the history effected by it. If a particular discipline is devoted to concentration on this collection of writings, then already from the standpoint of the material studied the theological question is the really appropriate one.

The Theological Question

The perspective of the question cannot be separated from one's own living relationship to the subject matter. Is the inner affirmation of the subject matter of the New Testament then the condition for the study of the New Testament? Schleiermacher spoke aptly to that point:

> Any extended occupation with the New Testament canon which is not motivated by a genuine interest in Christianity can only be directed against the canon. For the purely philological and historical gain of which the canon gives promise is not rich enough to attract a person to such an occupation. Still, even the investigations of opponents have been very useful, and will continue to be so in the future.[3]

Thus, productive scholarly activity in the field of New Testament in an antitheological interest is conceivable, but only within definite boundaries. Certainly, a person can interpret the Koran in a way that is historically correct without being a Muslim, although scarcely without one's own living relationship to religion as such. If, nevertheless, the theological question consists in reflecting on the coherence of the subject matter of Christian faith in the mutual critical interpenetration of traditional and contemporary experience, then, in view of this breadth of the hermeneutical horizon, the study of the New Testament cannot be fruitful if it is dissociated from the whole of theology.

Theological Understanding

The more deeply a person penetrates the interpretation of a subject the more strongly one's own relation to the subject matter makes itself felt. Therefore, the way in which one exegetes the New Testament reveals what sort of theologian that person is. Whatever texts Schlatter or Bultmann interpreted, their theology was always revealed. That is not illegitimate. Yet it presupposed that, when dealing with these texts, one is to pay sharp attention to what is unusual, in order to further one's own theological thought through discoveries that have a critical effect on it. Conversely, theological indifference and pallor scarcely further one's attention to the peculiarity of a text. Therefore, the more strongly a theologian must exercise self-discipline and the more it must also be in fact applied in historical work, the more strongly the cord is stretched that drives a person toward total theological responsibility.

3. Friedrich Schleiermacher, *Brief Outline on the Study of Theology*, trans. Terrence N. Tice (Richmond: John Knox Press, 1966), par. 147, p. 60.

3

The Study of the
Old Testament

THE CONTROVERSIAL CHARACTER OF THE CHRISTIAN RECEPTION OF THE OLD TESTAMENT

Just as it is uncontested that theology receives its Christian orientation from the New Testament, the question is debated as to how the Christian character of theology can also be sustained in the discipline devoted to the study of the Old Testament. Certainly, seen in the context of the whole of church history, the call to exclude the Old Testament from Christian theology remains very peripheral. The decision of the ancient church against Marcion was so decisive that it was only in the twentieth century, as it were under the protection of a monograph about Marcion, that the demand to exclude the Old Testament was taken up again in a more differentiated form. This was done in Adolf von Harnack's famous thesis:

> To reject the Old Testament in the second century was a mistake that the great church correctly refused to make; to preserve it in the sixteenth century was a fate that the Reformation was not yet able to avoid; but to conserve it as a canonical document in Protestantism since the nineteenth century is the consequence of a religious and ecclesiastical paralysis. . . . To make a clean sweep of it in this matter and to honor the truth in our confession and education is the great act which today—already almost too late—is required of Protestantism.[1]

Although the basis for Harnack's judgment has been prepared since the Enlightenment, this slogan remained without significant following from

1. Adolf von Harnack, *Marcion: Das Evangelium vom fremden Gott*, 2d ed. (Leipzig: J. C. Hinrich, 1924), pp. 217, 222.

the side of theology. The tidal wave of defamation of the Old Testament in terms of race and world view, which was arising at the same time and temporarily had its greatest broad-scale effect in Germany, contrasted deeply with Harnack's liberal approach and hindered a differentiated discussion of his thesis. From a Christian perspective that massive anti-Semitic and neoheathen attack upon the Old Testament, furthered by political pressure, had to be countered with such decisive opposition that this induced suppression of the problems that were uncontestably present. At the same time, the investigation of the Old Testament also experienced an upswing that, for a time, even gave it a leading role in the concert of the theological disciplines. Corresponding influences from the Old Testament have recently been effective, especially in systematic theology. They have provided the impulse to projecting a theology of history or the justification for slogans for a theology of revolution.

Thus, the idea that theology should rigorously rid itself of the Old Testament has never been given serious significance, either historically or in the present. Yet it also cannot be asserted on the contrary that an unproblematic Christian reception of the Old Testament prevails. Even when this seemed to be the case during the time of the unbroken domination of ecclesiastical tradition, methodological problems divulged difficulties that were to be overcome in this field. This was all the more true when the study of the Old Testament was constituted as an independent discipline as a result of the historical-critical approach.

THE STUDY OF THE OLD TESTAMENT AS AN INDEPENDENT DISCIPLINE

One can speak about the study of the Old Testament as an independent discipline only for the period barely covering the last two hundred years. The consequences of this innovation must be considered against the background of the customary Christian treatment of the Old Testament.

THE CHRISTIAN RELATIONSHIP TO THE OLD TESTAMENT

The Old Testament, although not under that designation, is common to Jews and Christians. Islam also lays claim to this tradition in a derived way. This fact is certainly significant in the history of religions and considerably expands the historical effectiveness of the collection of writings that emerged from the people of Israel. Yet this connection is much less important than the bond between Jews and Christians through the same sacred texts. Who has the greater right to it? Here, as is so often the case, what is common is the object of conflict. Taken strictly, division already exists over the question of the definitive form of the text. For Christians the Greek version that came from diaspora Judaism, the so-called Septuagint, was taken as the inspired text. Correspondingly, the scope of their canon was broader, also embracing the Apocrypha. In contrast, Judaism broke off its opening toward the surrounding world of Hellenism under the impact of Judaism's political catastrophe and in delimitation vis-à-vis Christianity, and it fell back exclusively to the Hebrew original text and to a narrower demarcation of the canon. It was only with the Reformation and humanistic influences contemporary with it that this conception of the canon found entry into Christianity, so that the difference now has become significant as a point of controversy within Christianity. Certainly more important than the question about the ultimately valid text was the question about the ultimately valid meaning.

For primitive Christianity, proof from Scripture played a decisive role in profiling Christianity vis-à-vis Judaism and in the separation of the church from the synagogue. It belonged to the original form of Christian theology. However, even when the relation to Judaism, which constantly shadowed church history, lost topical interest, proof from prophecy remained central to the Christian understanding of the Bible and to its own self-understanding. The task of a Christian treatment of the Old Testament stamped the theological mode of thought to a strong degree. Especially with regard to hermeneutics, the problem of the interpretation of the Old Testament worked as a constant goad precisely because the difficulties were so apparent. It evoked and kept alive methodological and theological reflection. That drove people into extremely fruitful investigation, but it could also seduce people into a forced apologetic if not even into a type of pious deception.

Ambiguity

The Christian treatment of the Old Testament was discordant from the beginning. Due to Christianity's emergence from Judaism and due to the path into Hellenism paved in advance by diaspora Judaism, the Old Testament was a self-evident, existing reality and initially the only sacred Scripture of the Christians. Nevertheless, from the beginning it did not have sole authority. The Scripture and the living Lord belonged inseparably together. This unity, however, did not lack contrast. The antitheses of the Sermon on the Mount, "you have heard that it was said to the men of old. . . . But I say to you," the Pauline antithesis of Moses and Christ, the setting aside of the cultic law, the dissolution of the certainty of election through belonging to the Jewish people—those are the most conspicuous symptoms of the contrast between the old and the new. That Jesus, nevertheless, is confessed as the Christ and those who believe in him regard themselves as the true Israel, that early Christian writings are saturated with literal citations from the Old Testament and innumerable suggestions of its language and conceptual world all underscore the indissoluble connection. However, precisely when the principal accent falls on continuity in the schema of promise and fulfillment, the antithetical undertone still cannot be ignored: the provisional is overcome, the final has come.

How is this connection presented in the texts themselves? That the Old Testament is present in the New is an incontestable fact. Although it has very diverse aspects, this provides the connection with a decisive affirmation. Yet what is the situation with regard to the New Testament in the Old? The test of the justification of the Christian incorporation of the Old Testament lies in the capacity of this affirmation of a connection to move in the other direction. This is true not only of its quotation in detail but also of its total reception as a part of the Christian canon of sacred Scripture. Laying claim to the Old Testament must have support in the Old Testament itself if it is not to be to the disadvantage of Christianity.

Harmonizing Methods

Augustine expressed the problem and his solution in a formula: "The New Testament is concealed in the Old, the Old Testament is revealed in the New" ("Novum testamentum in vetere latet, vetus testamentum in novo patet").[2] How does this revelation of what is hidden, this awakening of the Spirit that by itself slumbered unrecognized in the ancient letters, take place? The idea is that this took place in the appearance of Jesus Christ as the fulfillment and the intended meaning of the Old Testament. To speak with 2 Corinthians 3, where Paul in turn refers to Exodus 34 in a form of Midrash, the veil that lay over the Old Testament in its reading in the synagogue is thereby set aside. However, how is this assertion to be verified in the Old Testament texts? Three procedures

2. The citation, which is always transmitted in the literature in this form without a reference to the source, is probably, as my colleague H. D. Altendorf suspects, a modification from *Quaestionum in Heptatechum*, Bk. II, par. 73 in *Corpus Christianorum: Series Latina* (hereafter *CCSL*), vol. 33 (1958), p. 106: "Many strongly indicated things of the Old Testament pertain more in fear just as of the New Testament in delight, although the New may be concealed in the Old and the Old revealed in the New" ("Multum et solide significatur ad uetus testamentum timorem potius pertinare sicut ad nouum dilectionem, quamquam et in uetere nouum lateat et in nouo uetus pateat").

were offered for that. Certainly in the history of interpretation they are met seldom in pure form but mostly in various mixtures.

The selective procedure restricts itself solely to those statements that appear to lie on the level of the New Testament. To a certain degree, people have always preferred those texts through which they felt directly addressed and which could be adopted in their literal understanding without further ado. Of course, the idea of a religious evolution initially emerged only in recent times and even then never seriously led to the attempt to reduce the Old Testament to a nucleus directly acceptable to Christians. Such an undertaking obviously could not be carried through.

The allegorical method, in contrast, reinterprets everything that does not fit with what is Christian to give it a Christian meaning. To be sure, that was coupled with the claim that the only true meaning of the text intended by the Holy Spirit as the author of the Holy Scripture was thereby brought to light. Already in the second century the so-called Epistle of Barnabas offers grotesque examples of such a procedure. For example, the prohibition against eating pork means that a person should not associate with people who are similar to swine, namely, those who forget the Lord in abundance and remember him only when in want (Barn. 10:3). This method was too arbitrary for the church to sustain itself by it, even though the church gladly made use of it for edifying embellishment in details in conjunction with typological methods.

Typological exegesis basically allows the historical meaning of the text to stand, but it appeals to the idea that in the movement from promise to fulfillment in salvation history the historical events for their part also represent future realities in advance. Enriched by allegorical tools, this theory of a double meaning of Scripture, the literal-historical and the spiritual meaning, dominated the traditional interpretation of the Old Testament. The development to the fourfold meaning of Scripture resulted from the threefold division of the spiritual meaning with respect to the dogmatic contents of faith, the appropriation suitable for life, as well as eschatological reality. To be sure, there still was dispute about the degree to which the literal sense of the text itself was to be conceived as a prophecy of Christ or, especially in the Psalms, as the speech of Christ himself.

These methods rest on the presupposition of a complete concord of both Testaments as a result of their derivation from the same author. Without possessing the New Testament as a hermeneutical guiding principle, however, this is not recognizable and the Jewish understanding of the Old Testament cannot be disputed exegetically, and certainly just as little by the mere demand that such an allegation be recognized.

THE INTENSIFICATION OF THE PROBLEM BY HISTORICAL-CRITICAL INTERPRETATION

Distancing from Christianity

The independence of biblical theology vis-à-vis dogmatics had to result in a division into two disciplines under the banner of historical methods. This in turn had to work itself out in a way that was the most sharply etched in relation to the Old Testament. Certainly, historical-critical study of the New Testament also required the revision of familiar conceptions of what is Christian. However, in any case these texts remained within the domain of Christian history and language. In contrast, historical-critical study of the Old Testament transposed it unavoidably into a historical and linguistic domain that was different from the specifically Christian one. If the sacred hermeneutics related to dogmatics gives way to the principle that Holy Scripture is to be read like any other book, then the interpretive rule that everything is to be harmonized as the statement of a single author is no longer applicable if the historical facts speak clearly against it. The justification for using later texts, in this case from the New Testament, as the norm of interpretation also falls away. The alienation from the traditional ecclesiastical interpretation in this case amounts to the demand to deal seriously with the Old Testament as a non-Christian book. Now it is not remote from the theologian to deal intensively with non-Christian literature for the sake of theology. Nevertheless, in this case the demand that the Old Testament be distanced from what is Christian is so momentous because it involves the domain of the central source of theological knowledge, the biblical tradition itself. Does not the study of the Old Testament thereby automatically fall from the number of the central theological disciplines? And is not its canonical significance invalid if, at best, it is only advocated in dogmatics while seeming to be without effect in the field of Old Testament studies itself?

Distancing from Judaism

The impression that the Christian claim to the Old Testament thereby hopelessly gets the worst of it in contrast to the Jewish understanding is certainly hasty. The historical-critical method of itself is by no means to the advantage of the orthodox Jewish understanding. They also interpret this collection of writings from the perspective of a total understanding that is more recent than the Scriptures contained in that totality, namely, from the Rabbinic understanding of the Torah. The continuity of physical descent cannot in this case be separated from the continuity of the tradition and doubtless secures a primary claim to this book for Judaism. However, this continuity of physical descent by no means guarantees that the genuine coherence of the whole has been perceived.

HISTORICAL WORK ON THE OLD TESTAMENT

This intensifies the question of whether one can expect anything at all beyond historical distancing from historical work in the field of Old Testament. Or is a starting point along this path still offered for the study of the Old Testament as a theological discipline?

The Infrastructure of Old Testament Studies

The inner-disciplinary division of New Testament studies has *mutatis mutandis* its correspondence in the Old Testament. The need for specialization is even more intensified by the fact that in comparison with the New Testament the size of the Old Testament is three times as large and the period during which it emerged was ten times as long. The fact that it is embedded in the history of the Near East easily gives the study of the Old Testament the character of a special discipline in the philosophical faculty, namely, oriental studies. What people customarily designate as the theology of the Old Testament presents much more difficult methodological problems than the corresponding New Testament field. If the latter poses the problem of whether it succeeds in going beyond a *history* of early Christian theology, in the Old Testament it is intensified to the question of whether a person must be satisfied with merely an Israelite history of *religion*. Already to use the concept of theology for the phenomena of the Old Testament, and, thus, to characterize the mode of conceptualization and thought expressed in it, appears to be an anachronism in contrast to the situation within the New Testament. Nevertheless, if the term "theology" in this context is traceable to the *formulation of the question* under which the Old Testament is discussed, then a Christian interest is betrayed. For neither a purely history-of-religions investigation nor a Jewish reflection on the whole of this body of Scripture would formulate its task as a *theology* of the Old Testament. Is there, however, a justification for such a formulation of the question?

The Relevance of History in the Old Testament

The theological interest in the Old Testament should in no case impair the strength of the historical question. The viewpoint under which the Old Testament is established as a theological discipline in any given case ought not to give preference to particular phenomena according to one's own choice at the expense of unruly multiplicity. Also, the characteristic orientation of the Old Testament to concrete actualizations of life ought not to be forced to conform to traditional doctrinal types. The unavoidable problem of the total coherence of the Old Testament cannot be solved from outside by means of a philosophical construction. That would weaken what is undoubtedly characteristic of the Old Testament, namely, its eminent relation to history. The fact that the Old Testament is full of history also was not concealed from the traditional dogmatic view. Historical-critical investigation has here—even more strongly than with the Gospels—made us aware of the historical process that has led to the formation of historical traditions. The analysis of the Pentateuch in terms of the history of traditions is an unparalleled example of that. Constructions of history that lie within the layers of traditions are perceived as such by historical criticism. But at the same time they are seen as the deposit of an extraordinarily lively event in tradition which is both expressed and hidden in it. That provides one indication of the way in which what appears only to destroy the theological character of the study of the Old Testament can itself contribute to overcoming the dead end.

THE UNITY OF THE OLD TESTAMENT

The question of unity is much more difficult for the Old Testament than it is for the New Testament. That is not to be explained merely on the basis of the incomparably greater diversity of historical circumstances, literary forms, and religious conceptions and statements. The deeper basis is disclosed in the problem of the canon.

THE PROBLEMS OF THE CANON'S BEING CLOSED

A person easily falls victim to the delusion that the chronological sequence of the body of writings contained in the Old Testament and in the New Testament could also be carried over from the literary genesis of both to their canonization. Thus it would appear that the closed Old Testament canon was the prototype for the corresponding process by which the New Testament was brought to completion. Yet a person must differentiate. The collection of the writings that are now united in the Old Testament took place in stages. Initially the Pentateuch was canonized, a little later the second part of the canon under the catchword "prophets." A third complex, which above all contained the Psalms as well as wisdom and apocalyptic writings, was still open in the New Testament period. The problem is the inner basis that legitimates a definitive completion of this body of literature at all and the reason this collection of writings did not simply continue to grow.

In the case of the New Testament the situation was different. Faith in Jesus Christ carried within itself the character of definitiveness. To be sure, a living stream of witnesses of faith proceeded from the Christ event. However, this finally had to be protected against the danger of a degeneration of the tradition by collecting and canonizing the written testimony of a phase that was basic in a broader sense. The reason the borders were drawn precisely *so* gives impulse to many critical questions. However, inner appropriateness cannot be denied to the fact of such a completion in view of the coming of Jesus Christ.

With the Old Testament a corresponding inner substantive necessity is lacking. That Judaism at the turn from the first to the second century drew the canonical boundary of this body of writings definitively and relatively narrowly was to a decisive degree a reaction to Christianity, to which Judaism sacrificed a significant amount of its own wisdom and apocalyptic writings. The fact that the element of definitive validity in the Christian faith was taken up by Judaism—even though as a counter-move—could only strengthen a direction that had already been entered. However, the exclusive character of this direction had not yet been determined. Only now was the concentration on the Torah and the end of prophecy radically conceived. Thereby the canon was closed under the banner of the law, for which a definitive codification is, so to speak, natural. In contrast the canonization of the Old Testament for early Christianity (although within more broadly drawn boundaries), which was likewise coming to a conclusion, stood under a completely different banner, namely, the end of the formation of Old Testament tradition in view of the Christ event as its conclusion. Can this issue in understanding the final canonization of the Old Testament be tested by what constitutes the inner coherence of this body of literature?

THE QUESTION OF THE COHERENCE OF THE OLD TESTAMENT

Can a person specify for the Old Testament something like a "principle" or a "center" similar to the way in which Jesus Christ is the origin and center of the New Testament? Both testaments are surprisingly similar in structure in that they are deposits of an enduring process of traditions, to some extent a tradition of traditions. Both document a situation for which it is essentially inherent that the continuity of the tradition can be preserved only by entering into new historical and linguistic situations. If this process in the New Testament is defined by faith in Jesus Christ, in the Old Testament it is defined by the unity of Yahweh and Israel, the God of Israel and the people of God. That Yahweh and Israel are counterparts, belong together, and stand in contradiction is the red thread of the Old Testament, driving from experience to tradition and from tradition to new experience, and thus again to a new interpretation of the tradition. This process of tradition and interpretation prophetically stamped and formed the development of history to the point of viewing its completion. At the same time, in a type of prophecy turned backward, things from the past were more and more extensively incorporated and permeated by this tradition, beyond the patriarchal narratives to the primal history.

The movement of this interlacing of history and tradition cannot be thought of as an unambiguous development, whether as an increasing purification toward what is Christian or as a fall from the heights of the prophetic to legalism or apocalyptic. Nevertheless, symptoms of an irreversible inclination of this movement are unmistakable. The contrast with the New Testament makes this clear. In the New Testament the coming of Jesus Christ as the final revelation contains everything, even though it must initially be grasped and made explicit as such. In contrast, the relation between Yahweh and Israel is such that the question of who Yahweh is in truth and who Israel is in truth always drives further toward a transcending of their realized relationship. Therefore, as the event of tradition continues, the uncertain features are intensified. The experiences of contradiction, which point beyond themselves, open new perspectives, and just in this way they have the character of promise. A particular understanding of election stands in tension with the tendency toward what is universal. Israel as a political entity and as a religious community came increasingly into conflict. Cultic piety was certainly closely entwined with the prophetic piety concentrated on word and faith, and yet stood in an unclarified relation to it. On the one hand the individual came into consideration religiously only as a member of the people, and yet on the other hand the individual was as such a responsible person before God. The way the relation to the world and the relation to God permeated each other tended, on the one side, toward a mixture that moves into the neighborhood of the heathen religions. On the other side it tended in the direction of a distinction that, however, attained just as little clarity as did the relationship between suffering and confidence in God, judgment and grace, law and promise. According to Paul the Old Testament lacks clarity, and he grappled with the relation between the tradition of the law coming from Moses and the tradition of faith coming from Abraham. This characterization corresponds surprisingly with the historical-critical analy-

THE STUDY OF THE OLD TESTAMENT 35

sis. Also, the idea that the question as to who Yahweh and Israel in truth are should be answered together by means of the question about who Jesus is corresponds to historical observation.

"OLD TESTAMENT"—"NEW TESTAMENT"

A person needs to be aware that the identification of old and new covenant with a particular complex of tradition creates misunderstanding. One could say that the Old Testament is more than the old covenant and the New Testament is less than the new covenant. If one keeps this in view, the relation between the two can still be clarified with these names. The Old Testament is the Christian designation of a non-Christian book. That does not accomplish its transformation into a Christian book, but the relationship in which it stands to the New Testament, seen from the perspective of the latter, is made precise. Yet the Old Testament should not be placed thereby into a relationship that is foreign to itself. That is expressed in the fact that the conceptuality utilized in this distinction itself has its origin in the Old Testament. The Old Testament can be designated as such from the Christian side only because "New Testament" is the Old Testament designation of this primitive Christian book. The Old Testament already suggests the turn from the existing covenant to a new one, which makes the existing covenant the old one (Jer. 31:31 ff.). A substantive footing can be added to this linguistic one. The tensions in the Old Testament, which are full of contradictions, point beyond themselves to something new, where what is unclearly intertwined would be distinguished and reconciled in a liberating way. In that way the Old Testament expresses something that does not come into consideration as a mere historical prefigurement of the new. Rather, the Old Testament must be present as the enduring substantive prefigurement of the New if, on the other side, the New is to be preserved in its specific and continuing newness. Since the New Testament by no means attains validity of itself as that which makes all things new and which never becomes obsolete, the Old Testament is not rendered obsolete by the New.

THE STUDY OF THE OLD TESTAMENT AS A THEOLOGICAL DISCIPLINE

If one has a correct insight into the relation of both Testaments to each other, a person can expect nothing from a dogmatic regimentation vis-à-vis Old Testament study. The conflicting character of the Christian relation to the Old Testament is rooted in the conflicting character of the Old

Testament itself, which in turn points to the conflicting character of the human relationship in general to grace and truth as it has appeared in Jesus Christ. This tremendously complex situation, which is rich in interconnections, must be given space in an open treatment of the texts of the Old Testament with the highest degree of sensibility for its relation to the Christian faith. Allowing oneself to be repeatedly surprised through discoveries is more fruitful than possessing an exhaustive dogmatic formula for what is to be discovered in the Old Testament. Nevertheless, at least the directions requiring particular attention will be indicated.

BIBLICAL HISTORY

In the Old Testament the relation to God is strongly integrated into the context of history. This should not mislead us into isolating the complex of biblical history and surrounding it with a halo foreign to it. Rather, historical conditionedness is to be fully taken into account. This allows the way the Old Testament talks about God to be as unsystematic and contradictory as historical life itself. Yet it does so in such a way that in the midst of it all the basic situation of being before God is repeatedly announced. Further attention should be given to the power of God that permeates history. Precisely because this deals with concrete life, it cannot be conserved, and it prohibits a direct adoption of a past manifestation of life. Finally, and above all, the tendency of the relation to God to transcend history is to be considered. It is already expressed in the dependence of the event upon the word, and it points to the eschatological dimension. The biblical history itself is a simply unavoidable witness for that.

BIBLICAL LANGUAGE

A person must pay attention to the peculiar linguistic spirit of the Bible. Without the linguistic background of the Old Testament, the New Testament remains incomprehensible. The latter is a document of a translation from Hebrew into Greek, which certainly was prepared for by the Septuagint, but which opened a new world only in the power of the subject matter of the New Testament. In addition, elementary categories of talk about God are accessible only from the Old Testament. Even if they receive a different accent in the context of the New Testament, this process from the Old to the New Testament still is to be followed. This is all the more fruitful since penetration into the religious language of the Old Testament, which is not the language of abstract conceptuality, necessitates considering the relationship to the situation and history. It thereby preserves an encounter with the language of faith in its corporeal character.

BIBLICAL TRUTH

The study of the Old Testament deals with biblical truth in an excellent way because it introduces and trains theological thought in the turn from the old to the new. This does not happen in such a way that a person has to become a Jew first in order to become a Christian. Rather, it is true because the Old Testament is basically human precisely because it speaks of God in a singular way within the world of religions and gives space for the contradictory character of life within this talk of God. Apart from this background the miracle of the reconciliation of the world with God, which the New Testament proclaims, threatens to become pale and cheap.

4

The Study of Religion

THE HORIZON OF THE STUDY OF RELIGION

When the study of religion is discussed immediately after both biblical fields it appears to be given the rank of a discipline that is an aid to exegesis. In fact we meet a multitude of foreign religions within the Old and New Testaments, such as, for example, the Canaanite cults vis-à-vis Israel or the Hellenistic cults as counterparts of primitive Christianity. The worship of the true God necessarily conflicts with the worship of false gods, and the gospel with every other message of salvation. Biblical, Christian faith cannot be expressed apart from polemical contact with the world of the religions. It is also apparent in biblical texts that faith in Yahweh as well as in Christ is susceptible to foreign influences. As a result the decisive debates are switched over into the midst of Israel and Christianity as the struggle about the purity of the faith. This faith cannot be made explicit at all without getting into the issue of diverse conceptions.

To this point it is obvious that people always were aware that the Bible is embedded in its religious environment. Nevertheless, what became apparent in the study of the Old and New Testament through the pioneering work of the so-called history-of-religions school at the turn of the century and what since then has become a generally recognized instrument of historical biblical studies as the method of the history of religions goes considerably beyond that. It has now become clear that what was regarded as revelation, and therefore was thought to be removed from all historical dependence and analogy, also depends on the religious environment and on forms and laws of religious life. Thus this dependence involves the core of what is biblical itself. Particular attention was thereby paid to those aspects that, especially against the background of the understanding of Christianity dominant at that time, were experienced as shocking. Examples were the mythical character of central biblical conceptions, above all in the primeval history and in Christology, irrational

39

features in cultic life, or eschatology, especially in its alienating apocalyptic expression. Seen from the perspective of the history of religions, the emergence of Christianity appeared to be a syncretistic phenomenon.

Even though the study of religions initially influenced theology only through the biblical fields, the consequences for the other disciplines were also considerable. The most marked was the impact on dogmatics. Its biblical foundation, which was regarded as unconditionally valid, was shown to be historically conditioned in its innermost aspects. At the same time our vision was opened to the worldwide significance of other religions in the present. In the face of them Christian theology no longer knew itself to be in the position of incontestable missionary superiority. The challenge of the other religions also could not be weakened by interpreting the phenomenon of secularism, which was equally worldwide, as an indication of a religious disintegration that was approaching anyway. This diagnosis and theological speculation in preparation for a religious slump may turn out to be deceptive. Whatever the case may be with regard to religionlessness, theology would not take its confrontation with the present world seriously if it were to avoid the contemporary world of religion. The Christian segment of the world's population is somewhat less than thirty percent, and certainly will decrease further as a result of regional differences in population growth. If one considers this fact, then even the ecumenical movement—with or without Rome—can appear to be an expression of a Christian provincialism in spite of its breadth.

The claim of the study of religion reaches still further. It does not merely increase the phenomena that enter the theologian's field of view and require consideration. The approach of the study of religion does not simply fit in with theology. It increasingly comes into competition with theology. Christianity itself, and theology together with it, now becomes the *object* of consideration in the study of religion. Through religious studies theology is neither increased by a further discipline nor supplemented by a discipline outside of theology, but rather is placed in question as such. Because the horizon of the problems covers such a wide expanse, broad contexts must be alluded to in the interest of forming a judgment.

CHRISTIANITY AND THE RELIGIONS

CHANGES IN CHRISTIANITY'S ENCOUNTER WITH OTHER RELIGIONS

The great transformations in church and world history are reflected in the changes through which Christianity's encounter with other religions has moved. The extent to which these changes are to be tracked back to circumstances as well as to new thought can be allusively considered in a rough sketch.

Primitive Christianity

The movement out of Palestinian Judaism into the world of Hellenistic antiquity determined the direction of the further development of church history. This process should be understood from the fact that the motivation to world mission derives from the gospel itself. Formally described, it was based on a new religious reality that broke the structural schema of the religions at that time. The certainty that through Jesus Christ the distinction between Jew and Gentile had lost its religious significance deprived the religious characteristic upon which the contrast between Jew and Gentile was based of its power. This characteristic was the localization of the sacred and the profane in fixed realms, as well as the provision for security before the divine through particular cultic acts. Due to the way in which Christian faith experienced and testified to the reality of the sacred, the addition of Christianity to the existing religions signified more than merely the emergence of one more religion. At the same time, it was a religious critique of religion that touched the root of all religions.

The Early Catholic Church

Nevertheless, Christianity itself became established as a religion with forms of life and institutions that endured historically. Together with sharply distinguishing itself from powerful religious phenomena at that time, like the emperor cult, Gnosticism, Manichaeism, and Neoplatonism, there also was an intensive integration of religious borrowings into Christianity. These borrowings were partly from the Gentile environment and partly from the Old Testament–Jewish tradition. Christianity emerged from antiquity as the privileged religion without competition. The leading role with respect to politics and culture fell to it. In the missionary encounter with the religions of the Germanic and Slavic peoples, these religions proved inferior from the start. As a result, the existence of other religions did not pose a serious challenge to Christianity through the Germanic and Slavic religions.

The Middle Ages and the Beginnings of Modern Times

In contrast, in Islam a serious competitor arose again for the first time to which wide areas of the Roman Empire were lost. Throughout the Middle Ages, Islam formed the opposition to the Christian West both politically and culturally in which people experienced the confrontation with a contrasting world religion. That promoted an intensified rational penetration into Christian doctrine with an apologetic purpose, as well as tendencies toward an enlightened religious harmonization whose earliest impulses go back to the intellectual atmosphere at the court of Hohenstaufen emperor Frederick II. Certainly the path that led from there to the idea of tolerance in the Enlightenment was a long one. The expansion of the geographic and ethnic field of view since the discovery of America and of the sea route to India and East Asia affected the relationship to other religions in conflicting ways. On the one side, a new pressure toward mission was awakened. On the other side, what was religiously familiar was robbed of its obvious character and was relativized through the insight into completely different sorts of phenomena.

The Last Two Centuries

That a genuine interest in the history of religions was awakened first in the nineteenth century rests on the convergence of two factors: the global expansion of the West, in which colonization and mission went hand in hand, as well as the development of the historical mode of thinking in the strictest sense. Only then did the phenomena of primitive religions as well as such a significant major religion as Buddhism enter clearly into our awareness and become the object of empathetic engagement. At the same time, however, the perspective on the problem shifted. Secularism, as it accompanied development of technology, also thrust the non-Christian religions into a crisis. In part quasi-religions in the form of nationalism and communism streamed into the vacuum, and in part new constructions emerged from the womb of the ancestral religions. With that the study of religion grew far beyond the modest role of a theological supportive discipline with apologetic and missionary purpose. It attained explosive timeliness in view of the contemporary political and intellectual constellations of power.

CHANGES IN THE USE OF THE WORD "RELIGION"

For Christianity the discussion with the problem of religion was constantly a test of its self-understanding. This discussion is sketched in the changes in the use of the word "religion." This outline is punctuated with characteristic catchwords.

True Religion

The ancient linguistic use of *religio* is divided between two principle meanings: "religiousness" as the inner attitude of pious awe and "cult" as the institutionalized form of worship of God. What fundamentally changed with the gradual absorption into Christian usage was that the phenomenon of religion moved into the horizon of the question of truth. *"Vera religio"* occurs for the first time in Augustine.[1] Of course, for a long time there was so little urgency for the concept of religion to be used for reflection on non-Christian religions that *religio* was free for specialized usage within Christianity. Within the linguistic domain of medieval Catholicism it was used as the designation of life lived according to the rules of an order, thus of a stage of perfection organized in various expressions. Later in the age of the confessions it was used as a generic term for the conflicting religious parties. However, already under the influence of humanism people increasingly used the general concept *religio* again and correspondingly talked of the *religio Christiana*. In the orthodox understanding, afterward as before, the term represented the *vera religio*, while all other religions, together with malformations of Christianity itself, fell under the concept *religio falsa*.

Natural Religion

The concept of the true religion could become the lever for a critique of the orthodox understanding in two ways. On the one hand, the pious life could be claimed as the true religion over against the prevalence of doctrine, so that religion became sharply contrasted with theology. Or, on the other hand, in contrast to the authority of revelation, the truth of religion could be found by measuring it against general rational truths and grounding it in them. This also promised to overcome the unfortunate division between the historically oriented religions in favor of a religion that was anchored in the nature of humanity and was the sole religion appropriate to it. Both of these usurpations of the concept of true religion —crudely formulated, the pietistic and rationalistic variants—that were critical of tradition made talk about true religion questionable by their consistency.

Positive Religion

Schleiermacher saw through the natural theology of the Enlightenment as a pale abstract concept, which missed the character of religion as such. Only the historically defined, so-called positive religions deserved to be named as such. However, an absolute claim to revelation no longer

---

1. *De civitate Dei* 10.3.47, in *CCSL,* vol. 47 (1955), p. 276. *De vera religione*, Bk. I, in CCSL, vol. 32 (1962), pp. 169–260.

bestowed the predicate of truth on only *one* religion, but a broader concept of revelation was associated with the reality of historical life itself. Hence, the relation between historicity and truth became a burning problem in matters of religion. Schleiermacher connected both under the aspect of the reference to life. The orientation to the totality of what is human, which is intended by the concept of feeling, became the criterion of what is essentially religious, in distinction from metaphysics and morals. At the same time, this orientation offered a standard for ordering the multiplicity of types of religion, so that the question of truth remained tied to the concept of religion in a careful way. Hegel, who also was oriented to the positivity of religion, in contrast connected historicity and truth under the aspect of the universal-historical process of the development of the idea of religion. Through rising out of the medium of representation into the speculative concept, religion initially comes philosophically to the truth. Thereby its own historical inclination is fulfilled. Since then, in a way that has been relatively independent of the further course of endeavors in the philosophy of religion, the historical study of religion has experienced a considerable upswing as a fruit of this orientation to positive religion. But this has largely taken place under a suspension of the question of truth.

Religion as Negativity

In a combination of motifs drawn from Schleiermacher and Hegel, Feuerbach maintained the question of truth in such a way that he sought to unveil religion psychologically as "nothing other than" the self-revelation of what is human, which has been projected into an objectifying conceptualization. The further critique of religion, which defined the essence of religion as negativity, derived from this. In the Marxist version, religion was the ideological justification of bourgeois society, "the opium of the people." In Nietzsche's version, religion gives rise to the inner violation and crippling of humanity. In Freud's version, religion was interpreted as an illusory objectification of and compensation for unsatisfied desires and unmanageable anxieties. The positivistic-sociological classification of religion as the stage of human childhood, which is ultimately overcome by passing through the metaphysical stage to the scientific stage, can be connected with these analyses. From the side of theology, in contrast to the manifold attempts to found theology upon the concept and phenomenon of religion, the critique of religion was also finally utilized. The attempt was made to correspond to this critique by means of a theologically based concept of religion as essential negativity. Influenced by religious socialism, the early Karl Barth interpreted religion as the original sin of humankind, which was opposed to the revelation in Christ. At least according to a superficial conception, Dietrich Bonhoeffer interpreted the emerging religionlessness as basically conforming to the innermost intention of biblical truth. These extreme examples underscore the theological urgency of the theme of religion.

PROBLEMS WITHIN THE STUDY OF RELIGION

The study of religion stands before difficult questions of academic theory in ways that are different from theology but no less difficult. What is the situation with regard to its self-understanding as a science and its encyclopedic wholeness?

QUESTIONS OF METHOD

The definition of the object of study already causes great difficulty, as is indicated by the vast number of formulations posed for this purpose and, even more so, by the frequent resignation with regard to this issue. Even if a person renounces setting up a normative idea of religion from the start and wants to be content with the most open general concept possible, the constitutive viewpoint through which the concept of religion is to be limited remains contested. Such a viewpoint should provide space for all the phenomena that are to be considered and yet not allow the total picture to flow into indefiniteness. Does, for example, the concept of God necessarily belong to it? Or mythical modes of speech? Or is the orientation to the totality of life and reality a sufficient characteristic? Is it sufficient to remain with the phenomena of the history of religions that are uncontested? Or does the definition of religion have to also take into account crypto-religious phenomena, which, if need be, even understand themselves as antireligious? But how then are generalizations to be avoided that would sacrifice the historical profile of what previously was considered as religion?

The problem of categories in the study of religion borders these questions closely. May a person generalize expressions derived from Christian tradition like "faith" or "church" without further ado to make them basic concepts of religious study? This generalization often happens naively and also scarcely can fundamentally be avoided. Or is a corresponding expansion of terminology taken from primitive religions like "tabu," "mana," or "totem" protected from interpretive distortion? What justification and what danger lies in the preponderance of archaic phenomena within the study of religion? What is the situation with regard to the usability of general historiographic categories, as, for example, the concept of development or a concept of religion already stamped by secularization? The latter in any case has become widely removed from the premodern understanding of religion, if not even from a genuine understanding of the subject of religion as such. The methodological idea would be the combination of an expansive comparative study of language with the study of religion. Furthermore, that would be the best weapon against the danger of an ideological stifling of work in the study of religion.

Nevertheless, a difficult-to-solve, fundamental problem remains. Should the conception of the critique of religion on principle be the unavoidable method of a scholarly treatment of religion? Doubtless it can sharpen our eyes for particular aspects of the subject. The distancing, especially from one's own religious connection, can at times further the observation of unfamiliar religious phenomena. However, that does not give an advantage to an attitude that is hostile to religion. On the contrary, a fruitful study of religion is dependent on a living relationship to the subject and on a loving empathy. Now, however, the intensive turn to the study of religion is mostly an ambivalent expression of alienation from and longing for the religious. Being well versed in many religions often has the reverse side that a person is no longer completely at home in a particular religion, or is no longer at home in it at all. Moreover, through the fact that the world of religions is made an object of study, what is religious is restricted to a special sector in the expression of human life. With that it is restricted to a concept of religion, which itself is already the product of the secularization of what is religious and its isolation from the totality of life. Instead of considering the whole of reality in a religious attitude, what is religious is investigated by virture of a nonreligious approach to reality and is classified within the whole of reality—possibly in a thoroughly respectful way.

These considerations suggest neither a particular solution to the problem nor the impression of a dead end with no way out. The intention is only to make the questions that belong essentially to the study of religion conscious.

AREAS OF WORK

To totally structure the study of religion is a questionable undertaking because two possibilities compete with one another: centering on the phenomenon and essence of religion, or the interest in a different kind of horizon for the subject matter within which religion only emerges as a subsidiary aspect. Of course, the various branches of the study of religion cannot be divided in a way that would correspond to these two possibilities, but to various degrees they tend in one direction or the other.

The central discipline that belongs unambiguously to the first group is the *history of religions*. It forms the unavoidable basis for all other disciplines in the study of religion. Without knowledge about how religious life has unfolded and taken shape historically, all the other approaches to the study of religion would be without an object of study. Religion cannot be constructed and invented. It can only be interpreted and critically investigated as something already given. It is more strongly dependent upon tradition than any other area of human life. The investigation of contemporary religious phenomena also necessarily leads one into the historical dimension, just as even empirical fieldwork can serve as an instrument that indirectly illuminates the history of religions.

The *phenomenology of religion* obviously belongs as well to the central disciplines oriented to religion. It is dependent on broad historical materials, but it does not proceed genetically. Rather, it seeks to define the total manifestation of religion through demonstrating structural commonalities and differences in fundamental religious phenomena in order to advance detailed interpretation by means of a more understanding grasp of meaning and more appropriate categories.

The *philosophy of religion* has reflection upon the relationship of religion to the consciousness of truth as a whole as its theme. Although it derives this theme exclusively from religion, whether or not it belongs to religious studies in the strict sense is contested. Its task has been understood very differently. On the one extreme, it is a philosophical discipline in which the question of God itself is discussed. On the other extreme, it is a theological discipline in which the manifold character of what is religious receives a Christian interpretation. Whether along one of these paths or in a different conception, such as that of linguistic analysis, in any case the philosophy of religion points in one way or another to a broader horizon of understanding. This is defined by the question of reality as a whole, within which religion is also considered. Certainly, a person can rightly doubt that the study of religion can rid itself of the question posed by the philosophy of religion without damage.

The *psychology of religion* and the sociology of religion belong to those branches of work within which the ambivalence between a primary and a secondary interest in religion appears with particular clarity. The former can be interested in a psychological illumination of religious phenomena as a part of religious studies. Or, as a part of psychology, in particular of depth psychology, it can primarily serve diagnostic and therapeutic tasks, for which the religious dimension is important only in a pathological context. Similarly, the *sociology of religion* can have its accent either in the investigation of the formation of religious communities and the interaction between religion and society, or its accent can lie in the context of more general sociological studies within which religious factors are observed only alongside other factors. Naturally, this does not result in sharp alternatives. However, the easy transition shows how difficult and probably also misleading it would be to project a strict and comprehensive encyclopedic program of religious studies. This can be illustrated finally in *religious education*. This has a meaningful function only if it is directed toward a particular religion, unless it is understood as mere information about religions in general. In that case, however, it would only be a special division of pedagogy or perhaps a theory of antireligious propaganda.

THE STUDY OF RELIGION AND THEOLOGY

PARTICIPATION OF THEOLOGY IN THE STUDY OF RELIGION

In its origins Christianity was already interwoven with the history of religions, and at present it is confronted by the world of religions. These viewpoints, which were already mentioned at the beginning of this discussion, mark the poles between which the theme of religion theologically attains universal significance and varies widely. It becomes acute in a most provocative way in all theological disciplines. This has already been indicated with regard to the biblical departments and church history. The same is true for the systematic disciplines: in fundamental theology for the question about what is essentially Christian and its setting in life, in dogmatics for the articulation of Christian doctrines, in ethics in view of the relevance of the relationship to God for the orientation of behavior, and in practical theology for the functions and living forms of the church. A person becomes aware of that not only through particular examples, but already associatively through the unavoidable entanglement of theology in questions of the philosophy of religion, sociology of religion, psychology of religion, and religious education. If the field devoted to the study of religion in theological faculties is at times institutionally coupled with missions, this could appear as a constriction of the subject matter unless the task of the study of mission is understood in a theologically comprehensive way, namely, as a task that deals with a subject that is also present in all disciplines.

If theology wants to profit from the enormous object lessons to be drawn from religious experience in the history of religions, and if it is also prepared to be challenged by the aggressive problems of religious reality, then theology must affirm the methodological independence of all the branches of religious studies. Theology must also engage in the observation of fact and the food it provides for thought in as unbiased a way as possible. To control the study of religion from the beginning by theological needs and directives or, correspondingly, to filter its results from the standpoint of what appears to be theologically acceptable and comfortable robs theology of a significant increase in knowledge and takes effect in a way that damages theology.

Certainly, as with all interdisciplinary exchange, whether with external fields bordering theology or in communication between theological divisions, the difficulty immediately arises as to how a person can responsibly participate in the work of others. What a theology can adopt from the wide field of investigation in the study of religion is normally quantitatively very modest and seldom attains real competence in the subject. On the other side, it is obviously dangerous in theology to use accidental results, assertions, or hypotheses uncritically as though they were finished building blocks. The best protection against that is that a person would acquire one's own experience by becoming involved with work in the study of religion at some point, although the insufficiency or absence of linguistic knowledge presents a hindrance that should not be underestimated. Besides, the treatment of the material in religious studies—whether it be the colorfulness of a historical approach or the dryness of contemporary statistical investigation—decisively depends on a general theological capacity for judgment that grants a person the necessary circumspection and soberness. That becomes clear in the question as to whether people are prepared to allow themselves to be challenged to self-critical, basic theological reflection by the subject matter of the study of religion. From the theological side it also becomes clear in the question of whether people are prepared to participate critically in the methodological problems of the study of religion. The labels that separate the disciplines should not deceive a person about the degree to which the question of competence is relativized in the concrete course of scholarly work and thought.

THE DISSOLUTION OF THEOLOGY INTO RELIGIOUS STUDIES?

The demand that theology must transform itself into the study of religion and, in any case, has a place in the circle of scholarly fields at the university only in this form was already advocated in the nineteenth century and has been made since then in repeated new attacks. Ernst

Troeltsch, the theologian of the history-of-religions school, rejected the transformation of theology into faculties in religious studies with surprising sharpness. As much as he insisted that systematic theology is to draw consequences from the viewpoint of the history of religions and that traditional dogmatic methods are to be subjected to a radical critique, the decisive difference for him remained that theology deals with *normative* perceptions in the study of religion. Therefore it would be an absurdity "to build up a theological faculty that had no official knowledge of normative religious truth, that had to hunt for it like an explorer for the North Pole." "For religion has no meaning and indeed ceases to be religion if its truth and content are treated as something distant and supposedly quite unknown, if it is regarded as a source of eternally debatable problems rather than actually given divine actions and powers."[2] It does not matter whether that already answers the problem sufficiently. Its importance for fundamental theology in any case contradicts the expectation that a solution could already be decreed from the side of the study of religion, whose status in academic theory is, as we saw, itself connected with considerable difficulties.

This much is certainly already clear: not only would theology lose its specific object of study and its unity if it were transformed into the study of religion, but by doing so it would also forfeit its right to exist at the university. For the field of study of a general study of religion or, more narrowly, of a discipline primarily investigating Christianity from the perspective of the study of religion would at best lead a warped existence if joint responsibility for the subject matter of Christian faith and for education for ecclesiastical service were fundamentally denied to it.

THEOLOGY OF THE RELIGIONS?

Talk about converting theology into the study of religion can also be turned around into the demand that the study of religion be transformed into theology. Very different things can be concealed behind the slogan about a theology of the religions, as is true for any formula about a "theology of. . . ." In this case it can be the justified desire to theologically reflect on the phenomenon of religion in its totality, rather than passing over it thoughtlessly. Or it can be the question, which is no doubt worthy of consideration, as to whether theology first and foremost can work out the definition of its object from the perspective of the phenomenon of

---

2. Ernst Troeltsch, *The Absoluteness of Christianity and the History of Religion*, trans. David Reid (Richmond: John Knox Press, 1971), p. 26.

religion, so that a theology of the religions would be postulated as a theological fundamental discipline. Pannenberg represents this conception today with the thesis that theology can again attain the character of a science about God precisely through such a foundation in the study of religion.[3] Certainly that corrects the contemporary self-understanding in the field of the study of religion in a way that challenges the study of religion as well as theology to critical counterquestions. It is possible paradoxically that both could encounter each other more fruitfully in the common affirmation of their deep difference than through that merging of horizons.

3. Wolfhart Pannenberg, *Theology and the Philosophy of Science*, trans. Francis McDonah (Philadelphia: Westminster Press, 1976), pp. 315, 358 ff.

5

Philosophy

THE PARTNERSHIP OF THEOLOGY AND PHILOSOPHY

In comparison to theology, the study of religion is a very recent phenomenon. Philosophy, in contrast, is older than theology. Furthermore, it has represented an integrating factor in the history of theology from the beginning. This partnership between theology and philosophy has shown many modifications. Its scale reaches from the most intimate interpenetration to the most external hostility, from a philosophy that claims to be theology to one that understands itself in the light of its contrast to theology, from a theology that seems to dissolve into philosophy to one that strives to free itself from any contact with philosophy. Between these there lie the attempts, in numerous combinations and gradations, to distinguish theology and philosophy in such a way that they remain in communication with one another.

HISTORICAL PARTNERSHIP

The temporal priority of philosophy and the constant partnership between theology and philosophy are only characteristic of Christian theology. The origin and classical period of Greek philosophy preceded Christian theology. As it was mediated through Hellenistic philosophy, Greek philosophy exercised such a formative influence that already from its earliest formation Christian theology bears within itself an explicit or implicit relation to philosophy and could not exist at all apart from this relationship. This assessment, however, requires a double explanation. This involves the word "theology" as well as the origins of Christian theology.

53

The Philosophical Origin of the Word "Theology"

The word "theology" was philosophically coined. It initially appeared in Plato,[1] and for him it meant "mythology." This also was the predominant meaning for the following time. Thus, it meant religious rather than philosophical talk about God, which was regarded critically by philosophy. Of course, there was a line of linguistic usage that ran parallel to this through ancient philosophy, beginning with Aristotle. In this line the concept of "theology" is claimed for the philosophical doctrine of God.[2] However, this usage became strongly established only in late Hellenistic philosophy, already as a repercussion from Christianity. It is particularly noteworthy in the facts of the conceptual history of the term that Greek religion did not produce theology in the sense customary to us, namely, as a thoughtful account given by religion about itself. The aspect of religious language that was externally designated as "theology," with an undertone of religious criticism, although this side of religion also adopted this designation as its own name, remained within the element of the mythical and cultic. Reflection on the question of truth was not raised from within itself. On the other side, Greek philosophy seen as a whole remained loyal to the external religious forms, in spite of the impulse that was critical of religion, and it retained a certain inner connection with the spirit of traditional religiosity. Nevertheless, philosophy was not able to think of the divine in such a way that it attained agreement with religion itself, analogous to the self-understanding of Christian theology. In the ancient linguistic usage as well as in the reality of ancient life, both lines, namely, mythical and philosophical theology, split and never attained effective reconciliation. Hence philosophy certainly took into itself the question of God, however, without rooting itself directly in a particular religion and being jointly responsible for that religion.

The Role of Philosophy in the Constitution of Christian Theology

The origin of Christian theology does not coincide with the Christian reception of this term. The close association of the term "theology" with its heathen religious understanding resulted in early Christianity's being very reserved vis-à-vis this term. In contrast, it was relatively natural to lay claim to the expression "philosophy," although with the critical accent "true philosophy." Greek-speaking Christianity adopted the word "theology" only in the course of a general inheritance from the conquered

1. *Politeia* B 379a, ll. 5–6.
2. *Metaphysics*, E 1026a34, K 1064b3.

heathen religions. Still, it limited the term to discussion of the nature of God in distinction from *"oikonomia"* as the discussion of his work in salvation history. In contrast, in Western Christianity the mistrust of the word "theology" continued to persist for a long time. The use of the term then changed in Scholasticism to the broadened significance familiar to us, in which "theology" means the systematically reflected totality of Christian doctrine. The idea of an *"episteme theologike,"* which goes back to Aristotle, was essentially influential in this change. The same was true of taking philosophy into service for shaping theology, which was also connected with Aristotle. Certainly, theology as a thoughtful account of Christian faith already existed since Paul, regardless of the question of how it was designated. It was made possible and necessary by the peculiarity of Christian faith itself, although those earliest beginnings were not entirely untouched by Hellenistic philosophy. The history of dogma in the early church impressively demonstrates the contribution made to the broader formation and consolidation of Christian theology through the more intensive discussion with philosophical thought that was initiated with Gnosticism and the apologists.

Changes in the Partnership

The partnership between theology and philosophy continued during the changeable history through which both have moved with each other. It is most obvious to think of mutual influences on one another. Among them the influence of philosophy on theology immediately presses forward. However, influence in the other direction was not lacking. Further, the interwovenness of their historical fate should be noted. Although their mutual relationship at a given time could be of very different kinds, as a whole one can observe a development in which both partners correspond to one another as well as together being suited to their time. In the period of the ancient church, the tendency toward a fusion of theology and philosophy dominated, without, certainly, leading to a suspension of the distinction. For Scholasticism, the growing distinction became definitive, without, however, breaking off the relationship. The deep change that took place for theology through the Reformation and for philosophy through the spirit of modern times brought a kind of new birth and mutual independence. In spite of theological tendencies toward the sharpest diastasis and in spite of the philosophical inclination toward an anti-theological attitude, even this change was not able to dissolve the relationships that were most closely established by history as well as by the subject matter itself. Without being able to hold particular dependencies of one discipline upon the other responsible, both theology and philosophy are embraced by a common temporal fate, whether they are disposed to be in solidarity or at enmity with one another. For the most part, educational high points benefit both. For example, both benefit and lose from a widespread unity and constancy of thought forms or from intellectual pluralism. The relationship to science also raises analogous problems for both.

SUBSTANTIVE PARTNERSHIP

Upon what does this close partnership rest? Do both have the same theme, which is stated differently because they proceed in different ways and do not draw from the same sources? The customary answers are not false, but they also are not sufficient: for example, that the contact consists in the question of God or in the universal question of meaning and thus in the question about humanity in view of the whole or reality; or that the distinction is to be defined as the distinction between the jurisdiction of reason and of revelation so that the difference, correspondingly, is between a critical and an authoritarian approach. The attempt at such a definition of the relationship meets many difficulties, which, however, provide further impulses to reflection about what theology and philosophy have in common and what differentiates them.

The Task of Defining the Relationship

Beyond features that are very general and indefinite, the relationship between theology and philosophy cannot be formulated neutrally and definitively. That is due to the relativity and interdependence of the factors involved. It is common to both that their nature presses toward clarity and definition in their execution. What philosophy is is a fundamental philosophical question that philosophical thought is to determine. Likewise, the question of what theology is is a fundamental theological question. The outline of a particular self-understanding of theology appears in the answer to this question. There is *the* philosophy as well as *the* theology only in the movement and dispute associated with struggling for the correct self-definition. That means, however, that the definition of the relationship between theology and philosophy falls all the more under the law of perspective. The self-understanding of philosophy betrays itself in the definition of the relationship to theology connected with it. The same is true even more intensively the other way around. The theological self-understanding becomes explicit precisely in the way in which it relates itself to philosophy. In both cases the understanding that philosophy and theology have of each other combines general and particular features of their own definition of their essence, as well as of their corresponding evaluation of the partner, which can deviate widely from the partner's own self-understanding. This complex hermeneutical situation with regard to the relationship between theology and philosophy rests on the fact that contact and difference with regard to the subject matter are inseparably interlocked. Therefore, for each, the definition of the relationship becomes a particularly fruitful challenge to reflect on its own subject matter.

The Interest in the Distinction

In spite of the problem of demarcation, interest in the distinction is something that binds philosophy and theology together. Yet at the same time the difference in the subject matter appears in the fundamentally different orientation of this interest.

It is clear that from the perspective of philosophy value is primarily placed on a mere contrast, which underscores its own independence and superiority. Normally no positive interest in the existence of theology is at stake. To the extent that philosophy devotes specific interest to theology, it is incorporated as a segment into philosophy. But in so doing it is set off polemically against "theological" theology, which as such cannot be received philosophically.

In contrast, from the perspective of this "theological" theology there is an interest in the existence of philosophy that is necessitated by the subject matter. Even in the period when Christianity absolutely dominated culture and an independent philosophy was actually extinguished, theology accepted philosophy as a task that was distinct from itself and was meaningful alongside itself. But even when the situation of an ecclesiastically domesticated philosophy ended as a result of its emancipation from theology and the possibility of a sharp antagonism between philosophy and theology arose again, theology could by no means be uninterested in a philosophy that was hostile to it, regardless of theology's critical relation to such a philosophy.

This divergence in the relationship between the two disciplines expresses the fact that philosophy tends toward a unified understanding of reality into which theology also is integrated according to the standards of philosophical judgment. For theology, in contrast, the understanding of reality appropriate to Christian faith is defined by a fundamental distinction that confers on philosophy the right to independence alongside theology without dismissing the engagement with philosophy from the totality of theological responsibility. From the perspective of theology the distinction between the two "kingdoms," anchored in the understanding of the gospel, is actualized in the relationship to philosophy, whether one interprets that distinction with Scholasticism in the sense of nature and grace or with the Reformation theology in the sense of law and gospel. That distinction involves a fact that evades philosophical appropriation.

The Different Relationship to History

This indication of the innermost core of the difference joins with another observation that seems more external. The distinction between theology and philosophy becomes clear in their relation to history. Not that it is adequate simply to describe the circumstances antithetically with formulas like "eternal word of God" and "transitory human word," or "divine instruction" and "human wisdom," or "historical revelation" and "timeless rational truth." What is correct in such formulations can only be defined on the common basis of a historicity in which the absolute truth presses into language. However, within this framework, a characteristic distinction is apparent. Theology is related to a completely particular tradition and shares responsibility for the continuation of this event of tradition. Certainly, theology understands this as a consequence of the fact that faith has its enduring basis in Jesus Christ and history has its ultimate destiny in him, not as an arbitrary particularism. Philosophically this appears as a claim to absoluteness that cannot be reconciled with the openness of the search for truth. Theologically a person cannot be content with this characterization without indicating and explicating the difference in the understanding of truth itself. This is connected with a broader difference. For its part theology is only an indirect expression of the truth represented by it, namely, as explicit reflection upon what occurs in proclamation and prayer as the basic event of the church and Christian existence. Philosophy, in contrast, claims as such to be the form in which the truth attains its highest possible presence. That which in the subject matter of theology is divided between the endeavor of theology and the word event that it serves is indistinguishably united in philosophy. Therefore, with regard to its relationship with theology, philosophy has its counterpart not in theology but, and in a certain respect primarily, in the lived reality of Christian truth itself.

PHILOSOPHY AND HISTORY

The viewpoint of a close partnership between theology and philosophy comes into the foreground so strongly only from the theologian's perspective. From the standpoint of the philosopher, talk of such a relationship is occasionally accented, but then mostly with a polemical intention.

However, the relation to theology largely plays no role for philosophy. The interest of theology in philosophy, however, is not conditioned at all by whether the latter, in whatever manner, is explicitly oriented to theology. For that reason, the significance of philosophy for theology can only be fully gauged if a person unconditionally enters into the peculiarity of philosophy without interposing a theological filter. The fact that the relation to history is especially suited as a point of access for doing that corresponds to the difference between theology and philosophy already established in this regard. But it also corresponds to the way in which philosophy on its own terms initially presents itself.

The Study of the History of Philosophy

The question about the nature of philosophy initially directs our attention to history, since it is precisely history that provides information about philosophy. The phenomenon of philosophy is principally connected with outstanding thinkers as well as with philosophical directions that are named either for heads of schools or according to ontological or methodological principles, like Idealism, Nominalism, Positivism, Structuralism, and the like. Such designations or firm names fix one's memory on a complex of teachings, which more or less bear the character of a system and make an impression on one's mind primarily through particular basic concepts. For the outsider that is the predominant impression of philosophy: a multiplicity of thinkers, modes of thought and ideas, which are interwoven with one another in a pattern of historical influence. Thus philosophy presents itself as something that is historically given. The study of philosophy becomes the study of the history of philosophy.

Close at hand lies the objection that access to philosophy is blocked precisely in that way. Not only is it tiresome to incorporate a mass of memorized material from the history of philosophy into one's mind, but it even seems to be a hindrance to the purpose of philosophical thought. In whatever way a person might get rid of the presumed historical ballast, one constantly only creates all the more new difficulties. The more one renounces a general overview knowledge in favor of developing a point of emphasis, the more one becomes aware that the tendency to minimalism makes dealing with the history of philosophy even more unproductive. Ignoring historical connections makes difficult or even hinders one from entering into a single place in depth, and already makes the selection of that place questionable. If one pleads that preference be given to an engagement with contemporary philosophy, one would be correct in that its complete neglect could be a symptom of an antiquarian interest in philosophy that contradicts its nature. However, one deceives oneself if one thinks that this correction can be brought about at the expense of history. By doing so a person is robbed of critical distance to his or her own present. To narrow one's horizon to what is modern endangers intellectual independence through the temptation to immediate acceptance. On the other hand, the demand to become aware of and to deal with historical distance is capable of greatly enhancing inner activity and making it more sensitive for the contemporary state of the problem. The desire to devote oneself to what is of particular immediate interest harbors the danger that, for the sake of pursuing what is up-to-date, one could become useless to the kind of old-fashionedness that at times is ahead of one's own time. A person attains the patience necessary for that possibility only through the study of preserved and enduring texts.

THE HISTORICITY OF PHILOSOPHICAL THOUGHT

To be sure, a person cannot accent the study of the history of philosophy without being confronted with the problem as to whether the insight into the historicity of philosophical thought does not threaten philosophical thought itself. Philosophy does not consist simply in a particular teaching that one can take over from or produce for another, but it consists in one's own carrying out of philosophical thought. If one keeps this awareness in view, the encounter with the history of philosophy supports precisely this conception. Involvement with philosophical texts is only appropriate to these texts if a person is led by them into the movement of his or her reflection and further thought. The history of philosophy is only pursued correctly by thinking philosophically. The "anarchy of philosophical systems"[3] already contradicts the attempt to mine this history like a quarry in order to borrow a philosophy or to piece one together eclectically. Yet it is precisely the confusing and contradictory multiplicity of philosophical positions and claims that awakens the impression that the history of philosophy as such contradicts the idea that a person can expect knowledge and truth from philosophy. However, instead of being driven to resignation, a person must ask what is to be understood as truth in view of the historicity of humanity and what the history of thought has to do with the development of the knowledge of truth. Thus, even under such critical intensification the history of philosophy does not release a person from philosophical thought but drives a person all the more sharply toward it.

3. Wilhelm Dilthey, *Gesammelte Schriften* (Stuttgart: Teubner; Göttingen: Vandenhoeck & Ruprecht, 1958–63), 8:75, 78.

Although the historicity of philosophy expresses a viewpoint that has not yet become an object of reflection in the historical sources of philosophy, it is precisely the fact of its Greek origin that provides explicit evidence of its historicity. Philosophy did not emerge arbitrarily everywhere in history. Certainly, a person may, in a broad and undefined historiographic linguistic usage, designate reflection about ultimate questions of life in other cultures with this term and, for example, speak of Chinese and Indian philosophy. However, Hegel was probably correct when he mentioned this at the beginning of his lectures on the history of philosophy as "preliminary," saying, "We only deal with it at all in order to account for not treating it at great length."[4] What is characteristic in the Greek awakening to philosophical thought can be defined in terms of its basic attitude, which is amazement that, not believing in authority or miracles, is not satisfied with finished answers but bestows a courage for a radical questioning after the whole. This questioning admits its own lack of knowledge but also recognizes one's own reason as the only convincing court of appeal. For that reason it is courage to freedom. Because of this spirit, philosophy throughout its entire history has remained obligated to its origin in the Greek world. To repeatedly return to that origin represents an unavoidable elementary schooling and inexhaustible source for the renewal of philosophical thought. By virtue of the origin, fundamental changes in philosophical thought do not stand in the way of its continuity. Such changes have occurred most incisively through the great changes in the historical situation resulting from the encounter with Christianity as well as the entry into the modern period. Under both influences the awareness of the historicity of philosophical thought intruded in different respects, thereby intensifying the question about the nature of philosophy—even to the extreme possibility that it may even have come to its end.

PHILOSOPHY AND SCIENCE

That philosophy was radically placed in question certainly did not only grow out of the problem of historicity and the resultant experience of relativity. Under this aspect the challenge to philosophy would only be modified. What was decisive was the way in which the problem of scientific method, which increasingly concentrated on the demand for the exactitude of experience that is capable of being stated mathematically,

4. *Hegel's Lectures on the History of Philosophy* (1892), trans. E. S. Haldane (New York: Humanities Press, 1963), 1:117. G. W. F. Hegel, *Sämtliche Werke: Jubiläumsausgabe* (Stuttgart: Frommann, 1927–40), 17:151 (hereafter, *Jub. Ausg.*).

was coupled with the problem of historicity and the resultant experience of relativity. With regard to the present crisis in understanding philosophy, therefore, the question of its relation to science is of decisive significance.

PHILOSOPHY AS THE EMBODIMENT OF SCIENCE

The formation of the word *"philo-sophia"* originally designated theoretical interest in general, without limitation to a system of wisdom in distinction from a system of knowledge. The distinction between *sapientia* and *scientia* may not be mixed in from the beginning. Although Plato conceived philosophy narrowly as the discipline devoted to the idea, which is what is truly real—corresponding to what Aristotle called "first philosophy"—the broad Aristotelian linguistic usage according to which philosophy is science [scholarship] in general prevailed for a long time. In spite of certain impulses in that direction, neither in antiquity nor in the Middle Ages did people arrive at a real separation and independence of individual sciences [scholarly fields] from the general understanding of philosophy as the total orientation toward the world. They were clamped together through the basic philosophical disciplines: logic as the teaching of the ground rules of language and thought, metaphysics or ontology as the teaching of the basic principles of being, as well as ethics as the fundamentals and principles of behavior.

THE EMANCIPATION OF INDIVIDUAL SCIENCES FROM PHILOSOPHY

The relation between philosophy and the individual sciences only became a problem in modern times. Beyond the emancipation of philosophy itself, together with the individual sciences, from the tutelage of theology—one thinks of Giordano Bruno or Galileo—it is easy to overlook another process of emancipation that was concealed within it: the independence of the individual sciences from philosophy. The battle against the prevalence of Aristotelianism in scholarly activity was only the historically conditioned first stage beyond which the path led to emancipation from philosophy as such. Instead of being anchored in a speculative knowledge that moved toward what is ultimate and total, the circumscribed experience, which, however, was opened to further discoveries, became the methodological principle. Initially, and in an epoch-making way, this was true in the natural sciences, but *mutatis mutandis* it was also the case in the historical sciences concentrating on what is specifically human. The intensive philosophical endeavors of the modern period, which displace one another with increasing acceleration, are largely determined by the attempt to bring the philosophical question to bear vis-à-vis the emancipated sciences. This question has to do not with individual beings but with being as such and in totality. This has happened and happens in the form of a two-track system that speculatively supplements the procedures of the empirical sciences, placing alongside the natural sciences a philosophy of nature, alongside historiography a philosophy of history, alongside jurisprudence a philosophy of justice, alongside experimental psychology a philosophical psychology, alongside linguistics a philosophy of language. However, it is a thorny problem whether or in what way the one can be of significance for the other; how can the philosophical endeavor further the empirical, and the empirical be found in the philosophical consideration? The principal trend seems to move more and more toward things that once seemed to fall within the responsibility of philosophy becoming a part of the field of competence of an individual science. Ethics and even logic have also become specialized in this way. The question of metaphysics forms the core of this relationship between philosophy and science, which has fallen into a crisis. Is metaphysics, as this was predominantly still represented in the great philosophical systems of the eighteenth and early nineteenth centuries, to be developed in a modernized form into a fundamental doctrine of science [scholarship]? Or has it come to its end because its statements are designated as meaningless when measured by a strict criterion of meaning? Or, paradoxically, has it only now become virulent in a dubious way as the unpenetrated background of the modern technical mode of thought?

THE PROBLEM OF THE SCIENTIFIC CHARACTER OF PHILOSOPHY

For philosophy, its relationship to science has become the question of its fate. It knows itself at least potentially to be held accountable for including all perceptions of reality. Therefore, it may not take shelter behind a humanistic residue, for example, by leaving the natural sciences out of consideration. Apart from the educational mastery of such a task, it gives particular pause for thought that philosophy seems to forfeit its right to exist if, for its part, it does not become relevant for the sciences. The tendencies in the face of these difficulties are diametrically opposed. Either philosophy from within itself abandons the claim to be a science, and contents itself with the supplemental role of a teaching about the view of the world, which assimilates the traditional fundamental problems of philosophy, particularly the problems of the meaningful whole and of transcendence—or philosophy is reduced to the theory of science and the analysis of language, whereby it pays the price for its own scientific character through the sacrifice of critically questioning the dominant understanding of science. In this way it is threatened with the loss of its connection with its own history of thought. Of course, it in fact may be precisely through the pluralism of thought, which appears philosophically so questionable, that the opportunity is offered for countermovements to arise against the one-sidedness, narrowness, and atrophy of the philosophical thematic—countermovements that would be related in a more comprehensive way to the fundamental problems as they break open within the individual sciences themselves. However, a person should have no illusions about the fact that for the foreseeable future the situation of philosophy will be extremely difficult and contested.

THE USE OF PHILOSOPHY IN THEOLOGY

The situation sketched makes the involvement of the theologian with philosophy, seen as a whole, extraordinarily difficult. Of course, common threats have come into view in relation to history and science. This could result in an approach to one another through the awareness of tasks that tie them together, and in fact this has partially taken place. Such developments should not be dismissed as purely tactical. The predominant tendency of contemporary philosophy certainly points instead to an intensification of the contrast to the point of alienation, which impairs the possibility of a conversation, if it does not make it altogether hopeless. However, a person must be clear about the fact that within contemporary philosophy there are also massive dead ends in understanding that are intensified through pluralism and specialization. This is even more true for the theologian, who can be a professional philosopher in the strict sense in the rarest cases. In spite of all that, theology would be poorly advised if it were to neglect or completely abandon its previous partnership with philosophy in favor of phenomena of immediate interest. The difficulties indicated, which appear in philosophy, are symptoms of the situation, which theology avoids to its own harm.

A PHILOSOPHIZING INVOLVEMENT WITH PHILOSOPHY

In a certain way a theologian must also be a philosopher. One cannot be satisfied with mere memorization or imitative adoption. Blind dependence on a particular philosophy is scarcely the result of a basic study of philosophy. It is rather a sign of the opposite. In any case, being involved with philosophy should preserve the theologian from a harmful and uncontrolled dependence. For that reason the theologian should also remain free from an approach that is antithetic in principle and that is not prepared to enter into philosophical thought. Precisely when a critical discussion with philosophy is involved, what is required is primarily an inner-philosophical critique. It is urgent to warn against hastily bringing the subject matter of theology to bear against philosophy, rather than patiently participating in wrestling with the reasonableness of reason. If a person takes into account the difficulties mentioned as they grow out of the contemporary situation for the theologian's engagement with philosophy, then what is always to be recommended most strongly is that one give priority to an absorption in classical texts. This suggestion is not intended to prejudice the pertinent task of a curriculum reform. It is, however, the way in which a person can acquire the ability to enter into discussion with other types of philosophy as quickly as possible, and in particular it is the way in which a person can avoid being left in the lurch when it is necessary to maintain a sober capacity for judgment in a new and confusing state of the problem.

DISCIPLINING THOUGHT

If a person attempts to state in a formula the function that engagement with philosophy has for theology, the viewpoint of a purely formal and instrumental use of philosophical reason is without a doubt insufficient. Certainly, if theology takes seriously the task of reflective thought, importance must be given to the unavoidable disciplining of thought. Above all this includes a careful treatment of language, the formation of concepts, and the connection of ideas, as well as a self-critical awareness of method. Yet the formal and material aspects of thought are very closely interwoven. The thought of the theologian must be disciplined precisely with regard to the fact that one is concerned about the accuracy of the theologian's aim in the encounter with the generally reasonable awareness of the truth. The conception of a generally valid philosophical substructure for theology that is to be thereby probed, also, certainly, contains a correct viewpoint. However, it simplifies the problem of the possibility of understanding when dealing with questions of ultimate importance in an inadmissible way, and it masks the controversy with regard to these questions that must never be eliminated. Nevertheless, if one is to give a reasonable account of faith in conversation with the voices of doubt and unbelief, which also make themselves heard within the theologian, one cannot avoid making strict use of reason, which does not authorize either its surrender to unbelief or its confusion with faith. For precisely that in which faith and reason *toto coelo* differ from one another must be made clear in the first place. In both respects, therefore, the use of philosophy in theology always includes an element that is critical of theology in the discussion with what is commonly assumed.

CONFRONTATION WITH THE SPIRIT OF THE TIME

Hegel defined philosophy as "its time grasped in thought."[5] If this definition is followed, theology must be exposed to the confrontation with reality in its most distinctively pronounced interpretation in order to provide space for *fides quaerens intellectum*, if necessary even under the most contradictory circumstances. If philosophy in its factual manifestation does not suffice for this task, theology cannot dispense with its joint responsibility in this respect. If, however, philosophy in its factual manifestation represents its time in a way that is all too hasty and lacking in distance, then it is all the more the case that theology cannot avoid falling into conflict with that philosophically as well. This would be the case whether the human understanding directed to the question of God is considered in a distorted way or is concealed and left to forgetfulness. As long as philosophy remains in contact with its own origin—in any case without this it would give up its character as philosophy—theology retains its partner. To be in conversation with philosophy in one way or another must serve to further truth.

5. *Jub. Ausg.*, 7:35.

6

Church History

THE DIFFICULTY VIS-À-VIS CHURCH HISTORY

It is obvious that nearly two thousand years of church history—a historical complex of singular breadth and many layers—must be the object of scholarly investigation and presentation. The theological necessity of this field alongside the biblical and systematic-practical disciplines is not immediately obvious. A deep embarrassment in the face of the church's history itself is betrayed in the theological embarrassment vis-à-vis the department of church history. The fact that ordinarily among theologians the church historian most easily enjoys a general reputation and that, at times, those who cannot manage theology seek a neutral refuge in this field seems to fit into this picture.

Certainly, the initial difficulties that burden the relationship to church history are predominantly external. The immense quantity of material is discouraging. One's own study of the sources and the consideration of the most recent status of the investigation does not bring one far. Even the professional church historians capitulate more and more before the exacting demand to be responsible for the whole course of church history and limit themselves to a segment of it. It is understandable that the student is inclined toward resignation from the beginning and seeks aid through a mere compendium. The more dry and more inflexible the material becomes, reduced to names, dates, and facts, the more tiring and hopeless the attempt to appropriate it becomes. The discomfort is intensified because of an antihistorical attitude that couples direct interest in the present with practical usability as an optical filter. The result is that one scarcely finds anything to be important and at best only allows one's

67

prejudices to be confirmed. To the degree to which the historical contours become blurred, there spreads the wearisome impression that everything is fundamentally alike and correspondingly indifferent. Goethe's verses then speak from the heart:

"Say, what does church history contain?
For me it comes to nothing in thought;
There is infinitely much to read,
What then has happened in it all?"
There are two opponents that box,
The Arians and the Orthodox.
Through many layers the same thing is heaped up,
It lasts until the final judgment.[1]

Goethe's other dictum is also assimilated with little difficulty: "The whole of church history is a mishmash of error and power."[2] Church history as a history of scandal becomes a favorite arsenal for a critique of the church and of Christianity, which speculates on the basis of historical ignorance in a double respect: it is amazed by presumed revelations and thereby at the same time it is masked by the tendentious treatment of the material. Such pamphlets require intensive study of church history whether one wills to do so or not.

However, this is opposed by many theological hindrances. Particular areas and aspects of church history are withdrawn from critical judgment in accord with one's ecclesiastical standpoint. Or one may perceive the entirety of church history with few exceptions as a history of a fall from the original purity and unity of the church. Of course, that can awaken polemical interest. Yet the view of this deformation does not quiet the desire for a norm. It is only strengthened by the fundamental suspicion that entanglement with the world impairs what is essentially Christian. Christianity's involvement with history appears unavoidably to be a source of secularization.

That poses a central theological problem for the question of church history. The various interpretations of church history correspond to typical possibilities for a fundamental understanding of Christianity, which are expressed in the history of the conceptions of church history. Therefore, reflection on the understanding of church history necessarily gets into its own movement.

1. Saying no. 176, in *Goethes Werke* (Hamburg edition) vol. 1, ed. E. Trunz, 9th ed. (Hamburg: Klegner, 1969), pp. 333–34.
2. Saying no. 178, in ibid., p. 334.

THE CONFESSIONAL CONCEPTION OF CHURCH HISTORY

The designation "confessional" is meant in a broad sense here. It is not, as is customary, limited to confessional churches as they have existed since the sixteenth century. While it includes this meaning, it is extended to include those conceptions that confess Christianity with an anticonfessional tendency and in their own way express this with regard to church history in an equally confessional manner.

THE CLASSICAL CATHOLIC CONCEPTION OF CHURCH HISTORY

Eusebius of Caesarea wrote the famous *Ecclesiastical History* at the time of the change that took place with Constantine. The deep upheaval in church history at that time provoked him to do so, and its outlines appear in the various stages in the development of the work. Apart from Luke's Acts this was the first undertaking of the sort. Until the end of the Middle Ages it remained the definitive presentation of the first three centuries, which was merely excerpted by later historiographers and supplemented for the later centuries, and Eusebius also pointed the way for that. While living under the conditions of the early Catholic church, he created the classical type of the Catholic conception of church history as a whole. Three basic features will be briefly accented.

Continuation of the Incarnation

In continuation of the incarnation, the church is a supernatural reality in the world and history. Its continuity is identifiable and is secured through apostolic succession. One principal concern is, therefore, to present the corresponding evidence for the great episcopal sees.

Washed Round About by Historical Change

As much as the church actually exists in history, in its essence it still is withdrawn from and stands above all historical change. It is not subject to change either as an institution or with regard to its dogma. What can be related about the church historically is solely related to the processes that take place around it and that intrude upon it from outside: the persecution withstood by the martyrs and the heresies, which were innovations against which the church teachers brought the ancient unchangeable truth to bear.

Eschatological Battlefield

Human actions do not finally determine the history round about the church. Rather, it is the scene of a battle between divine and satanic powers. Therefore, a nuanced assessment cannot be expected. Also, there can be no doubt about the outcome of history. The victory of the church under Constantine attained eschatological dignity and made visible the goal of church history in general.

Two things should not be forgotten in this characterization of what is typical: the high historical quality of Eusebius's work in spite of everything, as well as a modification of precisely what is typical in the development toward the Roman Catholic understanding of church history. In this modification the Papacy ultimately guaranteed ecclesiastical identity. Also, the concept of tradition assimilated the idea of development. With these qualifications the fundamental stucture, nevertheless, essentially remained the same.

The Classical Protestant Conception of Church History

The contrast between the Reformation and the Roman Catholic church necessarily also extended to the way church history was understood. The dogmatic claim of the papal church implied a historical assertion. As an institution its substance as founded by Jesus Christ himself extended back in unbroken continuity to Peter. Initially that required exegetical discussion of Matthew 16. Nevertheless, since the Papacy was declared to be anti-Christian, the battle against it also required argumentation from church history. When did this universal claim to primacy arise and through what did the falsification of church doctrine take place? Therefore, on the occasion of the Leipzig Disputation, Luther saw himself impelled to study church history. The large-scale "Magdeburg Centuries" was written at the high point of the confessional debates. This product of teamwork, inspired and directed by the Lutheran Matthias Flacius Illyricus, arranged the expanded material according to centuries. Again I shall limit myself to the characteristic view of the whole.

Interest Determined by Theological Controversy

The interest in church history was now primarily a critical one, and certainly it was an interest exclusively in the service of and within the boundaries of polemics in the theological controversy. The point was to demonstrate the deep cleft between the origin and the further history of the church. The essence of church history had therefore been reversed into the domain of the Antichrist. Thus the evaluative judgment was antithetic to the previous picture of church history.

The Succession of Deformation and Reformation

Seen as a whole, church history was presented as a history of fall, initially from the perfection of its origin and then anew from the Reformation. After the Egyptian darkness the light of the gospel emerged again in the Reformation. Nevertheless, it did not long remain unclouded and unfalsified as debates within Protestantism demonstrated. In view of the principal subject matter, there is as little historical development in this picture as in the early Catholic conception.

Dualistic Understanding of History

Thus the fundamental structure was no less dualistic than in Eusebius's picture of church history. Also, according to the classical Protestant conception God and Satan, Christ and Antichrist battle one another in church history. This situation was even intensified by the fact that while the continuity of church history was certainly not abandoned, it was understood as deeply hidden. Apart from baptism it was still only represented by the invisible chain of *testes veritatis* (true witnesses), the representation of pure doctrine.

THE PIETISTIC CONCEPTION OF CHURCH

With regard to its understanding of church history, Pietism set itself— *cum grano salis* (with a grain of salt)—equally in contrast to both the Catholic and the classical Protestant conception. The epoch-making work of Gottfried Arnold bore the programmatic title *An Unbiased History of Churches and Heresy from the Beginning of the New Testament until 1688 (Unparteiische Kirchen- und Ketzerhistorie von Anfang des Neuen Testaments bis 1688)*. It understood "unbiased" as "unconfessional" in the sense of being obligated only to Christ and not to one of the two great ecclesiastical parties. Of course, the understanding and execution of this intention is in its own way equally confessional and no less biased.

History of Decadence

Here also church history is judged as a false development from the viewpoint of a fall from the truth, but this takes place even more broadly than in the classical Protestant conception. Certainly the early Christian period of the first two centuries continued to stand in a radiant light. But a change for the worse set in very soon, indeed, much earlier than in the judgment of the Reformation. Irrespective of what a person owed the

Reformation, it was also evaluated critically, for example, with regard to Luther's later quarrelsomeness and his later retrogression behind certain initial positions, or with regard to Melanchthon's reintroduction of philosophy into theology.

Secularization of Christianity

The cause of the false development lay not in heretical doctrinal deviations or in the misuse and perversion of ecclesiastical institutions but in the dogmatism of formulated pure doctrine as well as in the institution of an official church. Both were symptoms of a secularization that had its most pernicious expression in the shift that took place with Constantine. The true church existed only among the born again. True Christianity does not consist in dogmas and institutions but in living personal piety.

Spiritualistic Leveling of Church History

This living Christianity forms a unity that cuts across ecclesiastical fronts and requires no demonstrable continuity. With provocative one-sidedness Arnold emphasized that it is especially found among the so-called heretics who were suppressed by the official churches. The essential element of church history was removed from history to the sphere of the subjective and spiritual. Interest in the great ecclesiastical and dogmatic debates was entirely lost in favor of a monotonous critique of every historical shaping of Christianity. Church history did not have the movement of a drama, but to a certain degree its activity was a constant running in place. Arnold himself formulated it this way: "There are different people but only one and the same show."[3] Goethe's statements cited at the beginning of the chapter arose under the impact of this picture of church history.

THE IDEALISTIC CONCEPTION OF CHURCH HISTORY

The idealistic conception impressively represented by Ferdinand Christian Baur is the final type to be mentioned. The inclusion of this as a confessional consideration of church history appears particularly problematic, since in his philosophically influenced view equal justice should be done to all phenomena. Yet its characterization as confessional is quite correct in a new sense. In a way different from classical Protestantism but

3. Gottfried Arnold, *Unpartheyische Kirchen- und Ketzer-Historien* . . . (1699; 1740), 1:359.

still in agreement with it, it is an emphatically Protestant conception for which the key to the total understanding of church history lies in the Reformation.

Necessary Total Development

In distinction from the rigid pictures of history in which finished and unchangeable entities, namely, the church, pure doctrine, or piety, are only raged round about by the waves of time, Baur wanted to grasp the essence of the history of the church itself in and as movement. Instead of merely gathering detailed material and furnishing pragmatic explanations for limited processes, the interconnected character of the whole now was to be grasped as essentially necessary.

The Self-movement of the Idea of the Church

In dependence on Hegel, Baur understood the movement of history to arise from the distinction between idea and appearance. The idea conceived as self-realizing is the mover in historical change. Even what seems perverted has a meaningful function as a necessary transitional stage. Also, what is to be greeted as true must be relativized to the conditions of its development. In the case of church history the moving force is the idea of the church itself. This in turn is nothing other than the Christological idea of the unity of God and humankind.

Periodization

For Baur, the periodization of the whole of church history results from the subject matter of Christianity, and as a result he was the first to reflect fundamentally on the epochs of ecclesiastical historiography. In contrast to pietistic subjectivism, the principal forms in which the idea of the church realizes itself are dogma and system as forms of the objective spirit. The essential content of the first six centuries of church history was the formation of the Christological dogma, while the Middle Ages concentrated on the formation of the Papacy. Nevertheless, it was necessary for this realization of the idea to again be dissolved and to be translated into the spiritual realm because too much was transferred into the material realm. The decisive change took place in the Reformation. Proceeding from it, this destruction and rebuilding again took place in two periods: initially in relation to the condition of the church and then beginning in the eighteenth century also in relation to dogma. In the freedom of the subject and the autonomy of the state—that sounds foreign to us—the

Christian idea comes to true realization. Similarly to Eusebius, the present became the eschatological goal of church history. "From the standpoint of the Protestant Principle, man can know himself to be one with God and therefore certain of his salvation only when he is aware also of being free in himself, and sees himself placed in the state in the sphere of an existence free from the absolutism of the church."[4]

CHURCH HISTORY AND GENERAL HISTORICAL STUDY

To the extent that theology is a scholarly field, in each of its disciplines it stands in close proximity to other scholarly fields. As a consequence the methodological similarity shared between them comes into tension with that which constitutes the specific character of a theological discipline. Understandably this conflict becomes particularly explosive in those divisions that are accorded a normative function for theology, no matter how this is understood, namely, the biblical and the systematic-practical fields. Here the competition with so-called secular fields—the study of antiquity carried out with the historical-critical method and the history of religions, as well as philosophy and the humanities—is most sensitively registered. On the other side, the problem is easily concealed by the fact that those disciplines already seem to include an uncontested reserve of theology simply by virtue of their material. However, this is different in the case of church history. Purely in terms of the material, there is such a close connection with general historical study that the conception of the sole competence of theology cannot even come up. In addition, in particular cases it is precisely theological motives that further a critical investigation of church history, as became clear in the Reformation and Pietism. The earliest signal of alarm was the demonstration by the humanist Lorenzo Valla that the Donation of Constantine involved a falsification of history that had had an uncommon historical effect. When later the history of dogma, the history of the canon, and even the history of the origin of the church were given over to the clutches of historical criticism, this produced uncomfortable problems for Protestant theology also. Nevertheless, in Protestant theology the conception was established as uncontested that church history was to be carried out in the same way as

4. Ferdinand Christian Baur, "The Epochs of Church Historiography," in *Ferdinand Christian Baur on the Writing of Church History*, ed. and trans. Peter C. Hodgson (New York: Oxford University Press, 1968), p. 250.

historical study in general. That aggravated the question about the theological significance of church history.

METHODOLOGICAL UNITY

The concept of secular history has become invalid to the extent that it is understood as the cautious self-limitation of a historical study that concedes to sacred history a methodologically special treatment for the sake of its particular mode of being. The history of the church itself is now subject without limitation, so to speak, to secular historical consideration. As a simplification one could say it is subject to a treatment according to the rules of a healthy human understanding. Formulated with Ernst Troeltsch, this is according to the fundamentals of criticism, analogy, and correlation.[5] That means that there are no authoritative prejudgments, no exceptions in principle, and no limitations of historical interaction. Of course, a person must be clear that this one historical method can be extraordinarily differentiated in its adaptation to the situation and that as its consequence we became aware for the first time of the problems of involvement with history. Through coordination with historical study in general, all the problems that open up in our relation to history in general became virulent for church history: the meaning and limits of the demand to be without presuppositions and to be objective, the significance and unavoidable character of subjective interest, the inexhaustible character of historical interpretation, the ambiguity of the genuine moving force of history, the question of the peculiarity of specific historical contexts as well as of the relation between the perceptible fragment and the hidden whole, and whatever further problems there may be of this sort with regard to hermeneutics and the philosophy of history.

THE DISTINCTIVENESS OF THE OBJECT

The adaptation to general historical study does not contradict being concerned to grasp the distinctiveness of church history through an appropriate definition of its object of study. Every area of historical study requires a corresponding consideration. Of course, a person should not hastily use the distinction between "general" and "special." The decisive aspects for that distinction overlap. Every consideration of history treats a segment of it. Even what is called general history is determined by the

5. Ernst Troeltsch, "Über historische und dogmatische Methode in der Theologie," in *Gesammelte Schriften*, vol. 2, pt. 2 (Tübingen: J. C. B. Mohr, 1922; Neudruck: Scientia Aaalen, 1962), pp. 729–53, esp. p. 731.

preference for a partial aspect (ordinarily the political). There is no absolute schema for dividing the whole of history into partial areas. Church history is characterized not only by its chronological and global extent but above all by an unusual integration of every imaginable dimension of historical reality. It presents an incomparable historical cosmos in which a principle inheres that presses toward universality in a way that is otherwise never encountered in history.

The material of church history covers a broad area in which the most diverse historical interests—political or cultural, intellectual or economic —intersect with the theological interest. But this does not yet define the specific perspective that constitutes church history as such. The obvious difficulty in orientation offered by the concept of the church is, on the one hand, correctly taken into account by the expression "history of Christendom." On the other hand, this difficulty is hastily avoided if this means that the aspect of socialization is not dealt with adequately. Nevertheless, in both versions the basic situation remains the same. The historical diversity and controversy within the church or with regard to what is Christian in general have a common point of reference in the living relation to Jesus Christ as the origin of the church and the ground of faith. The specific approach of church history is indicated in this historical concentricity and the historical eccentricity based upon it. That is learned from the subject matter itself as a result of historical study. It is not an arbitrarily imported dogmatic assertion. In the midst of all the partial aspects under which church history may be considered, this general description provides the decisive theological viewpoint that must determine the perspective if the basic theme of church history is to be maintained, especially in the history of dogma and theology (whose demarcation vis-à-vis one another requires special discussion) or the study of confessions and ecumenics. If what is shown to be constitutive for the whole is maintained, then in church history it is not at all, or even primarily, theology that is theologically significant.

The Turning Points of Church History

One's total understanding of church history must stand the test of the consideration of the decisive turning points. With regard to the beginning of church history, it is unavoidable that the church historian overstep the boundary with the study of the New Testament and consider such questions as whether Jesus founded the church, how the transition took place from the preaching Jesus to the preached Christ, and what is to be thought of Loisy's paradox: "Jesus foretold the kingdom, and it was the church that came.'"⁶ Other principal turning points are the emergence of the Catholic church, the Reformation, and the entry of Christianity into the modern period. This results in two large periods, each involving epochs of expansion and transitional phases. They can be distinguished as the Christianized and the secularized time. The physiognomy of both periods is determined by a difference in the situation that involves the relationship of Christian faith to the environment and the latter to Christian faith, thus involving the polarity of concentricity and eccentricity. Of course, the fact that primitive Christianity and the Reformation do not fit into this schema warns us against a one-sided emphasis on such a twofold division and provides a reason for critical questions. Does the Catholic and Constantinian era lie in a legitimate continuation of primitive Christianity or is there a contradiction? Is the significance of the Reformation exhausted in forming the transition from the Middle Ages to modern times, or does it establish the validity of something that transcends both periods of history?

CHURCH HISTORY AS A THEOLOGICAL DISCIPLINE

It appears to me to be decisive for understanding church history as a theological discipline that this is made possible neither by some additional aspect nor by a selective procedure, and thus in one way or another by a dogmatic principle that is not mediated historically. Rather, the understanding of church history as a theological discipline results from the way its fundamental structure and the unlimited fullness of its manifestations are related to one another in the circumstances of church history.

THE HERMENEUTICAL ASPECT

What I have designated as the polarity of concentricity and eccentricity in view of the unity of the reference to Christ and the reference to the world can be called the basic structure of church history. This is a hermeneutical situation. How origin and continuation, unity and multiplicity, identity and change are related to one another can be conceived and considered most appropriately under the category of exegesis. A person should not misunderstand that, as is frequently the case when the formula "church history as a history of the exegesis of the New Testament scripture" is critiqued as though this declared Christianity to be a book religion and in

6. Alfred Loisy, *The Gospel and the Church*, trans. Christopher Home (London: Isbister, 1903; Philadelphia: Fortress Press, 1976), p. 166.

an extreme way reduced the living fullness of church history to a sterile process of scriptural erudition. If the association of text-related proclamation is evoked by the category of exegesis, this is done only to make one aware of the specific mode of the church's historicity in this model, which is certainly essential for the existence of the church in history. This involves the necessity, inherent in the peculiarity of Christian faith, of tackling constantly new historical situations in the power of its orientation to its ground and at the same time of calling forth a—broadly understood—linguistically creative event that preserves its identity only in continuing historical responsibility, the tradition only in a living process of transmission, and, so to speak, the text only in ever-new verifications in the context. The fact that nontheological factors play a role in church history to such a high degree is, therefore, theologically most important. Certainly that poses the question of whether "entering into" does not perhaps become "being lost in." The hermeneutical aspect does not suppress this question, but precisely keeps it awake.

THE ASPECT OF EXPERIENCE

Nothing would affect the theological significance of church history more detrimentally than if a person sought to master it systematically instead of benefiting from the enormous influx of experience. This is centrally true of the phenomenon of the church itself. What the church is cannot be derived from abstract doctrinal statements about it to the extent that these are not mediated by a historical perception of the church and are exposed to critical examination from that perspective. Church history is full of experience, whether a person remains with what is biographical or institutional, with liturgical forms or individual piety, with the riches of language or the deeds of love that speak for themselves as well as the suffering that bears witness to hope, with the proclaimed and lived faith but also the faith that is falsified, silenced, and weak because it has become far removed from life. Even if a person devoted a whole lifetime to the study of church history the whole could not be exhausted. However, what finally matters here is not completeness but the openness and devotion with which the individual and the concrete is perceived. The readiness for assimilation necessary for that grows to the degree that a person is moved to relate faith to experience and thus to let it take effect in life.

THE ASPECT OF TRUTH

The way in which the certainty of received truth is connected with constant questioning in search of truth is very impressively presented in church history. In this process, which does not cease as long as life and history endure, one certainly finds both the suppression of the truth, for which church history offers frightening examples, and the shining of truth with an illuminating power across the centuries. In relatively rare situations in which the question of truth is most extremely concentrated, from case to case the basic questions of faith are formulated with a precision and answered in such a decisive way that the following generations cannot get past it. That can be illustrated in the emergence of the dogma of the ancient church and in the basic perception of the Reformation. We would forfeit what is necessary for our own theological thought if the presence of such events did not provide a depth, set standards, and challenge and encourage us to our own theological responsibility. Certainly a person cannot speak of an increase in the truth of Christian faith in church history, but one can speak of an increase of knowledge in engagement with the truth of faith. To participate in that is essential for the contemporary theologian in two respects: one should become aware of the limitedness and relativity of one's own theological attempts at knowledge, and thus one should manage the claim of truth exactingly against oneself and modestly toward others. This experience of one's own historical conditionedness and limitedness through the occurrence of an enormous expansion of one's horizon should be merged into an openness for dialogue and an awareness of one's own theological responsibility. Engagement with church history helps a person do this. It is not only the most comprehensive theological discipline, but through its orientation to the interpenetration of truth and history it is particularly suited to adhere to a theologically disciplined engagement with all theological disciplines.

7

Natural Sciences and Humanities

THE PLACE OF THEOLOGY AT THE UNIVERSITY

The customary but strongly contested category "natural sciences and humanities" does not apply to an individual discipline or a particular complex of sciences but indicates the total spectrum of sciences [scholarly fields]. That calls our attention to the problems in understanding scholarship in general, as it exists quite apart from theology, as well as to the question of the place of theology in the totality of scholarly fields. Since according to the idea, the university represents this totality, the relation of theology to the total scholarly context takes concrete shape primarily in its institutional pratication in the university. Nevertheless, two fundamentally different aspects should be distinguished in this matter.

SEEN FROM THE PERSPECTIVE OF THEOLOGY

A general characterization of the attitude of theology toward the total phenomenon of scholarship scarcely seems possible because this attitude is influenced to such a large degree by cultural and institutional conditions and is subject to historical change. At any rate, such a characterization should not consist in a mere assertion of principle but must reflect the historical factors that have led to contradictory solutions. Of course, one should at least specify the necessary direction along which theology must move in order to give account of its relation to scholarship as a whole if this is to be the subject matter of theology.

Openness to All Scholarly Fields

All too often the church and theology have closed themselves to the progress of scholarly knowledge and have suppressed the truth until the artificial dam bursts again and the stream of true insight can no longer

81

be stopped. This process, of course, simultaneously has constantly been reflected as discussion within theology and the church with the roles people play changing with time. For that reason it seems difficult to justify the assertion that theology is fundamentally open to all scholarly fields. Nevertheless, it is necessary to consider the following principal viewpoints for an assessment of the factual course of events that is historically adequate to the subject.

One thing to be considered is that the cultural relationships of Christianity in each case present a most complex alloy of specifically Christian impulses and general cultural and historical factors. A correspondingly differentiated approach, which takes account of the importance of factors deriving from other sources and of the play of forces embodied in Christianity, is especially difficult for phenomena within the era of Christianity's political and cultural predominance. The fact that what is Christian is interwoven with the general conditions of a time and that they mutually stamp one another calls for caution with regard to what is credited to or charged against Christianity in a particular case. The more deeply Christianity enters into the time in which it lives, the more it shares its own historical responsibility with all the contemporary historical powers.

Second, with respect to all cultural activity a distinction that has particular importance for the relationship of theology to scholarship should be noted. The individual living act of producing something must be considered in its relation to the whole of life. That becomes particularly acute in the motivation to and the reception of cultural achievements. Since faith primarily involves a person's orientation to life as a whole, its relationship to scholarship lies principally in its influence on the impulse toward scholarship and in the processing of its results. Although the freedom for soberly perceiving and investigating created reality has its source in Christian faith, Christianity's genuine interest does not lie in that. Therefore its characteristic influence also does not consist in releasing a passionate drive toward scientific investigation. Certainly that sort of influence is not excluded under particular circumstances. The decisive contribution, however, is that Christian faith resists an unrestrained and reckless independence of scientific activity vis-à-vis the totality of life. In contrast, the principal accent is reversed with regard to the acceptance of what is disclosed by science. Although Christian faith shows that the misunderstanding and misuse of freedom in the sense of a boundless and unrestrained use of the power of knowledge is hostile to life, it is interested without qualification not in asserting its certainty by suppressing what contradicts it but in maintaining itself by processing every uncomfortable perception of the truth.

If one takes account of these discriminating suggestions, then, without suppressing the facts that seem to speak against it, one can say the following about Christian faith: because Christian faith knows itself finally to be decisively concerned with the truth and bound to the truth, confrontation and agreement with the total awareness of truth belongs unalterably to its living character. The inner necessity of theology as a responsible accounting for the truth of Christian faith is based on this, so that theology as such already implies openness to a comprehensive concern for the truth. Meeting and communicating with all scholarly fields must be affirmed by theology as things that fundamentally belong to its own constitution. How this affirmation in principle is to be practiced appropriately is an issue that must ever be struggled with anew in the history of theology.

Freedom in Institutional Perspective

Belonging to the university offers the possibility of a universal encounter with other scholarly fields. However, it does not guarantee that corresponding use will be made of this opportunity. The beneficial effects of coexistence in the association of the university include above all the public character of the teaching arrangements, a certain external control of the call procedures, the comparable character of examination requirements, the personal contact between teachers and students across disciplines, the accessibility of the most diverse scholarly facilities, the opportunity for interdisciplinary organization, participation in general responsibility of university politics and scholarly organization, as well as other things. This results in an influence that is not to be underestimated, even though, as is usually the case, communication lags far behind what is desirable and the possibility is not excluded that in this environment, in spite of everything, theology may still lead a ghetto existence.

On the other side, organizational disassociation from the university and the establishment of one's own centers of teaching and research is not a compelling reason for altering in the least the characterized engagement of theology with the totality of scholarly fields in principle. Theology does not attend to the other scholarly fields only because and as long as it is represented at the university. Rather, if theology understands itself correctly, it does this on its own initiative and can do nothing other than fundamentally affirm its existence at the university. Whether theology can remain there depends on theology itself only insofar as there is a corresponding readiness to accept the challenges from there in free discussion. For its own part, there is no sound basis for theology to initiate a retreat from the university as long as its independence and its specific task are not hindered by organizational measures, and the freedom for conversation with other scholarly fields is not impaired by ideological conditions in a way that amounts to the demand for self-abandonment. Experience shows that when this critical boundary is reached, and whether in a given case it has already been overstepped, it is contested at a particular time within theology itself. This is due to the wide latitude inherent in the question of evaluation involved, but it is also due to fundamental theological conceptions and not the least to pseudotheological self-deceptions.

SEEN FROM THE PERSPECTIVE OF THE UNIVERSITY

Quite apart from the way the situation is evaluated from the side of theology, those conceptions and powers that are authoritative for shaping the university at a given time can determine whether or not theology remains at the university.

The Structural Change in the University

The university is a creation of medieval Europe at the turn from the twelfth to the thirteenth century. Since the sixteenth century it has been transplanted to other parts of the world and to other cultures. Originally, then, it was a Christian institution that was relatively autonomous and was governed by the cooperation of spiritual and worldly authorities. Its heart was formed by the theological faculty. Alongside theology, jurisprudence and medicine together with the faculty of arts—the forerunner of the later philosophical faculty—which was arranged before the higher faculties as a lower stage, led their own existence. Nevertheless, together they formed a spiritual unity. This by no means was solely a result of the general regulative function of ecclesiastical doctrine, the predominant segment of the spiritual profession among the teaching staff, and the religious ordering of life that permeated everything. The common bond was above all the Scholastic understanding of scholarship in its tradition-bound orientation to the harmonized authority of Christian and Greco-Roman antiquity.

The formal structure of the university, as it still can be perceived in the neohumanistic conception of the university in the shape given it by Humboldt, has persisted with astonishing continuity through deep changes in the understanding of scholarship and in social relationships. To be sure, apart from the legal consequences of secularism, the relationship of the faculties to one another changed. The former primacy of theology was reduced to a decorative honorary advantage or was completely lost, while the philosophical faculty experienced an increase in rank but also a division as a result of the increasing differentiation of the scholarly fields. The establishment of academies and other scholarly institutions, a development already begun in the eighteenth century, reduced the previous special position of the universities because in various respects the latter did not show themselves equal to the new demands. Nevertheless, the idea of the university has demonstrated a tenacious hold on life up to the present discussions and experiments in university reform, even though with the changed circumstances problems have arisen whose scope is not yet calculable: how can quality keep pace with the quantity of teachers and students rising by leaps and bounds; how does the connection between teaching and research continue to be realizable under these conditions; what still constitutes the binding unity in the wake of progressive specialization; how does education come to its right beyond training; and in what way can academic freedom be politically guaranteed and its social responsibility be protected against a distortion into an ideological politicizing of scholarship.

The Tendency to Exclude Theology

Both the predominant concept of scholarship as well as strong political tendencies do not appear to allow a favorable prognosis for the persistence of theology at the university in the long run.

Prior to the positivistic understanding of scholarship, the idealistic understanding already, as Fichte's discussions prior to the founding of the university of Berlin show,[1] could deny theology the right to exist at the university or make it dependent on conditions that would mean the end of theology. The arguments in the theory of scholarship that were brought against theology with various nuances reproached it with dogmatic prejudice on one side and deficient exactness on the other. In addition to the second objection, the demand to be without presuppositions compels theology to compare its own specific situation with respect to the problem with those general aspects under which *mutatis mutandis* other scholarly fields are also exposed to analogous objections. The critique drawn from

1. J. G. Fichte, "Deduzierter Plan einer zu Berlin zu errichtenden höheren Lehranstaldt, die in gehöriger Verbindung mit einer Akadamie der Wissenschaften stehe" (1807), sec. 22, in *Idee und Wirklichkeit einer Universität: Dokumente zur Geschichte der Friedrich-Wilhelms-Universität zu Berlin*, ed. Wilhelm Weischedel (Berlin: W. De Gruyter, 1960), pp. 57-58.

the theory of scholarship can only be met through critical participation in the discussion about the understanding of scholarship. An unacceptable compromise solution would bisect theology and claim its historical disciplines as acceptable scholarly fields for the university, while systematic and practical theology would be banned from the university as "ecclesiastical."

The cultural-political viewpoint of the separation of church and state can, radically applied, lead to different consequences. In the United States, for example, where a religiously colored idea of tolerance is authoritative, there can be departments of religion at the state universities, but not theological faculties (divinity schools), while these obviously have the right to exist at private universities, which are mostly denominational in origin. In Communist countries, in contrast, two solutions are encountered: the pushing aside into purely theological academies or seminaries as well as the maintenance of state theological faculties. According to the circumstances, both possibilities offer advantages for ideological and political control, influence, encasement, and choking. Under the conditions of democratic freedom and religious tolerance in countries with traditionally strong ecclesiastical majorities, the maintenance of state theological faculties is justifiable as long as the society places value on furthering Christianity, at least in the form of seeing to it that, in view of the public influence of the churches, the spiritually responsible office-bearers receive a fundamental education that is appropriately related to the present status of scholarship and education. Of course, the practical function of the state theological faculties is connected with the training for ecclesiastical service. As soon as their aptitude for that would be denied from the perspective of the church, they would also become superfluous from the perspective of the state. In contrast, it would overstep the competence of political authorities to use arguments from the theory of scholarship in favor of the abolition of theological faculties. The legal problems of a state church, which derive from the existence of state theological faculties in particular, especially in relation to the question of call, are nevertheless substantial and require a high measure of political tact by all participants, which a democracy does well to exercise.

THE DISTINCTION BETWEEN NATURAL SCIENCES AND HUMANITIES

The need for a fundamental distinction in the area of scholarship is the consequence of the competitive tendencies released by the dissolution of the Aristotelian-Scholastic understanding of scholarship. As strongly as the

common emancipation from theological as well as a particular philosophical predominance cooperated in this dissolution, the open ontological,
epistemological, and methodological problems immediately awakened the
desire to provide security for the various scholarly fields vis-à-vis one
another. Although the natural sciences, seen as a whole, were the decisive
power driving things forward, the interest in a demarcation distinguishing
the disciplines initially had its justification in the theory of scholarship—
one can think of the efforts from Descartes to Kant. It was only after the
breakdown of the idealistic theory of scholarship that the so-called humanities, which had been pressed onto the defensive, sought to establish and
maintain themselves as distinct from the natural sciences.

THE SCIENTIFIC METHOD

The methodological upheaval appears as sharply as possible in the contrast with the Scholastic scholarly procedure. In the latter, all scholarly
fields, including those devoted to natural phenomena, were based on the
accomplishments of antiquity transmitted in written texts. Thus all the
fields consisted primarily of the interpretations of texts. To be sure, a
pervading thread that was oriented to experience also ran through the
Middle Ages. Initially this thread was very weakly developed, but then,
especially in Nominalism, it showed itself to contain pregnant impulses
for the future, at least of a theoretical sort. Nevertheless, in terms of the
history of scholarship, the break in continuity doubtless predominated in
the rise of the modern natural sciences, as is perceptible in the initially
modest, rather obstructive role of the universities in this process. This
became the overture of a development that a person can pursue only with
the greatest suspense and admiration. The characteristic elements that for
the first time, even in comparison with antiquity, permitted the emergence
of the natural sciences in the strict sense shall be merely indicated.

Experience

The absolutely determinative function of sense perception, one's own
observation, and planned experiment is fundamental. This orientation to
experience is not really contradicted by the analytical procedure that moves
back behind the surface view to circumstances that are not accessible to
direct sense perception and that require a highly abstract formation of
theories for their interpretation, which as the case may be can lead into
what is completely nonconcrete. Equipment that is constantly becoming
more complicated serves not only to substantiate but also to expand and
replace sense perception. However, as indirect as that may be, the pro-

cedure always remains primarily subject to control by direct sense experience by means of securing data through measurement.

Mathematization

The decisive step to the mathematization of science is apparent in the significance of the function of measurement. Everything depends first of all on making what seems to elude measurement measurable, thus on discovering and producing the conditions under which it becomes measurable. By reducing everything to quantitative relationships and structures and by grasping it through the language of formulas, the subjectivity of the investigator is eliminated except in the most extreme boundary cases —although it is just this subjectivity in its capacity for rational abstraction that is the condition *sine qua non* of this mode in which "nature" appears. On the other side, the contingent in what is investigated—again except in the most extreme boundary cases—is dissolved into what is generally valid, so that the experiment becomes repeatable and natural events calculable and planable.

Applicability

Due to the possibility of reliable prognoses about what will happen under particular conditions, as well as of an effective intervention in physical, chemical, or biological processes, the connection between the natural sciences and technology is not merely accidental. The pragmatic applicability of scientific knowledge is a motivator of investigation that is constantly becoming more important. Already in the beginnings of modern science, a will to power paired with excessive curiosity was manifest. However, beyond that, the technological resources of power themselves became unavoidable instruments for investigation, which ultimately can only be advanced with an apparatus of complex design. In the wake of these developments the problem of the capability of planning and manipulating humanity and its future is posed. This fact has, certainly, hybrid aspects of the failure to distinguish between what can be done and what is responsible. Soberly considered, this is above all a consequence of the fact that the place of the formerly incalculable character of nature has been taken by the specter of the incalculable character of humanity, whose technology, which is capable of altering the future, places us before the task of mastering its consequences. In this respect, the prognoses for the future that are at least highly probable and the possibility of intervening certainly still diverge in a frightening way.

Success

The natural sciences have altered our world rapidly and have resulted in the threat of catastrophe that derives from the potential for annihilation, for damaging the environment, and perhaps even more for damaging inner personal life. While this certainly overshadows them, it does not reduce the enormous success that the natural sciences can put down to their account, the fascination that derives from them, and the position of great power they enjoy in economics, politics, and society. Compared to that the humanities play the role of Cinderella, in spite of all the contributions they also have to show. Apart from limited procedures their methods lack exactness and, therefore, are subject to a difficult, if not hopeless, situation with regard to understanding. In this field one can talk of continuous progress only to a limited degree. Further, the results largely lack pragmatic usefulness, which feeds the suspicion that this field represents an activity that is a luxury.

THE PROBLEM OF THE DISTINCTION "NATURAL SCIENCES AND HUMANITIES"

The Concept "Humanities"

The English term "humanities"[2] derives from Cicero's treatment of *humanitas* as the education of an orator. In the second century A.D. the grammarian Aulus Gallius identified *humanitas* with the Greek *paideia*, which designated the general liberal education that prepared a man for maturity and citizenship. For the Greek and Roman rhetoricians it designated the basic program of classical education, and it constituted the basic education of the Christian Middle Ages and included mathematics, language, science, history, and philosophy. Its use was revived by the Italian humanists in the fifteenth century, for whom *studia humanitatis,* associated with classical studies and thus eventually especially classical languages, was contrasted with *studia divinitatis*. Since the nineteenth century it has been understood in opposition to the sciences. In nineteenth-century Germany the theory of the humanities was developed, relating it to areas of study that were outside the reach of the natural sciences, although the boundary with the social sciences was not yet marked out. Above all, Wilhelm Dilthey gave the German word *"Geisteswissenschaften"* its particular stamp, with influences from

2. For the English term "humanities" see the article by Otto Allen Bird in *Encyclopaedia Britannica*, 15th ed. (1976), *Macropaedia*, vol. 8, pp. 1179–83. For the German see A. Diemer, "Geisteswissenschaften," *Handwörterbuch der Philosophie* 3 (1974): 211–15.

Schleiermacher, Hegel, and the philosophy of life, expressing the concentration on the human-historical reality of life. Later substitute concepts, like *"Kulturwissenschaften"* (cultural sciences), *"Gesellschaftwissenschaften"* (social sciences), or *"sciences humaines,"* as well as the earlier concept of the "moral" as embracing what is human as such, or Schleiermacher's concept of "ethics" that was oriented to the whole of history, express this concentration on the human-historical reality of life but did not prevail. More recent attempts have also sought to distinguish the humanities from the social sciences.

The Critique of the Distinction

The distinction between the natural sciences and the humanities is laden with problems due to the uncommonly rich and complicated history of the concepts of "nature" and of the human "spirit" [*Geist*] as well as to the multitude of various complementary concepts possible. What serves to justify the distinction can be turned around simultaneously into an objection against it. If one appeals to separate areas of reality, this encounters the suspicion of a dualistic understanding of reality. Whether correctly or not, this reproach has been cast at Plato's understanding of body and soul, Descartes's distinction between *res extensa* and *res cogitans*, or Kant's definition of the relation between nature and freedom. It is understandable that deterrent arguments against the conceptual pairing of "natural sciences and humanities" derived from the long-lasting exclusion of what is human from the possible objects of investigation by the natural sciences, for example, in the opposition to the theory of evolution, or from the effect of the concept of the human spirit in guarding against a full consideration of the corporal and material conditions of historical reality, for instance, in an abstract understanding of the history of the human spirit. However, such objections still continued even when the viewpoint of a dichotomy was limited to two kinds of methodology, as when W. Windelband[3] distinguished between nomothetic and ideographic procedures, or Wilhelm Dilthey[4] between explanation and understanding. One can hardly overlook the ontological question about the basis of the methodological dualism. Also, a strict distribution into different scholarly areas appears to be questionable in view of the difficulties of methodolog-

3. Wilhelm Windelband, "Geschichte und Naturwissenschaft" (1894), in idem, *Präludien*, vol. 2 (Tübingen: J. C. B. Mohr [Paul Siebeck], 6th ed., 1919), pp. 136–60, esp. p. 145.

4. Wilhelm Dilthey, "Ideen über eine beschreibende und zergliedernde Psychologie" (1894), in idem, *Gesammelte Schriften*, vol. 5, 4th ed. (Stuttgart: Teubner; Göttingen: Vandenhoeck & Ruprecht, 1964), pp. 139–240, esp. p. 144.

ical demarcation. This is fully true in view of the possibilities not yet exhausted for expanding mathematical procedures into the previous domains of the humanities through systems analysis, information theory, cybernetics, or structuralism. This is to say nothing of the question of the place of mathematics or of a logic amalgamated with it in that schema of academic fields.

The Enduring Difference

In spite of such objections against tearing asunder what belongs together, the distinguishing aspects cannot be eliminated. Certainly everything that is experienced as real also has a component capable of being investigated by the procedures of the natural sciences. However, solely from this perspective a person will not do justice to the whole of reality, not even in a scientific respect. Once one is freed from the agonizing suggestions posed by the customary terminology "natural sciences and humanities" in order to grasp through observation the differences that contradict a monistic leveling, one encounters such fundamental distinctions as that between the universal and the individual, mechanical connections and connections involving responsibility, measured and experienced time, or the cybernetic function of a code and the human capability of language. The need for making such indications precise summons us to grasp the mutuality and interpenetration together with the difference, and vice versa. Instead of the problematic ideal of a unified scholarship, this suggests a flexible treatment of the methodological question in relation to the subject matter. It also provides an insight into the unavoidable lack of precision in the demarcation of scholarly fields as well as into the need for openness in the concept of scholarship. Nevertheless, a bipolarity remains that does not exclude a large number of points of contact and overlap. To provide a crass and extreme illustration, the so-called natural sciences are historical and as such are the object of study in the humanities. This in turn is a process in the brain and, as such, is an object of study for the natural sciences. As usually happens by necessity, as long as no other more persuasive terminology is found, a person will comply with the customary mode of expression and thus be required to reflect critically about its problems. This should result not in the isolation of disciplines from one another but, on the contrary, in an interdisciplinary opening toward one another, even though it is difficult to take account of the understandably loud contemporary call for such an interdisciplinary openness under the present conditions of scholarly work in a way that is not merely declamatory but understands the subject matter.

THE RELATION OF THEOLOGY TO THE NATURAL SCIENCES AND HUMANITIES

For the sake of its universal features, theology experiences the contemporary difficulties in communication between academic fields in a particularly marked way. This is underscored by the contrast to the situation in high scholasticism in which knowledge could be surveyed and the approaches and modes of conception were broadly compatible. The change by no means rests solely upon the fact that because of its theme theology has moved to the periphery and appears to be a stranger among the academic fields. In a time of scholarly overproduction, pluralism, specialization, and alien technical languages, the difficulties of a general scholarly interchange do not take effect in a less burdensome way for theology. For theology, the contact with other scholarly fields does not merely represent an additional task, which is taken up, for example, by an organization devoted to interdisciplinary conversation or by a double major, to the extent that this is undertaken not as a flight from theology but for the sake of its fruitfulness for theology. The total task of theology is unavoidably carried out in manifold contact with the most diverse scholarly fields. Therefore, the results of information and critical conversation contribute to the advantage of theological work itself, while a broadly scattered extratheological interest without corresponding concentration is not useful for anything at all.

THEOLOGY AND THE HUMANITIES

If, with the reservations presented, a person recognizes some justification for the division into the humanities and the natural sciences, then there can be no doubt that theology belongs to the first group. This neither minimizes theology's relationship to the second nor determines the manner in which theology belongs to the humanities.

Hermeneutical Dimensions

The depth and comprehensiveness with which theology is interwoven into the humanities is clear if a person calls to mind the principal dimension of the hermeneutical problem that methodologically unites all the humanities. It extends to the engagement with history as the constantly open future that coagulates into the past, a past that, beyond direct aftereffects, remains effectively present for the future as a remembered past. Therefore it extends further to engagement with language and responsibility for it. Consequently it finally extends to human existence amid the surging of social reality and individual existence, of creation and destruction, of meaning and meaninglessness, and of negation and affirmation. Theology as such participates in the domain of historical and cultural studies—in the breadth of all imaginable aspects and combinations—together with the corresponding reflection on what is fundamental. Theology cannot be carried out without a sense for history, without a knowledge of languages, and without interest in everything human.

The Question of Truth

Theology's participation in the areas and modes of work of the humanities, however, does not take place either in arbitrary selection or in blind acceptance. In its orientation to the theme defined by the Christian faith, the procedure of theology is, on the one side, exposed to control by corresponding nontheological disciplines (for example, in historical questions) and, on the other side, required to be in conversation with them (for example, with regard to the appropriateness of categories for interpretation). In both modes the question of truth asserts itself. Theology should not be subject to any veiling or self-deception, and it must allow itself to be subject to the claim of truth of its subject matter. In view of what conscientious investigation demonstrates to be correct, theology has to give an account of what is ultimately involved in history, language, and human existence in a way that is appropriate to Christian faith. Thus theology confronts the humanities through concentration on the question of God with the radicality of the question of truth, and thereby it simultaneously demonstrates where the object of theology has its place in the reality of life.

THEOLOGY AND THE NATURAL SCIENCES

The appearance of solidarity between theology and the humanities before the onslaught of the natural sciences corresponds to the situation only to a very limited degree. The genuine conflicts emerge for theology in relation to the humanities, while the relation to the natural sciences is burdened primarily by sham conflicts. It lies in their mutual interest to remove these false conflicts. The battle against the perceptions of the natural sciences on pseudotheological grounds and the defense of untenable positions in a protracted running battle betray a deep-seated theological defect, which bears the principal guilt for producing the inverse foolishness of the pseudoscientific battle with theology. In view of Christianity's interwovenness with culture, one must certainly guard against charging oneself with all the mischief in this *historia calamitatum* in which the decisive role has been played by th   ll too-human spiritual laziness.

Theological Self-Correction

There are questions that enter the theological thematic that have their origin in the natural sciences and that result in freeing theology from commitment to outmoded conceptions as well as to overcoming the false assessment and interpretation of these conceptions as alleged statements of natural science. Such questions touch the whole of dogmatics and in particular affect the doctrines of creation and preservation, miracle, and prayer. The doctrine of God and eschatology are included in that as the essential central themes. Thereby one should not underestimate the effort to rethink and transform the tradition of Christian faith on which generations have already worked. Nor, even more, should one underestimate the enormous benefit that can be expected from a corresponding illumination of what is essential. It is through this illumination that the genuine conflicts with the thought of the time initially can come into view and be settled.

The Common Responsibility

Theology and the natural sciences meet, above all, in two tasks that also require the participation of the other humanities for their accomplishment. Thus, this permits the hope of reattaining a universal interchange. The ontological problem must be tackled in order to restrain breaking our society apart into "two cultures,"[5] which is correctly feared. This requires an understanding of reality that grasps as "different but belonging together" what people customarily repeatedly tear apart by appealing to the formula "natural sciences and humanities" instead of considering them together in their distinctness. For theology this particularly involves a new consideration of the relation between the "book of nature" and talk of God. Second, the theme of ethics, which lies closer at hand, intrudes, since the natural sciences have raised virulent problems that are not their concern alone to solve. Whether theology can offer a contribution to that question depends on whether its competence is different from merely an ethical competence.

5. Charles Percy Snow, *The Two Cultures and the Scientific Revolution* (Cambridge: Cambridge, 1959).

8

Social Sciences

THE TIMELINESS OF THE SOCIAL SCIENCES

If nontheological subjects are considered at all in an encyclopedic overview of the subject matter of theology, then under the present circumstances the empirical social sciences have the greatest priority. This will not be disputed even by people who preserve a sober sense of proportion in the turmoil of the contemporary debates and do not regard philosophy, for example, as being disposed of by the social sciences and do not allow the transformation of theology's function to be prescribed from outside.

The social sciences stand in the final position among the four non-theological complexes that are inserted between the biblical and systematic-theological disciplines, which in turn are grouped around church history. That expresses the timeliness of the social sciences. Here the collision between theology and the scientific understanding of our time is doubtless the most sharp. At the same time, however, there is also such an obvious contact in the subject matter that it would be completely misleading to see the relationship predominantly or even exclusively as antithetical.

Like a flash flood, the social sciences in a short time have broken through the dams of the customary conceptions of scholarship and of the disciplinary divisions, inundated the universities and the general public, and effected a far-reaching change in interest, ways of thinking, and language. In the social sciences, science became a public phenomenon, an instrument for a mode of cultural revolution. It is too early to prepare a balance sheet as to what has been destructive and what has introduced a fruitful reorganization. It should not be surprising that this turbulent event has also drawn theology into its wake. How could it be otherwise if the question of what is human becomes thematic? If theology remained untouched by that, it would speak badly for its sensitivity to its relation to reality. That certainly does not exclude the possibility that false reactions predominate in this excited participation. It could provide a new example of how easily theologians fall prey to a falsely understood conformity to their time through fascination or panic. It is all the more urgent to enter into the problems that are not yet mastered so that a necessary task is not compromised.

Due to the difficulty of the task, a false reaction in the form of flight, whether *into* the social sciences or *from* them, lies close at hand. The high degree of topical interest is not directly beneficial to an appropriate approach to the subject. The absence of distance, especially in an emotionally laden situation, impairs a person's capacity for judgment, and, as a result of the lack of comparative possibilities, can mislead one into uncritically falling prey to whatever is offered. To usurp the word "critical" as a slogan also does not protect a person from that danger. With a more precise view of the matter, the appearance of a clear and determined subject gives way to the impression that the state of the problem is most difficult and the status of the discussion is most diffuse. A simple adoption of results is prohibited in view of the conflict with regard to the question of method and the immensely detailed material. Only the "long march" through thirsty stretches of intensive specialized work leads to a competent judgment.

For the theologian this situation is particularly urgent. The theologian's study, which is otherwise extremely demanding, now becomes burdened by an additional task in which, apart from a few exceptions, the theologian remains a dilettante, and as a result of which one is also threatened with the danger of becoming a dilettante in theology. On the other side, the whole of theology is at stake in this matter. If theology does not attain a clear relationship to the social sciences, this impairs not only vocational practice but also the integrity of theology itself.

In this situation a very brief treatment can do nothing more than attempt to present a few points for orientation within the broad field of the problem.

THE TASK OF THE SOCIAL SCIENCES

TERMINOLOGICAL

"Social Sciences"

The expression "social sciences" is of quite recent origin as a general concept for the empirical sciences devoted to what is human. The English term "the humanities" originally meant classical education and corresponds to the German concept *"Geisteswissenschaften."* It does not come into consideration as a direct model. In French the expression *"sciences humaines"* is common, but it primarily is also the equivalent of *"Geisteswissenschaften,"*[1] while the term *"sciences de l'homme"* is connected with the limited orientation to experimental science. It lies in the nature of the subject matter that the sciences dealing with what is human have a tendency toward an enormous expansion. While one above all associates the disciplines of psychology, sociology, and pedagogy with the catchword "social sciences," the sciences devoted to what is human also include history, the study of religion, jurisprudence, economics, ethnology, linguistics, behavioral studies, and so on, as well as everything that commonly falls under the concept of anthropology. In this area almost everything is in movement with regard to disciplinary structuring and interdisciplinary connections. This reflects the degree to which this enormous complex of fields devoted to the study of humanity is just now engaged in methodologically constituting itself. Thus, the process of fermentation also is sketched in the nomenclature. An investigation of the general concept "social sciences" would probably show that the origin of the term in this or that linguistic tradition is less informative than the crystallizing function of an available term within a particular situation. The question about what helped psychology, sociology, and pedagogy in particular to become enormously attractive in the last half of the sixties can only be grasped in connection with an analysis of the worldwide unrest that broke out among the younger generation during those years.

"Psychology," "Pedagogics," and "Sociology"

It is obvious that what has been joined together in such a powerful way is older than the general concept newly introduced. The customary nomenclature originated in various centuries. The expression *"psychology"* was coined by Melanchthon and is initially met as the title of a book at the end of the sixteenth century. This humanistic verbal creation pointed back to the classical Greek tradition, but it also had assimilated Christian elements and was occasioned by a new turn toward the human as well as by an interest in standard terminology. *"Pedagogics"* (to follow the chronological sequence) is a word coined in the eighteenth century. It was a product of the Enlightenment's enthusiasm for education and training. Kant was probably the first person to give lectures on pedagogics in 1776–77. The first chair of pedagogics was established at Halle in 1779. The term *"sociology"* was coined by the positivist August Comte during the

---

1. Cf. A. Diemer, "Geisteswissenschaften," *Handwörterbuch der Philosophie* 3 (1974): 213; It is characteristic that there is no article on "Humanwissenschaften."

1830s. He used it explicitly as a synonym for the previous expression "*physique sociale*," in order, as he said, "to designate with a single name the integral part of the philosophy of nature related to the positive study of the general laws underlying social phenomena."[2]

THE HISTORY OF THE PROBLEM OF PSYCHOLOGY AND SOCIOLOGY

The terminology only indicates particular phases in which an intensified and altered interest in these sciences was reflected in the effective coining of names. A person must dig further in order to characterize the history of the problem. Even though we are primarily treating the timely phenomenon of the so-called social sciences, we must call this background to mind so that we do not succumb to the deception that the subject matter is as new as the designation or as unified as it appears.

The Western Tradition

Psychology and sociology, to which the following discussion will be limited, originated in their modern sense in the nineteenth century. The significance attached to this event can only be grasped through the contrast with the conception of the soul and of human socialization that, up to then—through many changes and yet in a broad continuity—determined Western thought. Its roots lay in Greek philosophy on the one side and in biblical tradition on the other.

In the Western conception of the soul, as it was formed by antiquity and Christianity, two motifs—in the most extreme stylization—have been connected and have permeated one another in a way that was filled with tension. The one was an organic understanding of the soul as the entelechy of the body and therefore as the moving and shaping power of everything living. In its highest levels it participates in the world of the ideas and thereby in immortality. The task of the doctrine of the soul was to describe and classify the *psyche* as the principle of life according to its potentials. The other motif was a personal understanding of the soul that included a special place for the human being as the image of God and the indissoluble individuality of the individual. What happens in the heart and conscience in relation to God determines the death and life of the soul for eternity. In the wake of these two motifs, two principal problems have been posed more intensely on entering modern times: the relation of body and soul as well as the immortality of the soul.

2. Helmut Schoeck, *Die Soziologie und die Gesellschaften: Problemsicht und Problemlösung vom Beginn bis zur Gegenwart,* Orbis Academicus, vol. 1, pt. 3 (Freiburg, München: Alber, 1964), p. 173.

The understanding of the political arena was concentrated—correspondingly stylized—in two poles: the question of the appropriate forms of life in which the relationship between the individual and society takes shape, as well as the question of the source of legitimation, that is, of the authorization of the right to use power. In both poles the changes from antiquity to modern times manifest a similar tension-laden interrelationship of Greco-Roman and Christian heritage. This can be seen, on the one side, in the way church and state are distinguished and, on the other side, in the way the idea of natural law and the appeal to the divine will are related to one another. These points certainly also indicate the fissures at which, in modern times, the order of the Christian West broke up and the revolutionary transformation of social life set in.

The Upheaval in the Nineteenth Century

The question about the reasons that the change, which produced a far-reaching upheaval in the scholarly approach to personal and social reality, began about the middle of the nineteenth century can only be answered by way of suggestion. At that time the collapse of Idealistic philosophy and the victorious advance of the mode of thought of the natural sciences took place. Historicism and positivism established an attitude that was decidedly critical of metaphysics. Furthermore, the technological application of the natural sciences produced its first powerful effects in the beginning of industrialization and the resulting change in the social structure. Together with that, secularization made rapid progress. The traditional religious and ethical bonds partly disintegrated and partly were altered in an increasing process of emancipation. The previously supportive social institutions suffered an increasing disappearance of authority. All this directed attention to the signs and deep causes of processes of crisis in general, and, in addition, it produced a basic necessity for illuminating investigation in order to make it possible to take action to set things right. For the retrospective view that predominates today, the turn to modern sociology and psychology is perhaps too one-sidedly connected with the names of Karl Marx and Sigmund Freud. Nevertheless, they were the great movers in whom the characteristic features are perceptible with particular clarity.

The realities treated by these sciences are no longer understood as substantial realities whose properties and manifestations are to be described, but they are understood as processes in which human existence itself, threatened by estrangement and repression, is at stake. The concept of society critically called into question the category of order and especially the concept of the state that had previously determined social thought. In German the word *"Seele"* (soul) is, of course, retained in many words along with "psyche." However, it no longer covers the understanding of the processes of consciousness and of becoming conscious to which psychology is now oriented. In both cases the interlacing with what is bodily and material is decisive. In the understanding of social reality, the ideas have changed their status. They have moved from the historical driving force into an ideological superstructure. Also, mental processes no longer are considered apart from corporal reality. In both respects, therefore, the practical aim is decisive, which is already indicated by the origin of these disciplines in economics and medicine. That is the reason they are primarily oriented to pathological phenomena of social and psychic life, such as exploitation and estrangement, hysteria and repression, as well as to social revolution and psychotherapy. Thereby humanity became the object of science in a new way. Rather than merely being the given and describable subjects who investigate the world and shape the environment, people are considered in terms of the apparently paradoxical combination of the unreserved perception of their own existence as it is conditioned by nature and the environment, and an unrestrained determination to intervene in the social and mental processes of human reality itself to transform it. Corresponding to the model of the natural sciences, one makes human life calculable and manageable for sociological and psychological techniques by going behind the phenomena to the ultimately determinative elementary powers and laws, to the material means of production and conflicts of interest as well as to sexuality and the structures of drives. They also have in common a predominantly antireligious tendency as a result of the polemical relation to what was traditional.

Differentiation in the Twentieth Century

In their further development in the twentieth century, psychology as well as sociology experienced an extraordinarily strong differentiation. This was caused by many strains that may be schematized as follows. The tension between a psychological and a sociological approach, which demanded attention in many of the already existing sciences, became apparent, and they became independent branches of science. A polarization emerged between the trend toward a fundamental science, which embraced all cultural phenomena and, coupled with a claim rooted in theory of scholarship, was supposed to replace philosophy, and a special mode of investigation that proceeded in a strongly empirical way. A difference became apparent between more observational findings and general theoretical interpretation and an interest that was more strongly directed toward practical use in therapy and management. A functional subdivision intruded that was governed by special areas of application (such as the psychology and sociology of religion, behavioral psychology, the sociology of knowledge, and so on) or by various methods (such as hermeneutical or experimental approaches). Finally a splintering took place as a result of differences between schools and directions, such as, for example, the battles between orthodoxy and revisionism within Marxism as well as within Freudianism or the conflict over positivism within the German social sciences. The permeability of the boundary between the two disciplines, for which social psychology stands as an example, rendered the situation more complex rather than simplifying it.

COMMON BASIC FEATURES

Although they are so diverse within themselves, the social sciences demonstrate certain common basic features. Of course, these can only be defined as tensions, whose conflict must be considered if the makeup of the social sciences is not to be simplified in one direction or another.

The Method of the Natural Sciences

The affinity for the method of the natural sciences played a decisive role in the emergence of modern psychology and sociology. However, highly divergent tendencies stand out that, under various designations, revive the methodological conflict between the natural sciences and humanities within the social sciences themselves. One extreme is formed by experimental psychology, working with measurable tests, and social statistics, involving methods of working up data and calculating probability. The other is formed by the analysis of existence or critical theory (*Kritische Theorie*). As sharp as the contrasts may be, they contain elements that prohibit tearing them apart. Even a psychology that is explicitly oriented to the humanities and hermeneutics cannot bypass the aspects that can be scientifically understood if the totality of what is human is not to be missed. In turn, an extremely physical or mathematical approach must be expanded in the direction of the hermeneutical problem if it is to be included in a theoretical construct that applies to what is human. Thus it comes down to a methodological syncretism with various nuances. In Freud, for example, this emerges in a particularly significant way as the wide polarity between a decidedly scientific beginning and marked mythical elements of thought. The line back to primitive stages of human history and the way that that history functions in his concept of phylogenesis complement the eschatological-utopian components in dialectical materialism. Characterizing this as "syncretistic" loses its pejorative ring if a person is aware that this is the result of a necessity in the subject matter that must be included in methodological reflection.

Empirical

The social sciences are distinguished by an insistence on what is empirical. This stands in legitimate tension to intellectual abstraction, which is easily subject to distortions. A very important example of this problem lies in the ontological implications of psychological and sociological conceptualizations like drives, mechanism, and so on. The aim toward uniformities, structures, and laws, which is justified in a certain respect, stands under the banner of a generalization that should not suppress the constitutive element of the individual in what is historical. Attention to psychological or sociological processes and connections must preserve the tension between a justified objective distancing from an immediate connection with life and a sympathetic comprehension of and association with the meaningful coherence of living processes. Intensified reflection on human existence as it is carried out also represents a certain burden in each case. The leavening of our general awareness and of colloquial language by elements from the vocabulary of the social sciences creates the acute problem of how to preserve or reestablish a healthy functioning of the unconscious and how to safeguard what is obviously in concern for the other person. That is not directed against the growth in practical knowledge made possible by the social sciences. What matters is that what is empirical in human life is transferred into life itself in such a way that it benefits living experience.

Soteriological Intention

The social sciences claim to offer not only proximity to life but help for life as well. Where this tendency that is soteriological in the broadest sense involves humankind it can hardly be rejected as inappropriate. Of course, it again conceals within itself considerable factors of tension. People widely trust simply in the soteriological effect of enlightenment. Like the natural scientist a person attempts to get "behind" things. A person pursues an unmasking of consciousness in order to reach the substructure of the relationships of production, concealed by an idealistic superstructure, or in favor of the reality of drives hidden beneath illusions or repressions. Trivialized to a general removal of tabus and antiauthoritarian emancipation, this procedure lives from the opinion that through the strategy of unmasking, the correct insight will be established and will perfectly prevail on its own. This process, in which a person is brought to awareness with the goal of liberation, cannot be evaluated without providing space for the question of what humanity is in the broadest horizon. If, in psychotherapy, language itself becomes a therapeutic tool, an exceptionally important insight with regard to human existence is revealed. This presses us to the question about what is required for a psychotherapist, establishing trust, to release the patient's tongue and then not to guide everything that wells up from the subconscious solely into the channels of one theory. The social sciences also rightly live from substantive perceptions that were not initially produced by psychology and sociology. The more people realize that and thereby have their horizons expanded, the more they can do justice to humankind.

THE SOCIAL SCIENCES AND RELIGION

In its modern sense science does not speak of God. This has been called methodological atheism. Talk about God is neither contested nor battled, but it does not fit into an objectifying attitude toward reality that abstracts from a direct living relationship to reality. Nevertheless, when the occasion arises modern science treats religious phenomena very exactly. Religion appears within the social sciences in accordance with its fundamental assessment by the particular scientist and its place within that scientist's horizon of interest.

THE RELIGIOUS HERITAGE IN THE SOCIAL SCIENCES

While this situation is commonly given little thought, the way in which the religious world is expressed in the social sciences presupposes the fact that they owe a great deal to the religious heritage. With regard to psychology one should remember the degree to which religious phenomena have furthered inner personal experience and observation. The extent to which this is the case, especially of the Christian religion, is quite clear in Augustine, Luther, or Kierkegaard as well as in the practice of confession or mysticism. For sociology as well, one should not underestimate the degree to which the power of religions to build community and its radiation out into social relationships have sharpened our sight for the complicated mesh of social reality. Beyond this, certain leading ideas of the contemporary social sciences, like personality, partnership, or freedom, cannot be understood apart from their Christian background.

RELATION TO THE CRITICISM OF RELIGION

The multitude of neutral technical studies in the fields of the psychology of religion and sociology of the church is not really illuminating for the fundamental question about the way religion appears in the social sciences. It is more important to be aware that the emergence of the social sciences in the nineteenth century coincided both in time and in substance with the religious criticism of the left-wing Hegelians and positivism. In part that past continues to cling to the social sciences into the present. A person certainly must be discriminating in this question. The encounter between the social sciences and Christian faith stood under an unfavorable banner. Concepts drawn from primitive religions like tabu or fetish, with the appearance of what is typical of religion as such, became the categories in the social sciences for what is inhuman, and very often superstition or, at least, undifferentiated religious thought was used as the most suitable model for what is religious. These one-sided views bore heavy consequences. However, this should not hinder one from considering the justified aspects of a critique of religion as it is supported by psychological and sociological observations. In addition, one ought not to lose sight of the broad stream of psychological study that has advanced the interpretation of religious phenomena, as is the case with C. G. Jung or in the direction of the analysis of existence. Still, this should not induce a person to prematurely think the problem has been disarmed, which, as the contemporary crisis of religion, belongs to the present context of the social sciences.

THE SOCIAL SCIENCES AND THEOLOGY

SYMPTOMS OF THE CONTEMPORARY EDUCATIONAL CRISIS

The fact that the relationship between the social sciences and theology appears to be so distressingly difficult is not merely, and possibly not even primarily, the result of a religious crisis. Instead, what is involved is largely an educational crisis. It has various aspects.

Difficulties in Orientation

With the explosive development of scholarly production it is constantly becoming more difficult to be even only somewhat informed. The cleft between a superficial knowledge by hearsay, which is journalistically transmitted, and a discriminating understanding of the subject matter is becoming increasingly greater. Therefore the drawing power and the hectic character of what is fashionable is constantly becoming more powerful. This situation is sheer poison for the mental concentration and simultaneous breadth of horizon that theology requires to an extraordinary degree. The demand for meaningful possibilities for information about the social sciences and their integration into the study of theology is justified and urgent. Nevertheless, the efforts to do this would become hopeless if the acquisition of the knowledge attained by the social sciences were to take place at the expense of the theological treatment of this material and at the expense of the acquisition of the knowledge that is the indispensable presupposition for the theological capacity for judgment.

Difficulties in Understanding

The task of the hermeneutical mediation between such different linguistic horizons as that of the social sciences and that of the theological tradition is more difficult than the acquisition of sufficient knowledge about the social sciences. This critical transaction in both directions requires a philosophical education, the curtailment of which can only be harmful to theology. Even though it may have had some justification in the situation in which it arose, the vehement antipsychological and antisociological passions of dialectical theology left behind a disastrous helplessness and susceptibility of theology vis-à-vis the social sciences. In contrast, the subtlety with which, for example, Thomas Aquinas located Christian faith within the total network of the human expressions of life and interpreted it in the direction of its concreteness is impressive. This undertaking was deeply justified in its intention and must be tackled anew under contemporary conditions and guided by the theological insights of the Reformation, although it has been made extremely difficult by the contemporary educational situation.

Inhibitions of Inner Vitality

The aspects of the educational crisis also include what can be called the far-reaching phenomenon of an inhibition of inner vitality. This affects the capacity and courage to concentrate on what gives life and provides certainty, as well as the readiness and elasticity necessary for hermeneutical patience in conversation with history and with our contemporaries, which is dependent on that capacity and courage. However, this is a fundamental condition for the encounter between theology and the social sciences. This requires not only scientific education but also an education to true humanity.

GUIDEPOSTS FOR THE ENCOUNTER

What results or should result from the encounter between theology and the social sciences cannot be established in advance. As a conclusion we can only indicate *that* such an encounter must take place and *how* it correctly takes place.

Openness

It already amounts to a lot if a person refuses emotionally determined, all-inclusive assertions for or against the social sciences, or blindly follows the spell of a particular doctrine, or a nonorganic, merely external annexation of the material to the subject matter of theology. What is required is an expansive openness coupled with patience that allows a dialogue between the observed facts of human reality and the tradition of faith. This corrects the conception that this involves a task that concerns only practical theology and ethics, possibly to compensate for a lack of confidence in the subject matter of theology resulting from modernization or to force theology in general into the schema of a behavioral theory. It is obvious that a multitude of contacts with the social sciences necessarily intrudes into practical theology and ethics in particular. What is decisive, however, is that the encounter with the social sciences affects theology in all its disciplines and thus becomes a particularly urgent concern of dogmatics and fundamental theology. If an essential aspect of the contemporary experiences of reality is incorporated in the social sciences, then that poses not only the question about how we are to adjust to it in Christian behavior and the forms of ecclesiastical life, but above all the question as to how Christian faith enters into discussion with that reality and how it will stand the test with regard to it. Methodologically this has been seized by the slogan that the historical-critical approach must be supplemented by the empirical-critical approach. Certainly this does not insure a total theological integration of the social sciences as long as theologians do not recognize that what is involved are interdependent aspects of a single hermeneutical process of theological accountability. In fact a person cannot bear witness to and live the faith if it is not lived and witnessed to in the midst of the contemporary experience of reality.

Self-Criticism

Since both the social sciences and theology, as working processes, exist in a constant movement of self-correction, it is obvious that neither the former nor the latter can be the norm or the evaluating authority for the other. The critical process in the encounter between both fields must be reciprocal. This can best be taken into account through the observation that criticism is fundamentally always self-criticism, namely, the readiness to correct prejudgments relative to oneself as well as in relation to one's partner. After all, precisely for the theologian the critically fundamental figure of unmasking, as it is represented as the critique of ideology, is not unfamiliar from the perspective of biblical images of thought—one thinks of the phenomenon of *hypokrisis*. To that extent a critique of religion that is directed against Christianity is not fundamentally foreign to the theologian, even though the theologian at times needs to be reminded of it in a very uncomfortable and offensive way. That also includes vigilance vis-à-vis a suspicion of ideology that itself has become an ideological stylistic device.

Relation to Practical Knowledge

The social sciences correctly impress theologians because they have boasted of an advantage with regard to practical knowledge and make the theologians aware of their deficiency in this regard. However, if one is not to fall prey to deceptive suggestions, the encounter between the social sciences and theology requires above all a clarification of the concept of practical knowledge. Only under this condition do the decisive questions about the relationship between theology and practical knowledge, which is most extremely aggravated by the encounter with the social sciences, become discussable. Why must one speak of God in order to speak correctly about human existence? To what extent does the Christian talk about God as a gospel of freedom through faith do justice precisely to the facts that are impressively discovered by the social sciences but at times are also fatally buried? Why are other languages beyond the language systems of psychology and sociology required when, put differently, what is involved is living life and not merely analyzing it? Theology rests on the fact that the Christian linguistic tradition performs a service that cannot at all be exercised by the social sciences if they understand themselves correctly.

9

Practical Theology

THE KEY POSITION OF THE PROBLEM OF PRACTICAL THEOLOGY

Practical theology is the most recent of the principal theological disciplines. At the same time its designation and the definition of its task is the most controversial. It has been ironically characterized as "jobless" in the system of theological scholarship.[1] Yet something close to agreement exists in placing it at the close of the sequence of theological disciplines. An explicit basis is required for deviating from even this minimal consensus.

THE DEVIATION FROM THE CUSTOMARY ORDERING OF PRACTICAL THEOLOGY

At first glance the position at the end of the disciplines is immediately obvious. Practical theology evidently marks the transition from scholarly theology to ecclesiastical practice, from study to vocation. This can be coupled with contrasting evaluations. In one evaluation it appears as a descent from the heights of scholarship into the lowlands of a trade. In the other, it appears to be the goal of the theological ascent of the mountain, or, as Schleiermacher expressed it with the metaphor of the growth of a tree, as the crown toward which roots and trunk drive all the sap and powers of theology upward.[2] In the one case the scholarly

1. L. Fendt, "Die Stellung der Praktischen Theologie," in *Praktische Theologie: Texte zum Werden und Selbstverständnis der praktischen Disziplin der evangelischen Theologie*, ed. Gerhard Krause, Wege der Forschung vol. 264 (Darmstadt: Wissenschaftliche Buchgesellschaft, 1972), p. 314.
2. *Friedrich Schleiermacher, Brief Outline on the Study of Theology*, trans. Terrence N. Tice (Richmond: John Knox Press, 1966), p. 31. Further, idem, *Sämmelte Werke*, vol. 1, 13 (Berlin: G. Riemer, 1850), p. 26.

character of practical theology is called in question. In part it already stands outside of academic theology and therefore should be removed from the university to ecclesiastical seminaries. In the other case, as in Schleiermacher's understanding of theology as a positive science, the peculiarity of theology's scholarly character is connected with its inclination toward practical theology. Of course, these contradictions lose their expressive power in reference to the peculiarity of the discipline of practical theology as soon as one takes account of the complications on both sides. The conflict about the scholarly character of practical theology can to a certain degree become contagious. Along with that people have also regarded dogmatics as "ecclesiastical theology" in contrast to "scholarly theology" and have wanted to banish it from the university, leaving only the historical disciplines. A further consequence is the denial of scholarly character to theology as such, even to a so-called historical theology, because of suspicion about its practical, ecclesiastical purpose and connections. On the other side, while Schleiermacher was the real inaugurator of practical theology, he defined this discipline as predominantly technical and spoke out explicitly against establishing special academic chairs of practical theology.[3]

These initial observations already show how strongly the problem of practical theology, its encyclopedic place, and the detailed definition of its task is fused with the understanding of theology as a whole. If one pursues the reasons that led to the establishment of this discipline and to the founding of academic chairs for practical theology, then a person comes upon phenomena that affect theology as a whole: the disappearance of the obvious character of ecclesiastical reality and the increasing tension between scholarly and ecclesiastical interest in theology. Yet it is not only a scholarly interest critical of theology that can result in a lack of interest in practical theology. An accentuated turn toward the *subject matter* of theology can be coupled with a devaluation of practical theology even under the banner of a total understanding of theology as a function of the church. On the other hand, the recent shift in mood in favor of practical theology stands precisely under the banner of tendencies explicitly critical of theology and can be connected with an aversion to historical and systematic theology. All of that encourages the impression that the theme "practical theology" touches a seat of trouble for theology as a whole.

3. Wege der Forschung, vol. 264, p. 4.

Therefore it is meaningful, in contrast to the customary procedure, to treat practical theology at the place in our passage through the disciplines at which we cross a threshold that is decisive for the whole. We now begin a phase of our considerations in which what ultimately emerges from engagement with the rich historical material of theology in the simultaneous presence of other scholarly fields must become apparent, namely, what this immense expenditure amounts to, what the situation is with regard to the truth as the relation of theology to reality, and whether it furnishes anything from which and for which a person can live. The affirmation of the subject matter of theology and the affirmation of the call of the theologian condition one another and depend on whether and to what extent theology deals with something a person can answer for in the present and which also is necessary in some respect. Although this intensi-fication of the question also becomes acute in the remaining disciplines of dogmatics, ethics, and fundamental theology, it is most extremely intensi-fied in the problems that emerge in practical theology.

This choice of order certainly should not lead to far-reaching conclusions that depend on overtaxing the attempt at orientation. Of course, the guid-ing aim is an encyclopedic one in a limited sense. Yet the procedure adopted from the beginning is not suited to developing systematically the differentiation in disciplines and projecting an ideal architectonic structure of theology. This reflective report of the principal complexes should certainly benefit a meaningful engagement with the totality of theological study. Yet competition with plans for a curriculum reform remain far off and therefore also the claim to propose the sequence of divisions for a curriculum.

PRACTICAL THEOLOGY AS A CRITICAL SYMPTOM OF THE UNDERSTANDING OF THEOLOGY

It would be too narrow to discuss the problem posed with particular sharpness by practical theology only under the viewpoint of scholarliness, as much as that requires consideration. Further, it seems commendable initially to leave the concept of practice out of play and thus to proceed not from that customary designation and its implications but from the sub-ject matter itself.

Theology and Vocation

The argument that the purity of scholarship is impaired if the structur-ing of the scholarly field is affected by taking into account its practical application in a particular vocational activity and its requirements cannot claim general validity. Naturally the relationships are not the same for all scholarly fields. One also cannot contest the fact that considerations of this kind can be dangerous. Nevertheless, quite apart from theology, such considerations belong to the realm of factors that constitute scholarship. Pure striving for knowledge is an abstraction that, vis-à-vis the totality of life, can be carried on and justified within certain limits. However, the fact that the question of practical impact is posed in an elementary way even for the natural sciences is evident today in the aspects of these sciences that are disastrous as well as necessary for life. Even here one can no longer separate the task of investigation from responsibility for what is discovered. This is much less true in fields in which scholarship and life are incomparably more closely connected by the subject matter, as is the case, for example, in jurisprudence and medicine. The organization of the medieval university was oriented to the governing vocations and to the fundamental needs of society, so that along with judges, physicians, and teachers a place was given to the theologian, who was responsible for the saving truth. As much as the situation of the university has changed since then, the inner relationship between study and vocation, scholarship and practical necessity has not lost its justification. In spite of that, theology presents special problems in this regard.

Theology and Reality

The claim that theology deals with a reality that is of universal relevance and is concerned with a fundamental necessity of human existence —as distinct, for example, from medicine—cannot count on being recognized as obvious. Nevertheless, it would be insufficient to establish theology solely on the basis of the incontestable historically given fact and historical significance of Christianity, without simultaneously discussing the internal connection between the essential core of Christianity and a corresponding essential need of human existence. That includes the fact that responsibility for this essential connection between what is Christian and what is universally human is inherent to theology. Correspondingly, both human existence in its historicity and Christianity and its historicity together are the givens of theology and are its responsibility. Both aspects involve something historical in the sense of an event that is not finished but continues. Indeed, it is a mutually interpenetrating event of encounter—always only partial, although from the side of Christianity with a universal tendency—that is in process and that continues independently of the accomplishments of scholarly theology. That does not mean that theology is irrelevant for the development of this event of encounter. Theology participates in a particular way in responsibility for this event, but not in such a way that in theology something would be translated into reality for the first time. Rather, the reality of an event already found to be in process is accompanied by theology in a critical and helpful way. This event, seen with respect to the past as well as the future, always precedes theology as something that has already happened as well as something that is always grasped in the process of happening. If Christian faith no longer lived in the world and no longer continued to influence history through constantly carrying out the functions of church life and continuing the living forms of the church, then theology would be literally without basis. In all of its disciplines theology participates in this situation, but it is most directly reminded of it in practical theology. It is by no means obvious that this does not sever theology from the question of truth and make it positivistic. To give up its specific relation to reality as such for these reasons would of course mean rendering theology objectless.

The Encyclopedic Place of Practical Theology

To underscore the sense in which practical theology, which needs to be defined more closely, is given a key position in our passage through the theological disciplines and to indicate how it fits into the whole of theology, we take our orientation from the event of encounter between what is Christian and what is universally human, which is a given for theology. While under modern circumstances one cannot avoid a primary definition of the methodological difference between historical and systematic disciplines, it would be erroneous to understand only the former to be related to history. The investigation of the facts of the historical event of tradition and the investigation of the conditions and responsibility of the present event of tradition undoubtedly belong together hermeneutically, although this involves many tensions. In its own way and with various points of emphasis, each individual discipline participates in this total hermeneutical process. This happens in such a way that this process is effective as such in each discipline and thus each discipline becomes theology in its own area of work. Therefore, to isolate each discipline from the others represents an abstraction that does not correspond to the way they are actually carried out. With this reservation in mind, the classification of the historical procedure as applying to the biblical disciplines and church history easily results. In contrast, the disciplines that deal with the perception of the subject matter of theology in its contemporary form also fit into a methodologically similar complex. The subject matter can be organized in accord with the fact that in view of our contemporary reality one can ask about the life of the church, the truth of faith, and the appropriateness of ethical behavior. There results a certain correspondence between the historical and practical disciplines of theology insofar as both, each within its own field of vision, bring to view the reality of the church and the contingency of historical reality that is already given for theology. These aspects unyieldingly resist systematizing and abstracting tendencies and therefore are extraordinarily beneficial for theology.

THEOLOGY IN THE FIELD OF TENSION OF THE PROBLEM OF THEORY AND PRACTICE

It is not accidental that practical theology attracted to itself this designation which had previously been used with a different meaning. We must include a treatment of the history of the concept not only for that reason but especially since theology fell into the problem of theory and practice as a result of the terminology selected.

CHANGES IN THE UNDERSTANDING OF THE EXPRESSION THEOLOGICA PRACTICA

The history of the concept of *theologia practica* shows how closely the problem of this discipline is interwoven with the problem of theology in general.

Characterization of Theology in General

At the beginning of high scholasticism the question was posed within the framework of the Aristotelian understanding of scholarship about whether theology, to the extent that it was scholarship at all, was a *scientia speculativa* or a *scientia practica*. This formulation of the question involved the problem of verification. It includes the question of the basis of knowledge as well as of the purposes for which it exists, that is, of the goal of theology. Is theology ultimately oriented to the consideration of the truth for its own sake or to the good so that it initially verifies itself in behavior? Various answers were presented: it is only speculative, it is predominantly speculative but at the same time also practical, or it is predominantly practical. Of course, this schema was shown to be insufficient, so that alternative concepts like "contemplative," "mystical," and "affective" came into play. A person primarily interested in the inner effect of theology could place the viewpoint of the mystical or the affective in contrast to the speculative. Since the concept of the practical was related to human behavior and thus to what is moral, it was poorly suited to be the exclusive characterization of theology. When Luther, in contrast to the scholastic distinction, with a decisiveness previously unknown, expressed his opinion that theology is only practical and that speculative theology does not merit being called theology,[4] he burst the framework within which the problem of the theory of scholarship was treated and understood the concept of the speculative and, especially of the practical, in a way different from scholasticism. Practice now meant the actual carrying out of life as such, so that theology was designated as exclusively practical precisely for the sake of the primacy of the faith that defines and decides life.

The Completion of Scholarly Theology

In Protestant orthodoxy Luther's insistence on the practical character of theology was taken up in a very unsatisfactory way by developing a practical theology as the counterweight to a scholarly academic theology. This practical theology interpreted dogmatics in the direction of its edifying significance. For example, one could compose a *theologia practica per omnes articulos fidei* (practical theology of all the articles of faith) in which the viewpoints of the aesthetic and moral interlock. This brought one into a certain proximity to a Catholic genre of literature titled "*theologia practica*," which was primarily oriented to the problems of the practice of penance.[5]

Part of Scholarly Theology

The idea of practical theology in the modern sense as a sum of disciplines involving ecclesiastical action and instruction preparing a person for the activities involved in church leadership was initially presented by Andreas Hyperius in the sixteenth century, although not under this designation. It has only been since Schleiermacher that this term has been solidly connected with this area in the task of theology and that it has prevailed against the competing concept of pastoral theology. More recent proposals like "the theology of ecclesiastical action" or "the functional study of the church"[6] have not produced any terminological change so far.

---

4. *D. Martin Luthers Werke*, Tischreden (Weimar, 1912–1921), vol. 1, p. 72, ll. 16–24 No. 153 (1531/32); p. 302, l. 30 to p. 303, l. 3 No. 644 (1533).

5. Ernst Christian Achelis, *Lehrbuch der Praktischen Theologie*, vol. 1, ed. J. C. Hinrich (Leipzig, 1911), pp. 6–7, 9–10.

6. Cf. G. Krause, Foreword to *Wege der Forschung* 264:xix.

Although the term "practical theology" is somewhat directly illuminating, there are still difficult problems connected with it.

CHANGES IN UNDERSTANDING THEORY AND PRACTICE

The Aristotelian Understanding

An evaluation that theory has priority over practice was connected with the distinction between theoretical and practical scholarship, to which Aristotle added *"episteme poietike"* as a third possibility, which was directed toward creating something. There is an underlying idea that that far transcends a doctrine of scholarship, namely, the ideal of life that prefers the *vita contemplativa* to the *vita activa*. That already shows how difficult it is to fit the subject matter of theology into the Aristotelian schema without being exposed to its pressure. After all, the distinction between theory and practice could result in a distinction with regard to knowledge because the possibility of a pure theory was affirmed. This stood in contrast with knowledge related to practice, which obviously also contained theoretical elements.

The Modern Understanding

In contrast, it is characteristic of modern times that theory is valid only in relationship to practice. This characteristic is reflected even in the poorly thought through antithesis contained in the common saying "That may be correct in theory, but it is not good in practice" which Kant analyzed critically.[7] The contemporary concept of theory is reflected most clearly in its use in the natural sciences as an explanation of the coherence of experimentally attained experiential data. For that concept, of course, practice is unusable as a counterconcept. The left-wing Hegelians were concerned with defining the relationship between theory and practice for human behavior in a corresponding way. Marx in particular struggled against a speculative approach that would merely comprehend reality but did not produce its alteration. A theory of reality disposed in this way only served to fortify what already existed and therefore was dominated by practice in an ideological way. In contrast, practice was now to be emphatically understood as the task of establishing the unity of theory and practice by carrying theory as critical theory over into revolutionary

---

7. Immanuel Kant, "Über den Gemeinspruch: Das mag in der Theorie richtig sein, taugt aber nicht für die Praxis" (1793), in *Werke in sechs Bänden*, ed. W. Weischedel, vol. 6 (Darmstadt, 1964), pp. 125–172. Also in Kant, Gentz, Rehberg, "Über Theorie und Praxis," introduction by D. Henrich, *Theorie* 1 (Frankfurt am Main: Suhrkamp, 1967): 39–87.

practice. In order to subject the totality of historical reality to this conception of the problem of theory and practice, Marx carried out the equation of practice and productive work. That meant constricting the understanding of practice, which in turn corresponded to a narrowing of the understanding of theory.

THE USEFULNESS OF THE THEORY-PRACTICE SCHEMA FOR THE SUBJECT MATTER OF THEOLOGY

If a person takes the term "practical theology" seriously as the designation of an individual discipline, then the contrasting concept "theoretical theology" is suggested. This consequence has often been drawn with all the other disciplines being included under it. However, that has dubious consequences.

At a minimum, one should give weight to the fact that the word "practical" as it is customarily used in the theory of scholarship means the relationship of scholarship to practice, and thus again merely a theory of practice. One could discuss whether it might be more appropriate to bring the perspective of what is practical more strongly to bear by designating the actual accomplishment of speech about God in preaching, education, and pastoral care as practical theology as distinct from theoretical theology as it is carried out in a scholarly way. Then practical theology would be the practice itself, not the theory about it. That should not be understood, as is easily the case, in a devaluating sense, as though the high plane of pure theory were given up in favor of an accommodation to practice. Rather, correctly understood the concept occasionally used of applied theology (*theologia applicata*) must be considered as theology in the strictest sense as distinct from a theology that persists in an abstracting distance from concretely carrying out the message. Nevertheless, the concept of applied theology also suggests an incline downward from what is genuine to what is merely derived. In connection with the modern narrowing of theology to the process of scholarly reflection, the false conception arose that this theology creates something that is then merely applied in practice. To formulate it in a pointed way, preaching is not derived from theology, but theology from preaching. Yet this formulation of the distinction between theory and practice with respect to theology will scarcely prevail, even though to the extent that one uses this terminology it is the really appropriate way of making the distinction.

A more important consideration is whether the distinction between theoretical and practical theology within scholarly theology itself does not result in the abandonment of the relation of theology to practice as such rather than underscoring it. For Schleiermacher the aim of every theological discipline toward the task of church leadership was what made it theology.[8] The question arises as to what is involved with a special discipline of practical theology if all disciplines as theological disciplines are practically oriented. The answer can only be that practical theology presents the special theory of the forms of church leadership, while the other disciplines develop the theory of what constitutes the content of the practice of church leadership. Taken exactly, of course, the concept of practice should be expanded to include the reality of ecclesiastical life and thus the reality of life as such. For it is precisely there that the relation to practice that is genuinely constitutive for theology lies. In order to be clear about this one must be aware that the schema of theory and practice threatens to falsify the subject matter of theology in two respects.

The Relation Between Word and Reality

The erroneous impression could arise that not only theology as scholarly reflection but also the word to which theology is related and whose orientation to proclamation is constitutive for the living reality of the church is also a theory that must be transposed into practice. Rather, the proclaimed word is itself at least one decisive mode of ecclesiastical practice. Its relation to the reality of life as such has not been affected by the modern understanding of a scholarly theory that must then be carried over into practice. This does not establish a special case for theology. Rather, one can show in general that the relationship between word and reality is inadequately grasped ontologically when it is cast into the schema of theory and practice. The word event belongs to the reality of life itself, and indeed as that which, in a certain respect, initially constitutes reality.

The Relation Between Faith and Action

The situation is similar with regard to faith, toward which the Christian word is directed. Due to its literal meaning and as a result of its modern interpretation, the concept of practice has strengthened the tendency toward a narrowing in upon action. Nevertheless, the reality of life is not sufficiently grasped by the concept of action. It would be disastrous if in the face of the theory-practice schema Christian faith were to adopt the character of a theory of action and thus its verification would become a matter of morals and politics. Again this involves not an exception that is

8. Schleiermacher, *Brief Outline*, pars. 3–12.

claimed for theology but an ontological reservation vis-à-vis the theory-practice schema. If one attempted to think one's way into its Aristotelian understanding, that is, into the concept of a pure theory and the ideal for life of the *vita contemplativa*, this certainly would not correspond to the understanding of reality of Christian faith but would show itself to be a corrective to the present dominating conception of theory and practice that is worthy of consideration.

THE DEFINITION OF THE TASK OF PRACTICAL THEOLOGY

The critical considerations directed toward the designation "practical theology" do not intend a change of name. Even if such an attempt were fortunate enough to prevail, little would be gained by it. The definition of the task, for which precisely the questionable aspects of the customary terminology provide food for thought, must be developed from the subject itself.

ORIENTATION TO THE PRESENT TIME OF THE CHURCH

In a modified way the relationship to the present comes forward in all theological disciplines, indirectly in the historical disciplines as the unavoidable hermeneutical dimension, directly in the systematic disciplines as the question of truth. However, the relationship to the present emerges with particular penetration in practical theology. Of course, the dogmatic question of the truth of faith and the ethical question of the correct moral behavior are also related to the breadth of contemporary reality. However, while it includes these perspectives, in its orientation to the present time of the church, practical theology accents the particular domain of the present as it is shaped by history that claims to be the authentic representation of the Christian faith and that is interwoven with the contemporary reality of life in all its conceivable aspects, including political, social, and economic aspects. The field of the problem of practical theology is constituted by the question about how this exalted claim is to be answered for under these conditions and how it is to be practiced in the midst of such complexity. It extends from theological principles to detailed questions of technical practicality. As important as a corresponding basic reflection may be, in an uprooted present, practical theology discharges its specific task amid the cooperation of the disciplines only to the extent that it enters into its peculiar engagement in the present situation and takes up the concrete questions of practical ecclesiastical functions and modes of action. If it is not practical in this sense and persists too much in the "higher" spheres of theory, it then fails to provide what is essential.

The Basic Event in the Church's Contemporary Existence

The orientation to the present time of the church does not eliminate but intensifies the tension that the dogmatic concept of the church seeks to comprehend in distinctions like invisible and visible church, the universal and the particular church, or the church in the spiritual and legal senses. For no matter how the church appears, it is characteristic that it points beyond itself: to its historical origin with which canonical authority certainly is closely connected although not coincident; to the attributes of faith promised to it in spite of the contradictory appearances; to the universal unity regardless of the splintered and contested reality of the churches; to an anonymous Christianity beyond the organized church and conscious connection with Christian tradition. Although each of these relationships requires consideration in practical theology's orientation to the present, none of them is suited to provide the viewpoint that guides practical theology. This viewpoint cannot be derived from any of the antitheses present in contemporary ecclesiastical reality. However, it is also the case that no identification of the church can conceal the fact that the claim of the church always implies an element of nonidentity. Therefore, practical theology in any given case holds to one of the principal forms given the church by Christian history without putting on confessionalistic blinders. Precisely in the face of the tendency to blur what is Christian into anonymity, practical theology takes responsibility for the place at which and the way in which things are named by name.

An orientation to the event that is fundamental for the church in its contemporary existence is decisive for this task. Therefore its reference to its object is placed at the focal point. This event is not to be sought beyond the contemporary ecclesiastical reality, as, for example, the mere idea of the church, but it is to be met within it as its constitutive event. Thus a retreat from what is empirical is prohibited. One cannot construct the church in an a priori fashion, as it were from a neutral point, as though one were not dependent on the already given, historically determinate character of ecclesiastical existence as it is represented in the most elementary way in the succession of baptism and in the institution provided for gathering for worship. One is also simultaneously prohibited from uncritically falling prey to what is empirical without a sense for what is central and what is peripheral, what is healthy and what is sick. For the element of criticism directed at the church does not come from outside. Rather, the fundamental event of the church apart from which no church can exist is itself an occurrence that is critical of the church. At least it must be considered with a view to this as its intention. Of course, the expression *ecclesia semper reformanda* (the church reforming itself) can encourage a fanatical ecclesiastical docetism if it is understood in an unhistorical way. Taken precisely, however, it simply underscores the peculiarity of the church, which in its contemporary existence continues the event fundamental to it and in that way subjects its contemporary existence to criticism.

Perception of the Reality of Life

This orientation to the fundamental event in the contemporary existence of the church does not distract practical theology from the concrete reality of life but rather focuses attention on this reality in two respects that have to make use of all the suitable tools of empirical analysis and critical diagnosis. On the one side, it is necessary to investigate the actual practical reality of the church to ascertain which of its impulses and restraints derive from its function for life and its purpose for existence. On the other side, the totality of contemporary reality is to be investigated with regard to its relationship to that at which the fundamental event of the church aims. That appears to lead to the confrontation of individual items, but its intention is to test them with regard to their inner coherence. The fundamental event of the church cannot bypass the contemporary reality of life because it intends to and must tackle this life in its innermost core. The actual living reality of the church cannot claim to be something separated from life, because it must be wholly engaged with becoming the point of intersection between that fundamental event and the total contemporary reality of life. The fact that this connection is never guaranteed and is often disturbed is what gives such a sharp profile to practical theology. It must adjust the practical reality of the contemporary church from the perspective of the fundamental event of the church in such a way that the reality of contemporary life in general is disclosed, encountered, and altered. The more elementally one holds to the fundamental event of the church, the more free one becomes to perceive the situations into which it enters without disguising them. The more often one gives oneself in this way to the contemporary phenomena of ecclesiastical and common life, the more soberly will one recognize and evaluate their entanglement with one another or their distance from one another, their unavoidable difference from and tension with one another.

PRINCIPAL ASPECTS OF ECCLESIASTICAL LIFE

In order to explore the area of practical theology's task, the concept of the fundamental event of the church, which has remained undefined, may be illuminated by the conception of the church as the body of Christ. By doing so one should not turn away from the problematic associations with the word "church" to spiritual things, but it should provide an avenue for taking theological account of the historical corporeality of the church. On the one hand, the concept of the body of Christ expresses the distinction between Christ and the church as constitutive for its essence. On the other hand, it grasps the inseparable unity of things that appear to be contradictory with regard to the relation between the church and the world but that actually form a single living movement, like the systole and diastole of the heart, namely, assembly and mission. Even the instrumental definition of the relationship served by the formulations about the mission of the assembly or the assembly of the mission lags behind the fact that the body of Christ fulfills its mission to the world precisely by growing into the world. It serves the world in a freeing way by means of that which has happened and happens from God in the formation of the body of Christ in an event of liberation.

Ecclesiastical Functions

The living functions of the church have been attributed to a fundamental event through which Jesus Christ is mediated to the world in order to understand these functions as an emanation from the center of the church, not in order to confine them. This is a word event, not only because historical information is required for it to take place, but, together with that and above all, because the living truth of this information is fulfilled as freedom through faith and the task of opening this up can only be the affair of a powerful word. Against the tendency toward an unhistorical and abstract understanding of the word, practical theology has the fundamental ecclesiastical function of differentiating that word event with reference to the present under two aspects. It does so under the viewpoint of the form of the word, which embraces many forms of communication and infinite linguistic possibilities. It also does so under the broadly conceived viewpoint of the situation of the word, which primarily includes the corporeality of the community, the openness to the forum of the addressee, and service as the way a new life becomes effective in the midst of the old life.

Ecclesiastical Institutions

The differentiation of ecclesiastical functions coalesces and becomes institutionalized in fixed forms. In view of possible strains between traditional systems and the relation to the present, we are faced with the urgent task of taking care that the issue is decided neither by clinging to the past nor by seeking novelty, but by a sober concern for appropriately carrying out the fundamental event in the contemporary existence of the church. The area of practical theology's task divides according to the levels on which ecclesiastical life is embodied and assumes institutional forms of varying duration. It deals primarily with the institutional forms of the functions of the church's life centered on the word, namely, community worship, the occasional services oriented to the principal changes in personal life, as well as the form of pastoral care and mission, education and training. Closely connected with this, practical theology also deals with the institutional forms of socialization: congregations, broader organs of church leadership, special organizations for a *vita communis*, or ecumenical associations. Finally, also closely linked with that are the institutional forms of particular offices that essentially have the character of services. These should not be reduced to a single form, nor should the profusion of spontaneous services be suffocated by a form of monopoly. The problems that have become burning issues today for all the institutional forms of the church and that have been intensely discussed sociologically can only be resolved from the life these forms are supposed to serve. For that reason the isolation of these problems is not very profitable. That is also true of the discussion about the vocational image of the pastor. Being grasped by what is involved in the fundamental event of the church relativizes such problems and precisely for that reason makes possible new solutions that are simultaneously imaginative and sober.

CRITERIA OF ECCLESIASTICAL RESPONSIBILITY

Today practical theology is faced particularly with the danger of becoming a playground for theological fashion designers and their experiments. The fact that we sense the enormous pressure to tectonic alterations in the contemporary existence of the church and are on the lookout for new paths is not to be lamented. On the contrary, in itself it is a hopeful sign. Rather, what is unsettling is the fact that a deep uncertainty about the criteria has spread. This is a situation shared by all the theological disciplines, but it understandably takes effect in practical theology with particular severity.

Doing Justice to the Subject Matter and the Time

Rather than introducing the viewpoints concerned with what does justice to the subject matter and what does justice to the time separately and quite apart from each other, one criterion for appropriate engagement with all the questions of practical theology is whether the question about what does justice to the subject matter is profoundly considered for the sake of its intertwining with the present time of the church and in such a way that it becomes the question of what does justice to the time. Conversely, what in the subject matter of Christian faith can be said to do justice to the time can only be correctly considered if it becomes the question of what does justice to the subject matter. Of course, this piece of information is not comfortable, but it is basically obvious. It means that one's own participation in the fundamental event of the church becomes the criterion of ecclesiastical responsibility.

Freedom

Whether freedom is opened is not merely a formal criterion for all questions of ecclesiastical practice but a criterion that arises out of the content of the gospel. In its Christian understanding, freedom is recognized in the fact that as freedom from the law it makes a person willing for service to the weak.[9] The unity of faith and love as the substance of Christian freedom contradicts and withstands both forms of legalism that are disastrous for practical theology: traditionalism as well as progressivism.

9. Cf. Rom. 14 and 1 Cor. 8 and 10, as well as Martin Luther's Invocavit Sermon (1522) in *Luther's Works*, 51, trans. John U. Doberstein (Philadelphia: Fortress Press, 1959), pp. 70–75; *D. Martin Luthers Werke*, Kritische Gesamtausgabe (Weimar, 1883–   ), vol. 10, p. 3, ll. 1–64 = M. Luther, *Werke in Auswahl*, ed. O. Clemen ("Bonner" Ausgabe) (1912ff.), vol. 7, pp. 362–87.

10

Dogmatics

THE HORIZON OF THE MEANING OF THE DESIGNATION "DOGMATICS"

Intuitive, contradictory evaluations are connected with the word "dogmatics." On the one hand, it represents something firm and supportive in outlook amid the confusion of historical material, contradictory opinions, and vexing doubt to which theology is exposed, that is, not merely a "that is the way it was" or "that is the way it might be," but a "that is the way it is" and "that is the truth." That promises the clarity and certainty necessary for a person to come to terms with the subject matter of theology in such a way as to be able to make it one's own business. On the other hand, the word "dogmatic" is connected with the conception of something rigid, of an authoritarian claim of ecclesiastical dogmas, the acceptance of which finally leads to a *sacrificium intellectus*. That would contradict a fundamental condition for scholarly work, but it would also simultaneously contradict the Christian faith itself. As blind acceptance of a law of faith it would be changed into its opposite.

"DOGMATICS" AND "SYSTEMATIC THEOLOGY"

It is inadequate and hasty to take account of the deep-seated aversion to what is dogmatic by abandoning this word entirely and speaking of systematic theology instead. The designation "systematic theology" certainly does not lose importance as a result. Its terminological roots lie in the seventeenth century, when the concept of system found access to theology. Certainly, objections similar to those raised against the associations the word "dogmatics" commonly calls forth can be raised against the concept of a *closed* system. Nevertheless, in contrast to such a narrowing, the methodological demand contained in the idea of system cannot be given up. This is the demand to test the truth of statements by accounting for their connection with one another as well as with all other statements that can be of importance for their validity. To understand something is to grasp its coherence. Therefore the systematic viewpoint is a hermeneutical one, and the hermeneutical aspect is inseparably connected with the question of truth. Nevertheless, the concept "systematic theology" is broader than the designation "dogmatics." While the latter is used in a limited way of the coherent presentation of religious doctrine, thus predominantly being set off against ethics as the doctrine of moral behavior, the expression "systematic theology" has the tendency to embrace everything in theology methodologically oriented to the question of contemporary validity and to the testing of the claim to truth. Thus practical theology can also be counted as systematic theology if it asks not merely about pragmatic practicality but also about what is appropriate to the Christian truth with regard to the present ecclesiastical reality, for that exposes it to the question of truth in general.

Thus, if, at least in present linguistic usage, "dogmatics" constitutes a sector of systematic theology that is limited in content, the more comprehensive methodological expression does not suffice as a terminological substitute to characterize this particular task of Christian doctrine. Hence it would be premature to disclaim the expression "dogmatics" from the beginning, because this would avoid the necessity for reflecting on the implications of the meaning of this word. These implications already make clear some important dimensions of the problem associated with the discipline being discussed.

ORIGIN AND MEANING OF THE WORD "DOGMATICS"

Formal or Objective Understanding?

The term *"theologia dogmatica"* emerged in the seventeenth century, while its adoption as the German noun *"Dogmatik"* followed initially in the eighteenth century. What was new, of course, was not the area of work so designated. What can be regarded as dogmatics in retrospect had already existed for a long time. Nevertheless, changes in scholarly nomenclature seldom take place by chance. In this case the emergence of the new term was connected with an exceptionally large number of attributive neologisms to specify the most diverse aspects of theology. That began the crystallization of our present canon of theological disciplines, even though with a conceptuality that was still in part very unsettled. Thus *theologia dogmatica* was only one among other equivalent designations. However, it is symptomatic that in the two places where the expression is met for the first time, the one uses *"theologia historica"* and the other *"theologia moralis"* as the counterconcept.[1] From the beginning, nuances of meaning including both method and content appear. Dogmatics follows not the historical order but the order of the subject matter. Placing theological ethics alongside it underscores its orientation to the *credenda* as distinct from the *agenda*.

Now that certainly does not yet explain what is to be understood by "dogmatic." Does this adjective, which also had been used previously in theology, mean something formal, namely, something didactic or a particular mode of what is didactic, or does it express the object of teaching, namely, dogma or the dogmas? If dogmatics today is frequently defined as the science of dogma, there unavoidably intrudes the idea of particular statements that are historically given and ecclesiastically sanctioned, which form the object of scholarly study for the history of dogma. To what extent, however, is it also the object of study for a discipline of dogmatics that is to be distinguished from the history of dogma?

Occurrence Outside Theology

Certainly, the obvious explanation of "dogmatics" from a specifically theological concept of dogma appears to be questionable if one thinks about the use of the expression "dogmatics" outside theology. In connection with a distinction that goes back to antiquity, already in the sixteenth century people spoke of *medicina dogmatica* as the direction in medicine that set itself against the emerging empirical medicine. In jurisprudence "dogmatics" is still customary, for example, in the form of the dogmatics of criminal law, as a designation of a discipline for which what is definitive is not already given dogma but fundamental principles still to be acquired. In both cases the dogmatic form of thought is definitive, even though with different accents. In antiquity it was philosophically represented with an emphasis directed against skepticism, while in modern times, largely in the wake of Kant's criticism, it has been understood pejoratively and has been judged as dogmatic submission to unexamined teaching.

What then constitutes dogmatics in theology: the dogma, that is, dogmas as its object of study, or the dogmatic form of thought, or both?

1. See the Appendix "The Meaning of the Word 'Dogmatics,'" in my book *Theology and Proclamation: Dialogue with Bultmann*, tr. John Riches (London: Collins; Philadelphia: Fortress Press, 1966), pp. 109–13.

How does dogmatic theology react to the reproach of dogmatism? This question cannot be clarified further, apart from a discussion of the concept of dogma.

CHANGES IN THE CONCEPT OF DOGMA

"Dogma" in Its Classical Greek and Its Predominant Modern Usage

In classical Greek, *"dogma,"* which was derived from *"dokein"* (think, believe, imagine, seem, decide), received a double stamp as a result of two modes of authorization: a philosophical proposition that lays claim to truth, as well as a political decree in which an authoritative rule is established. In the religious realm, in contrast, it played no role.

The adoption of the term into Christian linguistic usage was dependent on the philosophical usage and competed with it. That reflects the orientation of Christian faith to the question of truth. The juridical nuance in its meaning was only secondarily connected with that. Still one must free oneself from reading the present common ecclesiastical understanding of dogma into the earlier usage. Two aspects constitute the present ecclesiastical understanding. Dogma is identical with a particular authority that alone is competent for such a formulation. This concept of dogma, which unites both stamps given it in the ancient linguistic usage, was only fully developed in Roman Catholicism in the nineteenth century. It corresponded to a historical use of the word "dogma" for the doctrinal decisions of the ecumenical councils of the ancient church. Certainly one already meets the characteristic connection between a formula for the truth and an authorizing authority in these decisions. Yet this situation was not yet contained in the word "dogma," at that time, although it was already used in various applications.

The Usage in the Ancient Church and the Middle Ages

In Greek theology dogma was predominantly understood as divine statements of revelation. However, it had to be explicitly characterized by corresponding epithets to distinguish it from the human *dogmata* of the philosophers. With the exception of a few authors who used the word positively as in Greek theology, Western theology in contrast used this foreign loan word almost exclusively as a negative designation of the opinions of the heretics. However, that only had slight influence on the usage in the Middle Ages, when the word "dogma" together with the adjectives derived from it are met very rarely. The fact that it was more widespread after the sixteenth century was a result of humanism, which reappropriated the usage of philosophy and the ancient church.

Various Strands of Conception in Modern Times

This was the source for the understanding of dogma as the subjective doctrinal opinion of the individual, which now constitutes broad reaches of the principal stream of theological linguistic usage. This neutral formulation was well suited as a historical category, so that the "history of dogma" was initially understood in this sense. Correspondingly, "dogmatics" can also be understood as the subjective doctrinal opinion of the individual. A relatively narrow line ran parallel to that which claimed "dogma" for the divine truth of revelation, yet in such a way that the identification with ecclesiastical decrees was decisively rejected. Thus Luther took up the catchword passed on to him by Erasmus in a sharp rejection of a skeptical attitude. Initially this produced little aftereffect in Protestant usage. In contrast, Hegel emphatically set forth a concept of dogma that was speculatively conceived, while in later Protestant theology up until Karl Barth one can follow a chain of attempts to bring the positive evaluation of the concept of dogma into harmony with an evangelical understanding of the word of God. Yet these attempts occupy a difficult position vis-à-vis the Roman Catholic formulation of the concept of dogma, which is characterized by demonstrability and to which the popular understanding of dogma extensive in Protestantism is oriented. In a certain way this is also true of the history of dogma as a historically limited phenomenon, as Harnack developed it. The theological critique of ecclesiastical dogma as a fundamentally unevangelical phenomenon, even in terms of the idea, converges with the common modern animosity against dogma. As a result of this, must this word and its derivative "dogmatics" be regarded as abolished?

THE THEOLOGICALLY JUSTIFIED INTENTION OF THE DOGMATIC

If one draws the balance on what has been said, no unambiguous finished results can be formulated on the basis of the diverse historical findings. However, certain points of reference emerge. The term "dogmatics" does not presuppose the concept of an authoritative, defined ecclesiastical dogma but was originally critically related to it. Dogmatics is oriented to the dogmatic form of teaching. To be sure, its character requires particular clarification and argumentation with regard to its theological content. Nevertheless, the extent to which and the relationship in which the word "dogma" is used is a question in itself. In any case it is not accidental that the segment of systematic theology that concentrates on statements of faith has drawn the designation "dogmatics" to itself. Some directions will be indicated for the inner connection that exists between Christian faith and dogmatic theology and the intentions that justify an appropriate theological use of the words "dogma" and "dogmatics."

FAITH AS AN OBJECT OF DOCTRINE

The terms "dogmatics" and "dogma" remind one that theology deals with God and for that reason with faith in the mode of doctrine. What the Christian faith has to say does not bear the character of mystagogy or of mere assertions of feeling but bears the character of a truth that can be publicly represented and discussed. To be sure, the Christian word is primarily not doctrine but witness. It expresses the truth that claims to stand the test of life in the face of the mystery of reality. For that reason Christian faith is capable of being explicated with regard to its connection with every experience of reality and perception of truth. This is precisely what "doctrine" means, namely, the development of the subject for the purpose of understanding it in the broadest possible horizon. Therefore, the derivation from its philosophical linguistic usage is important for the theological use of the terms "dogma" and "dogmatics." In contrast to the prejudgment that dogmatics separates theology from the general use of reason, it precisely obligates a person to a responsible appropriation of the relation between faith and reason. There is and must be dogmatic theology solely because it is appropriate to faith to engage in thought. It is not blind and thoughtless faith. It presses toward understanding and releases an inexhaustible wealth of ideas.

THE CERTAINTY OF FAITH AS DETERMINATIVE OF THE MODE OF STATEMENT

The concepts "dogma" and "dogmatics" can also express the fact that the teaching of faith is doctrine that is clear, definite, and to be represented with certainty. Of course, it already lies in the concept of doctrine as such that, within the framework appropriate to the object, it is anxious for the greatest possible clarity, definiteness, reliability, and that the person teaching stands by what is said. However, in view of the peculiarity of the basis for certainty in matters of faith this aspect requires clarification.

For the sake of the certainty of faith, a warning must be put forward against encouraging a dogmatism under a false appeal to this certainty. If skepticism means nothing more than the self-restraint that tests things, sober caution vis-à-vis hasty judgments, the justified consideration and weighing of all arguments, as well as the knowledge, which makes one modest, about the limitations, fallibility, and need of correction that belong to one's own insights, about the changeable character of experience and thought, and about the temporality of theology, then precisely this sort of skepticism should suit the theologian well. Knowing the dangers that especially threaten the theologian in this regard, one should take particular care not to adopt opinions unexamined, establish unfounded assertions, or cover one's own lack of knowledge by a loudly voiced pathos. The worst illusion to which the theologian can fall prey is imaginary certainty. One must be aware of and admit what is questionable and uncertain to oneself. Therefore the theologian should not avoid the most strenuous self-critical reflection and, if the case arises, should not shrink from the reproach of complexity. One also should take care not to get lost in the thicket of problems—"that by some evil spirit round and round is led, while fair, green pastures round about him lie"[2]—or conversely not confuse what is intellectually primitive with what is mentally elemental and hold the absence of problems for immediate clarity.

The element of certainty belongs in a certain way to Christian doctrine as it derives from its subject matter. The certainty that belongs to the essence of Christian faith itself must be incorporated into the mode of its doctrinal development. Christian doctrine can only claim to be such if it arrives not merely at problematic statements but also at assertive ones, that is, at judgments that express an unrestricted and unconditional reality and assert the truth. Of course, this avoids the charge of dogmatism only if account has been given of the extent to which this involves a ground of certainty that as such is not subject to scientific procedures of proof and if statements of faith that produce the basis of certainty are distinguished from explanatory theological assertions, for which no infallibility is claimed. Christian faith as such cannot be scientifically investigated with regard to its truth, but it can be so investigated with regard to its development. It does justice to its object only when it formulates assertive judgments through its connection with the basis for the certainty of faith. This is what is dogmatic in a Christian dogmatics. It implies the dogmatician's concern to move beyond a historically descriptive report to one's own judgment that is oriented to the subject matter, and in this way to provide help in thought and language for engagement with the statements of faith.

2. Johann Wolfgang von Goethe, *Faust*, tr. George Madison Priest (1941; Chicago: Encyclopaedia Britannica, 1952), pp. 1832–33.

ARTICULATION OF THE CONTENTS OF FAITH

The word "dogma" can indicate that at a given time what faith has to say can be condensed to a few statements or even a single one. Statements of this kind contain a clarifying, guiding significance that transcends even the change in times. One could call them fundamental statements of faith. We meet such linguistic events that form tradition outside the Bible in outstanding turning points in church history. The linguistic character of such elemental statements would certainly be misinterpreted if one wanted to add them all together and harmonize them into a system. They form a whole only to the extent that they interpret one and the same thing within each different horizon of interpretation. Each genuine statement of faith is *in nuce* complete The fact that faith presses toward a variety of statements does not result merely from the fact that it can only be expressed in a broken and incomplete way (which is valid only with reservations). Rather this is the case above all because faith becomes the inexhaustible source of the authorization of language. That we are to take account of an aggregate of statements, whose coherence is to be considered, is expressed by the concept of the articles of faith, which aims at a plurality of statements from the beginning. However, even in this case, it is an undividable faith that is articulated in different aspects. In each article the whole is present, but the whole is therefore at stake in each. This is even a criterion of what merits being called an article of faith: only that which speaks of the one thing involved in faith in such a way that a person would lose this one thing if a person explicitly denied this particular article of faith. Something can be an article of faith only if it expresses in a particular respect what is the one, decisive, and necessary thing, not what is individual, isolated, and supplementary.

RELIGIOUS DOCTRINE AND ECCLESIASTICAL CONSENSUS

Primarily the word "dogma," as well as the designation of the discipline as "dogmatics," reminds a person that it is suitable for theology to deal with the question of ecclesiastical doctrine. Dogmatics cannot represent mere private opinions. Dogmatics must attempt to express what the church has commonly confessed and believed even though it does so in one's own noninterchangeable mental handwriting. That is not directed toward statistical inquiry, although even that can be of interest dogmatically, but it is directed toward that which makes the church the church. Therefore, dogmatics participates in the inescapable and questionable character of confessional division. This is due not merely to the pragmatic basis of preparation for service in particular churches. Correct theology cannot further the elements of that which has a narrowing effect. It must strive to say in a particular way, even in an anticonfessional way, what Christian faith as such is. Nevertheless, in the fundamental confessional difference within the church the question about what it is that makes the church the church has been raised in such depth that one cannot be indifferent toward this difference without becoming superficial. The topical interest of this confessional difference certainly has been hidden under much historical debris. Yet as long as this difference has not been overcome by a deeper penetration into the subject matter of the Christian faith, dogmatics, quite apart from pragmatic viewpoints, will continue to give account of Christian doctrine with a fundamental orientation that is either Catholic or evangelical. For what is confessionally at issue is not merely particular doctrinal contents but the understanding of ecclesiastical doctrine itself and its relation to theology. Nevertheless, as the discussions about the development of dogma, even on the Catholic side, show, ecclesiastical doctrine can in no case be produced apart from theological concern about its identification and interpretation. For that reason, however, dogmatics conversely does not stand by its subject matter apart from a concern for an ecclesiastical consensus.

DOGMATICS AS A SEPARATE DISCIPLINE

The viewpoint that results from the name of the discipline is largely the sort of viewpoint that belongs to a fundamental theology. It calls attention to problems that strike upon the nature of theology as such and therefore will still return within the framework of fundamental theology. The fact that all theological work is touched by the dogmatic aspect raises more sharply the question about the justification of dogmatics as a separate discipline. By bringing the history of dogmatics into view, one also becomes aware of the deep threat to dogmatics that grows out of its own historicity.

DOGMATICS IN THE CLASSICAL FORM

From a very early time Christian literature included both a more exegetical and a more systematic explication of theological ideas, following either the course of biblical texts or the substantive structure of particular themes. Even in the second case an exegetical orientation to biblical texts predominated, while in the first case a dogmatic way of thinking predominated, for which each text became an entry into the whole of Christian faith. However, even presentations of Christian faith with a more comprehensive concern, such as the young Origen's writing *"Peri archon"* or works with a catechetical purpose do not fall within the genre we are accustomed to calling dogmatics. What began to be designated as dog- matics initially in the seventeenth century in orthodox Protestant theology arose—*cum grano salis*—at the turn from the twelfth to the thirteenth century. What is characteristic of this literature is threefold.

The strict *systematizing procedure* had in mind the aim at the broadest possible completeness and inner coherence of the statements of faith, a harmonization of the tensions and contradictions in the definitive tradition of the Bible and the fathers, as well as reflection on the revealed doctrine in the context of the whole of the awareness of truth, anchoring the revealed doctrine in that awareness of truth and simultaneously preserv- ing its distinction from nature and reason. This comprehensive undertak- ing could not be carried out without providing a *scholarly method*. The commissioning of Aristotelian philosophy, particularly logic and meta- physics, provided theology with the required methodological equipment and governed the procedure of argumentation that was reflected above all in the microstructure of the great systematic works. The fact that system- atic theology was rendered scholarly allowed it to become the definitive form of theology as such. Therefore the problem of the scholarly character of theology was concentrated on systematic theology. This resulted, finally, in a *hypertrophy of doctrine*, a multiplication of theological problems, the tendency to a degree toward an intellectual and theological imperial- ism, and the danger of self-deception about the historically conditioned character of an orthodoxy that understood itself as timeless.

THE REFORMATION'S CRITICISM OF DOGMATICS

The Reformation's criticism of the systematic theology of Scholasticism cannot be reduced to the formal viewpoint that the Scripture principle obviously meant that primacy must again be given to the exegetical pro- cedure in theology. Melanchthon's and Calvin's new impulses toward a dog- matics modified by the Reformation were fundamentally legitimate, even though they also disclosed the problems that appeared with such a radical departure from the tradition of dogmatic theology. The far-reaching return of the Scholastic style of dogmatics in classical Protestant Orthodoxy deserves historical understanding, taking into account the circumstances of the time. Yet to a large degree false developments that had been battled by the Reformation appeared again. The Scripture principle was certainly the foundation for the theological doctrine of principles, but its theological effect was dogmatically domesticated. The principal problem that the Reformation posed for dogmatics consisted neither in detailed dogmatic corrections nor in obvious methodological questions like the use of philosophy, but was a hidden question. Within the framework of the traditional dogmatic outline, was it possible at all to accent the concentration on the theme that is fundamental for theology in such a way that what belongs together in the event of word and faith is not taken apart and torn asunder by being cast into a sequence? Connected with this is the question as to whether there does not inhere in dogmatics a tendency toward self-representation and perfection that is difficult to harmonize with the serving function that should determine all theological work with regard to the situation of need in which it has its setting in life (*Sitz im Leben*).

THE CRISIS OF DOGMATICS IN MODERN TIMES

Even though the crisis into which dogmatics has fallen primarily has causes other than the Reformation criticism, there are nevertheless characteristic points of contact in the principal points. The emancipation of biblical theology, which was sharpened to a form of historical theology, created the dogmatic legitimation for its separation from dogmatics out of dogmatics itself by appealing to the Scripture principle. The break with the language of the dogmatic tradition appeared to be justified by the freeing process of the Reformation, which, seen from outside, equally presented itself as a process of shaking off the burden of tradition. The loss of the uniting obligation to the valid ecclesiastical doctrine presented itself as the consequence of the Reformation's struggle against ecclesiastical doctrinal authority, and the softening of confessionalism as the necessary continuation of the split in the confessions. Without a doubt connections of this sort exist; nevertheless, the crisis of dogmatics now began to encroach upon the roots of the Reformation's criticism itself.

By disengaging biblical theology as historical theology from the domination of dogmatics, the question arose about the extent to which biblical theology could be expected to share responsibility for the dogmatic task of theology as a whole. A dogmatics that now for the first time was degraded to being a special discipline could no longer exercise its original function in this isolation, while another discipline, such as exegesis for example, was not at all in the position, or willing, to step into the breach. The crisis of theology in general is sketched in the crisis of dogmatics. If with the consistent understanding of historical method the dogmatic method as such has been brought to a close, which according to Troeltsch's pitiless diagnosis defines the whole of the previous supernaturalistic theological thought, then the problem is posed as to whether, paradoxically formulated, there can be an—approximate to this understanding of dogmatic theology—"undogmatic" dogmatics, that is, a dogmatics that has taken historical-critical thought into itself. It is obvious that a process of reduction that would discard the ballast that has been dogmatically overcome in favor of the few things that still remain from the old dogmatic style is not sufficient. Rather, what was required after the collapse of the dogmatic doctrine of principles of Protestant orthodoxy was a new consideration of the foundations of dogmatics, of that which is the source from which its statements proceed and bestows the character of binding force and inner necessity. Again Schleiermacher was the dogmatician of modern times who introduced us to this problem in the most penetrating way.

PRINCIPAL PROBLEMS OF DOGMATIC THEOLOGY

The crisis into which dogmatics has fallen appears to drive the concern about it that leads us further into contradictory directions.

Since the whole is at stake it initially seems to be necessary to conceive a new, totally systematic outline. In contrast to that, it not only corresponds to the limited possibilities of a profound new approach but also appears to be most meaningful and fruitful to begin with individual problems and to compile dogmatic monographs instead of dogmatic compendia in order to grasp the whole from the details and in the details.

Another dilemma touches that. The dogmatic question of principles appears to be the most urgent, for without the clarification of this question there is apparently little promise in tackling the themes of substantive dogmatics. On the other hand, the isolated preference for questions of method threatens in dogmatics, as always, to produce idle motion, which can be hindered only by a resolute decision to give priority to particular questions of substance. Thinking that circles within itself must be opened to what is concrete in order to obtain initially the experience that is the basis for fruitfully discussing questions of method.

Finally, the critical situation of dogmatics seems to intensify its task of providing a contemporary account of Christian faith to such a degree that the viewpoint of immediate interest fully dominates. Nevertheless, there is little hope of attaining again in our altered situation a discipline of dogmatic theology that merits this name and can withstand the comparison with its history if a person has not become fundamentally familiar with the classical form of dogmatics and its problems. It is necessary to deal carefully with the dogmatic tradition precisely in the interest of our contemporary responsibility. With these reservations three crucial problems that affect the whole of dogmatics can be named.

STRUCTURE

The problem of how the biblical revelation, which was saturated with history, could be presented and discussed systematically was solved in an impressive way in the classical form of dogmatics. The general framework was formed by the universal salvation-historical outline in stylized lines running from the creation and fall through the Christ event to the end of all things. The salvation-historical outline related to the individual fits into this schema: a person participates in the creation and fall and in the soteriological event through repentance, justification, and sanctification with the whole oriented toward death and resurrection. Both were anchored metaphysically in a general doctrine of God that secured the universal relation to reality, as well as a formal anthropology, above all a structural psychology, and finally an ontology, a doctrine of categories, and logic as the medium of a comprehensive hermeneutic of the revealed reality. When the integrating power of the philosophical implements disappeared, this classical schema became problematic, because it did not measure up to the system-breaking power of history. The decisive difficulty did not consist in the fact that the salvation-historical sketch no longer coincided with the insight into the course and problem of a universal history. Rather, the essential question was how to make allowance so that the compulsion to an ordered sequence, of whatever kind, does not hinder the insight into the coherence and the interrelatedness that unites everything in the development of dogmatic statements. Yet the experience that one meets the whole in each of its points should not make one incapable of presenting the state of the facts in its inner movement and in the multilayered character of its factors.

PROCEDURE

The classical dogmatic procedure of proof from Scripture in fact always consisted in more than merely mentioning biblical proof texts. The hermeneutical problem implicit in it now requires a comprehensive treatment, not only with regard to the way the results of historical-critical exegesis of Scripture are to be brought into dogmatic work, nor only with regard to the way the various linguistic levels within the Bible itself and within the dogmatic tradition are to be grasped in their distinctness and transferences are to be made among these levels, but above all with regard to the understandability of this transmitted language in the context of contemporary language. The decision about that falls on the hermeneutical power of the transmitted texts to illuminate the contemporary experience of reality. Thus the hermeneutical problem is connected with the problem of verification. It involves the verification of dogmatic statements in the contemporary reality, but in such a way that this task on behalf of the subject matter of dogmatic theology cannot be carried through at all apart from engaging the question about what it is that brings this contemporary reality itself to the truth.

THE INNER LOGIC OF THE SUBJECT MATTER

If the goal of dogmatic theology is not the most complete summation of dogmatic statements possible, but the aptitude for arriving at dogmatic statements, then what matters above all is what it is that makes the capacity for judgment possible, one could say, a canon of dogmatic thought. Put in a way that is extremely broad and, although indefinite, is extremely provocative, one could formulate this canon as the advice to pay attention with equal attentiveness to the Christian tradition as well as to the contemporary experience of reality, and from time to time allow oneself to be driven from one to the other and to be drawn into a mutual critical conversation. The Reformation's distinction between law and gospel, which is oriented to Paul, leads one most deeply into the inner nexus of the subject matter—by treating the dialectic that is constitutive of it—to the extent that one succeeds in releasing this distinction from its isolation as a special topic in theology as well as from its solidification to a historical form of doctrine in order to deal with it as a guide for one's theological capacity for judgment. Seen in the light of the total tradition of Christian theology, the doctrine of the Trinity presents such a comprehensive canon of dogmatic thought. One can see the sense in which this is the case if one interprets the doctrine of the Trinity from the viewpoint of the appropriate talk of God. Contrary to the customary development of Trinitarian statements, the following principle for theological dogmatics emerges: talk about the Holy Spirit as the power that frees and makes everything new must be talk about Jesus Christ. And talk about Jesus Christ must take place as talk about God, so that talk about God becomes talk about humanity and about the reality that concerns humanity unconditionally.

11

Ethics

THE VIEW TO WHAT IS HUMAN

Ethics directs our attention entirely to what is human: to what is purely human, commonly human, and concretely human. It treats what is purely human because it deals with the behavior and action of people on their own responsibility, cast upon themselves as though there were no God. It treats what is commonly human because no responsible person is released from this responsibility and each in his or her own way participates in this general responsibility. It treats what is concretely human because the question of correct behavior and action is decided in particular situations and under constantly different demands and situations.

Now it would certainly be fatal for theology if this aspect entered its field of view initially and solely in ethics. What is specifically human, the viewpoint of what is generally binding, as well as the orientation to what is concrete, belong throughout to the subject matter of theology itself. There is, to be sure, a concept of theology that exclusively makes its ethical impact the standard by which it is measured. That poses the question as to whether it would not then be more consistent to give up theology completely in favor of ethics. In spite of all that, if the peculiar and irreplaceable character of theology consists in the fact that it is precisely theology that truly expresses for the first time what unconditionally concerns each person in his or her concrete existence, then this cannot take place independently of the ethical. Ethics, therefore, does not merely have the role of a subsequent area of practical application within theology, however such a role might be interpreted in detail. Rather, the phenomenon of ethics also and even primarily has the function of a horizon of understanding apart from which what the subject matter of theology is could not be made clear. The definition of the task of ethics as a discipline and its encyclopedic arrangement, of course, customarily stand under the perspective of the consequences of faith. Nevertheless, the problem of ethics runs through the totality of the attempt to render an account of faith. The more strongly the pressure into what is purely human, commonly human, and concretely human comes to its validity in the discipline of ethics, the more urgent it is to allow the experiences that come into view through that to be effective for the understanding of theology in general.

Thus, with the turn to ethics the question of the subject matter of theology is intensified. For it is not at all immediately clear what it is that allows a person to be theologically attentive in this field. For that reason it is advisable initially to restrain the theological question and to describe the phenomenon of ethics for itself as far as is possible.

THE PHENOMENON OF THE ETHICAL

Rooted in Human Existence

As everyone knows, the peculiarity of human existence consists in the fact that human beings have not been fixed on a particular mode of behavior. As distinct from the biologically programmed course of life of the other creatures, human beings have an incomparably broad field of play for the possibilities of life, but above all the capacity to alter themselves. Here immediately appear all the significant catchwords that characterize the situation in various respects from the perspective of the same root. The human being not only has sense organs (*Sinnesorgane*) but as the "*zoon logon echon*" (living creature having language) also, so to speak, has an organ of sense (meaning—*Sinnorgan*). Human beings of course belong to a species, but they are distanced from themselves as members of a species through consciousness and personal existence. Human beings are not limited to the exchange of signals with those like themselves, but possess language, which is capable of making everything an object and bringing it into conversation. People do not merely have an environment, but are open to the world, make their world for themselves, and correspondingly create their environment for themselves. Certainly, humans live under the law of heredity, but beyond that they have the freedom to transmit and to be engaged with tradition. Human beings are not merely temporal, but relate themselves to time and therefore live historically.

As a result of the space for play given to the possibilities for life, it is necessary for humans to shape life rather than simply living it and thus initially to actualize themselves. They *can* choose. They must determine themselves. And by doing this—even if it is done in such a way that decisions are avoided—who they are is determined. Although they can and must choose, they *may* not choose arbitrarily. The limit that that sets is quite different from the fact that they *cannot* choose arbitrarily. Limits are obviously set for the possibilities for choice through the resistance of given facts. People experience that equally in the narrowness and repetitive constraints in the customary circumstances of life as well as in the dizzying breadth of their advances into what is unaccustomed and uninvestigated. For in the reception of what is given, the challenge to a task is initially ignited, in the resistance of the material, the incentive to its formation, and the experience of a limit, the possibility of arguing with it. Even if the limit is shown to be fundamental or is in fact insurmountable due to the circumstances, and the vexing impression arises that no choice remains to a person, *how* one relates oneself to that situation still remains open. Thus, in dependence an independence makes itself known, which for its part is again the expression of an entirely different sort of dependence. People know themselves to be dependent on a judgment by virtue of which possibilities are offered to them and even intrude imperiously. There no one can exist any longer by appearance, and particular possibilities that are richly offered are prohibited. This is the root of the ethical.

THE DEMARCATION WITHIN HUMAN EXISTENCE

The realm of modes of behavior and action that are based on choice and thus, in an entirely general sense, are conditioned by judgment extends much more widely than the phenomenon of ethics. It embraces all activity that rests on a particular insight and is directed by it. Yet this viewpoint should not mislead a person into arranging together things that are categorically different. Every human action can move under the aspect of ethics, so that in that aspect fundamentally different viewpoints with regard to choice can meet and compete with one another. Of course, those points of intersection that allow the phenomenon of ethics to become imprecise are much more difficult. The sharp demarcation of ethics is certainly, historically seen, a later development, and certainly can also disappear again. Such manifestations into which ethics has sunk in the past and can repeatedly sink are especially custom, law, and religion. The connection ethics has with them can only be clarified if one takes account of the ambivalence of the relationship. For with regard to all the indicated directions a mixture is just as disastrous as a separation.

The convention of *custom*, which releases a person from decisions, conceals what is genuinely ethical and at times contradicts it. Nevertheless, within a culture, morality can scarcely be developed and exist without the help of corresponding custom. The *law*, which includes the potential of being able to carry it out—even in cases when the factual relationships of power render it impossible—draws the outer boundaries for ignoring what is ethical. However, since it is oriented to what can generally be controlled and if need be what can be compelled, it can neither guarantee what is moral nor replace it. Yet for its part it is dependent on being measured by the standard of what is moral, as well as being defined and corrected by it. *Religion*, finally, allows what is moral to be embedded in the totality of an understanding of the world and of an orientation of life as it derives from a particular manifestation of the holy. The danger lies in mixing cultic prescriptions into the understanding of what is moral as well as mixing moral achievements into the religious understanding of salvation. Nevertheless, the reservation intrudes no less as to whether a complete emancipation of what is moral from what is religious is able to preserve the purity of ethics that is proclaimed in this way, without falling into pseudoreligious dependencies or even damaging the content of ethics.

INNER STRUCTURES

The attempt to characterize the phenomenon of ethics by a few principal structures appears to shatter on the fact that the wealth of ethical phenomena can be interpreted as an inherently unified phenomenon only by means of an ethical theory that is already presupposed. This obvious suspicion can only be met by giving the problem of inconsistency explicit consideration.

Historicity

Historical changeableness, in fact, appears to be difficult to unite with the phenomenon of the ethical. What is supposed to be unconditionally obligatory threatens to disintegrate through the recognition of its historical conditionedness. The stability of a self-contained society seems to be the most favorable for the ethical: a culture, a political commonwealth, or, at least, a corresponding common way of thinking, that is, conditions that grant what is ethical the appearance of exclusiveness, unambiguity, and obviousness. We know the extent to which the disintegration of the Greek *polis*, or the encounter of the West with foreign cultures, or the confrontation of traditional morality with the changing relationships of the industrial age have unleashed a crisis in ethics which people easily experience as the disintegration of ethics as such. Of course, the complaint about a decline in morality that always accompanies the change in generations warns us to be careful. The fact that there are historical ups and downs in the area of ethics also is just as obvious as the fact that ethical crises of large extent often were the birth pangs of a new ethical consciousness. In any case, one cannot speak about the danger of a simple disappearance of ethics if it is true that the phenomenon as such is rooted in human existence. Then one can expect that the compulsion of what is given with human existence will provide for the ethical dimension to establish its validity.

That certainly does not remove the problems: contradictory evaluations of the same circumstances at different times (for example, in sexual questions), or the simultaneous contradiction of fundamentally different expressions of ethos in a pluralistic society, not to speak of the competing multiplicity of ethical systems. Precisely the fact that ethics in itself is controversial belongs to the phenomenon of the ethical. To harmonize ethics by reducing it to a consensus about ethical fundamentals that are inherent in human nature can scarcely be justified, and this is even less true of the expectation that further historical development will produce such a consensus. However, this does not provide space for the skepticism that in the field of ethics there are no points of convergence or possibilities for understanding at all. The uncontestable constants of human existence, as they are given, for example, in the elementary needs of life and human relationships, certainly have their primary constancy in the problems they produce, not in the solutions to these problems nor even necessarily in the formulations of the problems. For all that, these constants hold the breadth of variation in the divergencies in check, especially if a person distinguishes between the intention and the conditions for its realization. The perspectives that result from the equalizing influence of industrial society for the phenomenon of ethics remains an equally open and disturbing question. Neither the previously unknown degree of global exchange and the mutuality that helps civilize people nor the process by which the historical roots of traditional morality are dissolved can be left out of consideration.

Principle and Situation

In all its modifications, the phenomenon of the ethical is defined by the polarity of a basic insight that has binding force and the changing life situation with its problems. The way in which the phenomenon of the ethical presents itself depends not only on the peculiarity of the ethical principle but also, above all, on the mode of the relationship to the situation established in it. "Principle" is obviously used here in a very broad sense and means the fundamental experience that obligates a person, which defines an ethos. It is essentially inherent to the phenomenon of ethics that it does not present an accidental conglomerate of individual rules of behavior, but it is concentrically related to an initial impulse in which a total understanding of human existence is settled and from which it derives its orientation and motivation. That can be the divine authority of a law, the binding power of a particular living community, an image of self-realization, a utopian conception of the goal of history, the power of an idea of the highest good whether it be righteousness, freedom, love, or reverence for life, and so on. Whether explicitly or not, in each case the "should" is based on an "is," the imperative on an indicative, the task on a gift, even though the conceptions of this relationship can differ strongly. Together with that it is also determined how one comes from the "should" to the "will," how the perception of evil and the evaluation of its conquest are related to one another. However, how one moves from ethical insight to ethical action is not merely a question of moral strength. This poses a problem that is particularly pressing for the phenomenon of the ethical: the negotiation between the universal and the particular, the principle and the situation; the translation of the fundamental demand into the concrete demand, of the simplicity of the idea into the complexity of life. The spirit of an ethos is stamped by whether a casuistic norming or the flexibility of responsible freedom of discretion is decisive in this process.

Multilayered Character

Beyond the historically multiformed character of what is ethical, we must consider a further differentiation that gives rise to an internal multi-layered character. The idea of a double ethos as a special case of a double truth has been generally neglected, ultimately correctly, as not discussable. This should not lead a person to be deceived about the fact that this reflects an essential structural element of what is ethical. The fact that one thing may not be befitting for all may widely be attributed to the difference in the situations that determine people's lives, which also include circumstances that last a long time. Thus, a regional compartmentalization to various sorts of ethos related to a person's status and vocation can be justified as a result of various concrete conditions. Also the difference between aspects of individual and social ethics that becomes acute for each person can be explained in a corresponding way. Of course, this difference needs to be relativized, since the phenomenon of ethics as such, even in social ethics, can never be detached from the responsibility of the individual, while the individual ethical components cannot be isolated from their social aspect, since the human person as an individual always stands in intersubjective and transsubjective relationships.

In contrast, a more important question is whether the factual relationships do not furnish illuminating reasons for contrasting a freely chosen elite ethos with what is ethically responsible for everyone. That need not have the character of introverted arrogance, but it could be understood as a simple modification of the idea of vocation and service. Still more provocative and perhaps even more urgent is the question as to whether it may not be the case that for one and the same person there could be an acute distinction between participation in the public moral standard and claiming an extraordinary dispensation by virtue of a necessity of conscience that cannot be generalized—an extreme case of the ethical relevance of the situation. Nevertheless, a fundamental condition with regard to such possibilities in each case is that in spite of everything, it continues to preserve the unity of the phenomenon of the ethical in a defensibly higher sense.

Dead Ends

Finally, it is an essential fact for the phenomenon of the ethical that problems that are ethically not solvable and that transcend the horizon of the ethical break open in it and indeed are directly produced by it.

The Absolute Demand

Apart from the unconditional element ethics would be perverted into something merely pragmatic. The truth and presence of this unconditional element, nevertheless, is a theme that does not fall within the competence of ethical discussion. At this point ethics is necessarily entangled with more comprehensive connections to the experience of reality, namely, with religious or philosophical questions. That is all the more true if the unfulfillable character of the absolute demand is endured, and thus the discrepancy between the unconditional and the conditional is not hastily resolved in favor of the latter. It is inherent to the phenomenon of the ethical that it sets standards in relation to which people's behavior and action fall short, not just accidentally and occasionally but essentially.

Guilt

The failure of people in their moral fallibility produces consequences that reach further than that which can be eradicated in order to make it good again. The problem, for example, of reestablishing trust that has been destroyed certainly has an ethical aspect, but it points to dimensions that are not accessible to human actions. In view of the opaque and incalculable network into which human responsibility is interwoven, the consciousness of guilt has a counterpart that cannot be directly circumscribed. For what is violated does not absolutely coincide ethically with what it is that has been touched by the violation. However, the domain of the problem of guilt includes not only the failure that is fundamentally avoidable, but—and this is a most significant symptom of the phenomenon of the ethical—guilt that becomes unavoidable in situations of ethical conflict. To deny its character as guilt for that reason betrays an ethicizing endeavor to render the ethical phenomenon harmless.

Fate

Finally, problems that arise from the fact that the reality experienced does not correspond to ethical standards break out in the phenomenon of ethics. The questions of predestination and theodicy formulate different aspects of the problem, that people who are determined to act ethically find themselves exposed to contexts of reality that cannot be calculated by ethical standards and before which people as ethical beings are apparently powerless. How the unconditional character of the ethical can nevertheless be made compatible with that is a question that can be rejected or suppressed within the boundaries of ethics, but it cannot be answered.

PHILOSOPHICAL ETHICS

"Ethics" has existed since Aristotle. Not only does this term stem from him, but he also gave it its first systematic treatment, which had an extraordinary historical effect. As a consequence, the precise treatment of the phenomenon of ethics in its peculiarity is a philosophical action, and seen as a whole it also remains a peculiarity of philosophical ethics. It includes, therefore, from its origin and in its continuation an element of emancipation.

EMANCIPATION

The element of emancipation is a common feature of ancient and modern philosophical ethics, as different as these two principal phases may be within themselves and in relation to one another and as much as this kind of total judgment for that reason can only be expressed with reservations. However, it is clear that the ethical interest of classical Greek and especially Hellenistic philosophy was directed toward its strictly rational basis and permeation, as distinct from the traditional religious and political formation or morality. The same is true for modern philosophical ethics, in spite of the very different situation from which it proceeds in the Christian West. The viewpoint of emancipation certainly cannot be given a purely antithetic accent. The ancient philosophical ethics did not simply produce a break with what was traditional, but it preserved a certain spiritual continuity in a transforming process, which was caused by the collapse of the orders and the forms of thought that were no longer productive. Modern philosophical ethics also originally did not have a revolutionary pathos vis-à-vis the Christian heritage. Rather, in view of the confessional struggles over what was Christian, it saw itself compelled to place the principal elements of its ethos on a basis that was generally valid and thus to preserve them as effective in the disruption of the times. Thus, in both cases, if the viewpoint of independence tends to conceal these connections, it is still unmistakably the case that philosophical ethics does not produce the phenomenon of the ethical, but interprets it. Also, in relation to the ethos it represents, philosophical ethics feeds from an already lived ethos to a high degree.

AUTONOMY

In agreement with this general characterization, the concept of freedom, understood as autonomy, understandably represents a leading concept of philosophical ethics, even though in very diverse interpretations. The independence from external determination (in whatever form, for example, by the passions or a bestowed law) receives its exegesis through the inner dialectic of freedom and law (whether freedom is understood as agreement with nature or as self-determination under the categorical imperative). This autonomous understanding of freedom betrays a strong ethical optimism, along with its high ethical pathos. With relatively few exceptions this ethical optimism has been a common basic feature of philosophical ethics since Aristotle. The right and duty of self-determination rests on the presupposed integrity of human existence to which appeal can be made. The autonomy of the moral implies confidence with respect to its effectiveness. That does not exclude conflict that requires engagement and effort, but it promises that the problems of life will be mastered along an ethical pathway precisely under the banner of the most extreme legal strictness, as it fundamentally belongs to the idea of autonomy.

EVIDENCE

Philosophical ethics replaces establishment through authority with establishment through rational evidence. That corresponds to its intention to free the phenomenon of the ethical from the embrace of a particular religion and regional custom, and to provide it with its universal human breadth, and to demonstrate its strict universal validity. The basis is provided by a philosophical anthropology in which the viewpoint of rational evidence is anchored. Yet a dilemma appears in its wake. The attempt to comprehend radically the ethical phenomenon under the viewpoint of what obligates people unconditionally and universally leads to a formalization of ethics. It becomes difficult if not impossible to arrive at particular ethical content from this formalization. If, in contrast, the concern is directed toward questions of substantive ethics, then ethics is threatened either with the loss of what has general validity, which is replaced by value judgments that cannot be rationally derived, or with the loss of the strictly conceived ethical aspect as a result of the behavioral sciences. Of course, in their way the behavioral sciences support the need of a universally illuminating account, but they make it questionable whether behavioral studies or ethology can still result in a path toward a normative ethics. Thus the right of philosophical ethics to exist is threatened with denial altogether in the name of scientificness.

ETHICS AS A THEOLOGICAL DISCIPLINE

Theology would be ill-advised if it expected to gain from the fact that philosophical ethics has become questionable. The history of Christian ethics has been deeply impregnated by the influence of philosophical ethics. For the period of the ancient church Stoicism was of primary significance for Christian ethics, for Scholasticism Aristotelian ethics, which Melanchthon immediately returned to honor in Protestantism as well, while in the nineteenth century a comparable role fell to Kant. Correspondingly, theology has also participated in the crisis of philosophical ethics. That cannot be disposed of simply as the consequence of a harmful dependence of theology on philosophy. Certainly the strong influence of philosophical ethics has problematic aspects, especially if it is misused as an interpretive tool for central theological statements. Luther reproached the Scholastic adaptation of Aristotle as such a misuse. Nevertheless, there is a deep basis in the subject matter of theology for an openness toward philosophical ethics. To be sure, the great confessions are divided on the way in which this is established. On the side of Catholicism—in any case according to its normative tradition—the interest in the philosophical idea of natural law predominates. Through the Catholic concept of the relation between nature and grace this idea can be subjugated in detail to the claim of ecclesiastical interpretation. From the side of the Reformation an ecclesiastical regimentation of ethics is rejected. This is not due to general objections to an ecclesiastical teaching authority, but it is a consequence of a different conception of the theological relevance of ethics. It permitted and even required the uncensored voice of reason to be expressed in those things that fall within a person's own responsibility. That does not mean that everything that passes itself off as the voice of reason is recognized as such without contradiction, and above all it does not mean that one thereby allows oneself to be deprived of theological responsibility. Nevertheless, the latter does not have its direct competence in ethical questions, certainly also not in questions aside from ethics, but in the theological evaluation of the ethical.

THE THEOLOGICAL VIEW OF THE PHENOMENON OF THE ETHICAL

It is not because humanity is only a partial aspect of theology's theme that ethics does not receive the central role in theology. Rather, because humanity becomes the theme in a radical way with a view to its fundamental situation, the question of ethics is moved into a more comprehensive context through which it is on the one side intensified and on the other side limited. Theology as such is not ethics. This is expressed by the fact that what is directly given to theology and is considered by it has the character of gospel, for which human beings are considered exclusively as recipients, and not the character of law, which claims them in their activity. However, human beings come into consideration as recipients because they certainly live *in* activity but not *from* activity. Therefore the gospel is to be understood only in its relation to the law. Theology can be understandable in its specific difference from ethics only through its relation to the phenomenon of the ethical.

The intensification that befalls the phenomenon of the ethical in theology is concentrated in the understanding of sin. This word is a religious category, not a moral one. However, it is only correctly interpreted theologically if its relation to the ethical is strictly grasped so that people are sinners not as a result of ceremonial offenses but as a consequence of their failure to meet their moral tasks. This failure, however, does not consist in individual moral lapses. They are only partial effects of a perversion of a person's fundamental orientation to and evaluation of the ethical, or more correctly of himself or herself with regard to the ethical. The idea that what is religious consists in adding duties toward God to duties toward other people, and correspondingly offenses against God to offenses against fellow humans, does not correspond to the intention of the Christian understanding. One's relation to God does not stand alongside one's relation to the world, but it defines the latter as its decisive premise.

Anthropologically, this circumstance can be verified in the difference between human personal existence and the actions that derive from it and are determined by it. Sin in the genuine sense is not the failures in individual actions, which are always only partial, but the essentially total perversion of the person and therewith of the fundamental situation of humankind. Thus the theological intensification of the phenomenon of the ethical as it is expressed in the concept of sin does not consist in an introversion that considers the hidden sins of thought alongside the sins of action. Rather, it consists in the return to the root of all offenses, certainly not only of the individual moral *offenses* but also and above all of the false attitude toward moral *accomplishments*. According to Christian understanding, the fundamental sin is unbelief, understood as not wanting to be dependent on God. However, this understanding of sin also results in an extraordinary intensification of moral judgment in detail by relating all action to a single fundamental demand and measuring it by that demand: whether it carries out love. The intensification lies not in a multiplication of commands and prohibitions but in a radical simplification to a single command, love. Faith, as being incorporated into God's love, gives the freedom for love.

However, a limitation of the ethical dimension corresponds to this intensification that theology brings to the phenomenon of ethics. Precisely because it steps under that intensifying banner is this dimension reduced. It does not suffice to explain that by pointing to the moral weakness of humanity. This weakness exists, of course, but it is precisely humankind's moral strength that also comes into consideration under the viewpoint of sin. One cannot simply say that because people are sinners we cannot expect too much of them with respect to ethics. According to a theological judgment two things are correct. On the one side people can be promised nothing at all from the ethical with regard to their partial attainment of true life. On the other side the highest imaginable standard is established for the ethical, namely, love, which is the central concept of God's perfection. In terms of ethics, this love can only be a radiation from God's love, which has been received. Therefore, the ethical is limited to the concrete deed, and thus it is set free from the excessive demand that it provide the basis for people to create worth for themselves. This limitation to the concrete deed is accompanied by the limitation to the doing of love without personal claim. Love is set not on doing works that serve the doer by bringing praise but on works that best serve other people. Its goodness is dependent not on an abstract scale of value assigned to the possible contents for action but on the freedom to choose the helpful thing that is nearest at hand, even if it involves the most insignificant activity.

The limitation that befalls ethics in the Christian understanding of it takes effect in the fact that the social dimension is definitive for it. According to the Reformation conception, therefore, ethics has its genuine place in the so-called *usus civilis* or *usus politicus legis*.

DOGMATICS AND ETHICS

In order to understand ethics as a theological discipline, everything depends on the appropriate theological view of the phenomenon of ethics. One could say it depends on the dogmatic understanding of ethics. The great danger with regard to ethics as a theological discipline consists in the opinion that a particular form of the ethical as such guarantees its qualification as a theological discipline, and thus that ethics is a theological discipline by virtue of its own character. Rather, ethics becomes a theological discipline only when the character of independence, which adheres to it from its philosophical origin, is denied to it.

In contrast, however, the question of the definition of the disciplinary relation between dogmatics and ethics is of secondary importance. If a correct theological evaluation of the phenomenon of ethics is what matters and this results in an appeal to completely integrate ethics into dogmatics, this solution, in spite of its correct intention, is problematic for two reasons.

First, even such an insertion of ethics into dogmatics cannot conceal the fact that there is a distinction in themes, even if the transition in themes takes place repeatedly within the individual dogmatic loci rather than from one discipline to another. In favor of such a procedure it can certainly be maintained that it would help in treating the inner connection between dogmatics and ethics more strongly. Nevertheless, the danger of obscuring the distinction could also arise.

Second, and more important, in this case the ethical is threatened by being made Christian in a way that would short-circuit it as well as by being deprived of concrete experience. Theological ethics is not limited to a special Christian ethos. It does justice to its task only if it considers the problem of the ethical within the total breadth of what is purely human, generally human, and concretely human, and in doing so does not lag behind philosophical ethics. It has to treat ethics not only under the aspect of the fruits of faith but in its entire breadth under the aspect of the works of unbelief. That is, it has to treat ethics with regard for our joint responsibility for the problems of the ethical in a society in which what is Christian is no longer generally held to be valid, while the ethical surely makes the question of what is generally valid imperative. Only when theology exposes itself to the encounter with the detailed ethical phenomena as they crowd in today quite apart from theology and are guided by a clear theological perception with respect to the phenomenon of ethics can theology do justice to its task of venturing out upon the sea of contemporary ethical problems in solidarity with our contemporary times. The courage for such a boundless confrontation doubtless arises more effectively and comprehensively if a special discipline has been provided for it. Even the profusion of substantive questions can only be considered in that way. Yet this courage apparently to extensively step out from theology into the discipline of ethics stands in the service of theology only if a person remains mindful of the extent to which the engagement with detailed ethical questions as such has theological character.

THE ETHICAL EFFECTS OF CHRISTIAN FAITH

Without going into detail one can only state the general methodological rule for accomplishing the task of theological ethics. Everything that fundamentally belongs within the horizon of the ethical problem as it is conditioned by the circumstances of the time is to be subjected to two criteria: faith and love. According to Christian persuasion, these are the criteria of what constitutes the human as such. Ethical questions are treated theologically only when a person is able to give an account of how they are to be assessed in the light of faith and answered in a way appropriate to love. A Christian consensus in ethical questions in any case is by no means easier but rather more difficult to obtain than in dogmatic questions, and ethical commonality in ethical perception and decision also cannot be made the condition of commonality without further ado. Only the person who has lost the theological orientation with regard to the phenomenon of ethics can take offense at this insight.

12

Fundamental Theology

THE TASK OF FUNDAMENTAL THEOLOGY

One could expect that our course through the many divisions of theology would close with a comprehensive reflection on the whole rather than with an additional discipline. What was initially noted about the theme "the whole of theology" as a prelude in order to introduce the problem would now be taken up again and completed. The individual discussions that have taken place in between certainly allow us to recognize cross connections and repeatedly to ask about what is theologically constitutive and thus is common to them. In spite of that, a person will scarcely imagine that we have grasped the whole through having passed through all the stations along the way. Instead, the question is now posed all the more intensely as to how all this fits together into a single whole, especially if life itself is the touchstone rather than the ideal of a well-balanced architectonic being definitive for its wholeness. How does the tension-laden complex of theological study comply with the complexity of life? For it is probably correct to assume that it is precisely that which is capable of clearing up life that should tie the various aspects of theology into a unity. And how do I fit myself into the undertaking of theology? For its unity is undoubtedly fulfilled only in the living actualization of the theological vocation, not in a theory.

However, it is precisely the last discipline we are treating which deals with this theme that aims at the whole. It seems to be nonsense to think that the difficulty resulting from many disciplines would be removed by adding one more discipline and that the question of the whole should constitute a new special field. This presents a genuine dead end that should not be weakened too quickly. It shows clearly that the division of theology is not an expression of its perfection but the consequence of a necessity.

Reflection on the difficulties resulting from that therefore has the character of a service of necessity. Vicariously for all disciplines, fundamental theology has to watch out that theology does not come off the loser under the profusion of theological work. That would be the case if specialization resulted in becoming remote from theology rather than becoming absorbed in it. No matter how one may designate this service of necessity, which is intended to benefit the whole, it cannot fundamentally add anything new but only remember what has become acute in each discipline and should be perceived by each in its own way.

THE CONCEPT OF FUNDAMENTAL THEOLOGY
Talk About Fundamental Theology

The choice of the designation "fundamental theology" betrays traces of a particularly acute need in theology. What appears to be a mere loan word from Catholic theology, in which a discipline bearing this name has existed for somewhat more than a hundred years, appears in a different light as soon as a person follows the prehistory of the talk about theological fundamentals back into the theological controversies of the confessional age and also takes into account the extent to which the self-understanding of fundamental theology within present Catholic circles is contested and is in flux. Without going more closely into both of these aspects, the contemporary state of this problem within Protestant theology can be characterized as follows. For a long time the centrifugal effect of the emancipation of the disciplines within theology has been connected with the fact that the classical Protestant theological doctrinal principles have become untenable. Now, however, two things are new. This problem, which concerns the whole of theology, can no longer—as usually happened in the past—be adequately treated within dogmatics as its prolegomenon, for dogmatics itself has become one discipline among others, and, to be sure, a particularly contested and unsure discipline. Nevertheless, it is necessary to lay the foundation of theology in a way that takes explicit account of the disciplinary pluralism. Second, the various attempts to enter the breach with a new discipline have in part proved to be insufficient and in part merely partial. Therefore these attempts move partly toward correction and partly toward fusion.

The intentions in this respect, which were and are propagated under various designations, can be schematized as variations of what can be held to be theologically fundamental. If a person thinks primarily of the *basic principles* that form the normative elements of theology as revealed principles, then a theological *fundamental doctrine* lies at hand. At one time they were conceived as the elemental basic material of dogmatics. Conceived differently, this returned as the fundamental condition of orthodoxy in the program of fundamentalism in our century. If the interest lies in a supporting *foundation* that is able to establish the right of theology against the hostility of the times, then the task of *apologetics* moves into the foreground. It is concerned with a substructure upon which genuine theology can be erected. If, in contrast, a person constructs an *outline* that orders the mass of material and the directions for theology, which tend to diverge, so that it can be surveyed and attempts to make a synopsis of it possible, then one engages in the business of a theological *encyclopedia*. If one expects something similar from the *ground rules* of the disciplines, according to which theology must proceed, then the methodology often tied to an encyclopedia becomes independent as a *theory of* theological *scholarship*, in which the clarification of its scholarly character is supposed to furnish the fundamental concept of theology.

The Question About the Truth of Theology

All this contributes to the task of fundamental theology as it is initially being developed within evangelical theology. Not only are the aspects of encyclopedia and the theory of scholarship connected into a higher unity, but even apologetics, which has fallen into disrepute, and the dogmatic doctrine of fundamentals are considered to the extent that an element of truth is present in them. If a person seeks the highest viewpoint toward which all this converges, the question presses forward about what the situation is with regard to the truth of theology. Fundamental theology deals with the question about the truth of theology. The objection that this describes nothing other than the business of theology itself, which as such should give critical account of its truth, only confirms the total theological scope of fundamental theology. To clarify the objection by pointing to the various disciplines, which are nothing other than partial tasks within the theological procedure of verification, underscores the fact that fundamental theology should not be set on anything other than the correct execution of this total theological procedure of verification. By finding its own red thread, so to speak, in the problem of theological verification, fundamental theology does not take away participation in this task from the other disciplines, but they are expected to carry it out more than ever.

What it is that necessitates discussing the truth of theology in a fundamental theological way is opened by the question about the unity and necessity of theology.

THE QUESTION ABOUT THE UNITY OF THEOLOGY

The Phenomena of Dissent and Dead Ends

If freedom from contradiction is the formal characteristic of truth, then the problem of its truth becomes extremely virulent under the viewpoint of the unity of theology. Initially, the contradiction that befalls theology from outside does not come into consideration. Theology itself is so laden with contradictions that a person can ask about the right with which a person speaks of theology in the singular at all. Theology apparently only exists in the form of theologies that compete and strive against one another. Certainly this is something it has in common with all other efforts to deal with the truth. Of course, consensus, as a symptom not to be overlooked, plays a role in the discovery of truth, but an ambiguous one. That dissent exists is not a compelling objection against the truth of a statement, but it probably is a compelling objection against leaving it as a mere assertion. Concern about the truth is always concern about consensus, even if, when the need arises, it includes the courage to a decisive contradiction. As long as conflicting sides can still specify what the conflict is about, they are commonly attentive to the subject matter. The right, in spite of everything, to speak of theology in the singular is based on that.

A deeper difficulty lies in the fact that contradictions are met in the theological facts themselves. What can be charged against imprecise thinking can certainly be eliminated. The objections against the subject matter of theology that theology must consider, whether these objections are proposed from outside or arise from within, are certainly not the only motivation of theology, but they are strong ones. A theology that was free from this sort of contradiction and was satisfied with itself would already for that reason find itself to be outside the truth, both because it would misunderstand its actual relation to the world, and, especially, because it would leave unconsidered the dead ends that belong to the subject matter of theology. These dead ends are the expression of ultimate mystery. They do not allow thought to come to rest lest alleged ultimate contradictions be established in the wrong places. And where such contradictions in fact exist, one must consider the sense in which one can and must talk about contradictions at such places at all.

The Division According to Disciplines

The dissent in theological conversation as well as the dead ends in theological thought are essential motives toward fundamental theological inquiry about the truth of theology. Compared with that the phenomena that threaten the unity of theology and necessitate the question of the truth of theology that emerges within the field of tensions between the disciplines are of secondary rank. The division into various branches of work as such is already a consequence of the fact that theology has surrendered itself to the question of truth. Neither the fact of a multiplicity of theological disciplines nor its predominant division into systematic and historical ones justifies in itself the diagnosis that the unity has thereby been lost and as a result the truth has become unknowable. One should certainly not minimize the difficulties that incontestably result from the institutional structuring of the theological concern for the truth in various disciplines in modern times. That would contradict the interest in the truth just as much as the attempt to forcibly restructure the existing canon of disciplines into an external unity.

The threat to the unity and with that to the truth of theology originated from a false understanding of the facts. Certainly the organization of academic theology suggests the conception of an isolated existence of the disciplines. The bond that unites theology seemingly exists only in the external form of being organized as a faculty or as a department within the university as well as in the pragmatic purpose of educating people for ecclesiastical vocations. The fact that that involves an abstraction that corresponds to the factual situation only to a limited degree is all too easily concealed by the appearance of concreteness that arises through the personal representation of the disciplines within the academic realm. Yet even these symptoms—even though often symptoms of deficiency—show that no theological discipline carries out its work without a relationship to the others. The demand for interdisciplinary exchange—initially within theology itself—is justified because an essentially interdisciplinary character is effective in each theological discipline, even though often only in a rudimentary and undisciplined way. The extent to which this results from the subject matter of theology and the orientation that that provides to the interdisciplinary task is a question that becomes the question of truth in each particular relationship between the disciplines, for example between the study of the Old and New Testaments, or between dogmatics and ethics, or between biblical and dogmatic theology. The question of truth undoubtedly arises most sharply within this horizon out of the strain between the historical and systematic discovery of truth. A principal occupation of fundamental theology is to get to the root of this split and to conquer it through a return to the basis of the subject matter of theology. Its service to aid in correctly carrying out theology must allow us to recognize equally the functions of the separation into disciplines that further truth as well as ones that interfere with the truth.

THE QUESTION OF THE NECESSITY OF THEOLOGY

To assert that the question of truth is posed with the question of necessity appears dubious. Obviously, necessity is thought of not in a logical sense but in the sense of a compulsion that is appropriate to life. That could lead to the suspicion that the truth is postulated out of the need. Nevertheless, theology has reason, not only for its own sake, to pay attention that the understanding of truth does not lose its relationship to what is at stake in life. Vigilance vis-à-vis an intellectualistic, rationalistic, or empiricistic narrowing of the concept of truth and also an irrational emancipation of what is necessary for life from the question of truth belongs to the task of fundamental theology.

The Compulsion to Theology

Close at hand lies the impression that theology owes its existence to a compulsion that comes from outside and forces or misleads Christian faith to explicate itself theologically in an apologetic accommodation or defense. The history of theology itself as well as an analysis of theological figures of thought could offer ample examples of that. Nevertheless, such a total judgment for its part contains an element of violence. Apart from the suggestive power of the pejorative understanding of apologetics, we are warned to be cautious by the thought about whether such an uncommonly rich and lively phenomenon as Christian theology—it is not so only for the vulgar—could arise through external influences without at least a corresponding disposition of Christian faith cooperating with it. The question about the truth of theology as it presents itself in the light of the compulsion to theology allows the changeable interplay of factors conditioned by time and subject matter to occupy an important place for fundamental theology. However, this takes place not as the schematic contrast of fixed roles but as a process of integration, the interpretation and evaluation of which depends on the insight into the characteristic relationship between Christian faith and time. If the freedom of faith is the substance of its universal relation to the world and history, then one is encouraged to trace the compulsion of theology back to the freedom of faith. The preservation of the freedom of faith then would come into consideration as the basis for the necessity of theology and at the same time as the criterion of theology. In any case, it is a task of fundamental theology to comprehend the necessity of theology from its subject matter.

The Borders of Theology

If the connection between the fact and the subject matter of theology is so closely conceived, a person could fear that as a result of the freedom of faith theology would dissolve into the boundlessness of the relationship of this freedom to the world and history and thus be deprived of its relationship to the truth. In a different way, orthodoxy is inclined to identify theology with the claim of truth belonging to its subject matter to such a degree that the use of the word "theology" coincides with the knowledge of God as such and even bursts the boundaries of historical knowledge of God. One can profile the specific necessity of theology only by placing a limit on this phenomenon of theology oriented to the peculiarity of an account of Christian faith that is self-critical, methodologically pursued, and correspondingly communicative, that is, to scholarly theology. Fundamental theology has to discuss this problem of demarcation on various sides. First, there is the question about what scholarliness means and whether it is compatible with the subject matter of theology. Further, there are problems that arise from the fact that the boundaries in the direction of the life of faith remain fluid, for in the measure to which responsible thought belongs to the existence of the believer as such, a participation in theology, even though to different degrees, becomes unavoidable. For one thing, it is directed toward the account of faith that is required and expected of each person in order to reach a unanimous awareness of truth; for another, it is directed toward the particular total situation and what is required in order to confront it with a genuine Christian word; and finally it is directed toward the particular character of ecclesiastical service and its inherent charisma of vicariously taking responsibility for the Christian word for others. The necessity of theology certainly by no means coincides with the necessity of the subject matter itself, but must be derived from the latter and relate to it if the question about necessity is not to be detached from the question about the truth.

TO THE IMPLEMENTATION OF FUNDAMENTAL THEOLOGY

There can be as little deviation here as in the previous cases from the limited goal of merely offering help in orientation, which transmits a few impulses for thought. Nevertheless, a further step must be taken with fundamental theology for two reasons. It is the only theological discipline treated here that is in the position of being developed, at least in its evangelical form. The perception and experience that can be presupposed for an established discipline—as contested as it might be—is largely lacking here.

In addition, in this overview it falls to fundamental theology to consider the whole again from the perspective of the end. That corresponds to its own task as well as to the position that falls to it in the study of theology. The disciplines cannot—already not in the order selected here—be forced into a chronological order. To the extent that a didactic sequence cannot be avoided, it must still be compensated for by a no less important simultaneity, for in theology everything is connected with everything else and must, therefore, be able to mature together as much as possible. With this reservation, one could certainly say that fundamental theology preferably occupies the last place to the extent that it would be senseless to consider the whole of theology without already having attained a certain experience in engagement with everything that belongs to theology. Whether engagement with a subject is profitable becomes clear only by concretely entering in upon it, not through a prior process of general reasoning. It also does not help one's entry into scholarly work if one wants to settle the problem of method in advance, without already having risked one's own step and having acquired an appropriate knowledge of the material. A person cannot even pose a single question without at least knowing something.

Thus, since fundamental theology is a special case, we cannot avoid the question of its implementation. If in so doing nothing more than an inadequate catalog of problems results, that is satisfactory within the framework of an attempt at orientation that intends to invite the reader to further thought.

STRUCTURES OF THE PROCESS OF VERIFICATION

Fundamental theology investigates the process of verification. This arises from the fact that it deals with the question of the truth of theology. Therefore, it discusses explicitly and as a whole what should be accomplished in the concert of the disciplines. In a manner of speaking, fundamental theology is the study of the musical score of theology. Whoever wants to exploit this metaphor allegorically certainly does it at his or her own risk.

The discussion of the process of verification within fundamental theology has its center of gravity in the question about the subject matter, language, and—that toward which it all aims—the truth of theology. It treats, so to speak, the trigonometric point by which the survey of the terrain is oriented—a terrain that is linguistic and therefore must be investigated with regard to the relation between language and the subject matter, so that on the whole the question of truth can come into view. Even in this case it cannot treat a sequence in which one thing would be definitively settled before the next. Although these principal viewpoints cannot be isolated from one another, they nevertheless describe an inner inclination that the discussion has to follow with the necessary circumspection. In doing so it should be just as clear that the question of the subject matter has the primacy as that the aim is at the question of truth.

Since all disciplines participate in the process of verification reflected by fundamental theology, they appear in fundamental theology as partners in the discussion, not as mere objects of discussion. Fundamental theology should be broadened to a total theological conversation that can never be only an inner-theological conversation. From the perspective of its subject matter, a universal horizon has been established for it within which essentially all the important voices that were represented in my overview of the nontheological departments are expressed. In the light of the presence of all other theological disciplines, fundamental theology is not basically distinct from these but is distinguished from them only through the degree of explicit reflection. The more this becomes a matter of specialization, the more fundamental theology endangers itself.

The primacy of the subject matter, which defines the total inclination of the field, must also be established in detail. Corresponding to the double meaning of "subject matter" as something that is already given and something that is given as a charge, the tasks always are to be developed that derive from the subject matter and that consist in comprehending for the first time what that which is given is in truth.

THE SUBJECT MATTER OF THEOLOGY

The Christian Character of the Subject Matter of Theology

The fact that theology was developed as Christian theology is neither to be justified positivistically nor to be made comparatively clear by means of relativizing it to a general genus "theology." Rather, it must be illuminated by demonstrating how theology emerges from what is essentially Christian. This is attained on the one side by considering the biblical witness within the broadest possible relationships, with regard to the history of Christianity, the world of the religions, and the rational grasp of reality, and on the other side through the strictest concentration on the question of the fundamental situation of human existence.

The Universality of the Subject Matter of Theology

For the sake of the universality of this context which has not been proposed arbitrarily but which Christian faith for its part claims, theology is not merely the science of Christianity in the sense of describing it historically. Theology is a critical explication of what is to be asserted on the basis of Christian faith about the interrelatedness of the experience of God, the world, and the self in confrontation with all relevant traditions and experience.

Fundamental Distinction

This interrelatedness of the experience of God, the world, and the self has happened in the appearance of Jesus Christ and thus has become capable of being proclaimed. It has become definitive for life in the faith that has its counterpart and its basis in him. It takes place as an event in which what has been confused, perverted, and spoiled is set right through all things coming into their correct relationship with one another. Therefore the process of distinction is decisive for theology. Theological thought has to carry out this distinction in such a way that it provides room for the distinction that sets things right to take place in and on the reality of life itself. The soteriological character of the distinction that does not separate but sets things in their right relationship can be seen in fundamental concepts of Christian language like faith, love, hope, reconciliation, and redemption. This distinction requires that we elaborate leading fundamental distinctions like that between God and the world, time and eternity, nature and grace, death and life, sin and forgiveness, or law and gospel. Theology's relation to reality is determined by the way in which the fundamental distinction is grasped, and thus it determines the setting in life which the subject matter of theology has.

THE LANGUAGE OF THEOLOGY

The Language of Faith

The only way the subject matter of theology unfolds is through the language of faith, but the subject matter does not coincide with the language of faith. Language includes the difference between language and the subject matter as well as the difference between language and language. Fundamental theology has to pursue the following connections: the reason the word has the fundamental significance for the subject matter of theology, not in competition with the reality of life but as the way in which it becomes real by coming to truth; that the biblical tradition provides the inexhaustible source of the language of faith, and familiarity with it is the principal task of the theologian, although one never attains it; the reason the one thing that is at stake in faith can and must be expressed in words in an unending multiplicity of statements and linguistic possibilities;

and the extent to which the living character of the language of faith is constituted by the fact that it constantly moves in the field of tension between traditional language and contemporary verbal responsibility.

The Hermeneutical Responsibility of Theology

Theology is related to the event of tradition of Christian faith, which is found in process prior to and independent from theology. Theology bears responsibility for this event remaining identical to its own intention by and through entering into constantly new situations and linguistic spaces. Therefore its business as a whole is hermeneutical. Nevertheless, the hermeneutical task of theology is curtailed and distorted if it is dominated by the conception that it only deals with the translation of a text out of the past into the present and with the problems that then result from the change of context. It then becomes customary to speak with Lessing about the "nasty broad rifts," which are to be overcome. Lessing himself thought he was not able to leap over them.[1] Yet the problem Lessing posed is constantly misunderstood when it is treated this way. It was not the difference between past and present that represented the unbridgeable rift for him, but, as he expressed it, the difference between accidental historical truth and eternal rational truth, in other words, between historical observation and valid truth that has the power to move the heart and make a person certain. When this problem is considered, hermeneutical attention is directed to the connection between language and experience in such a way that traditional language is interpreted with regard to the experience expressed and addressed in it. With that the hermeneutical approach attained a breadth that orients what threatens to break asunder into historical and systematic theology toward its unity.

The Critique of Theological Language

I cannot share the idea that the modes of procedure represented by hermeneutics and linguistic analysis, which are often treated as competitors today, represent a genuine alternative. Of course, it still requires considerable effort to set both traditions of thought about language in relation to one another in such a way that their mutual responsibility for language becomes clear and fruitful. In fundamental theology this is of great importance in view of the need to grasp in a differentiated way the relationship between general colloquial language, religious language in general, and the

---

1. G. E. Lessing, "Über den Beweis des Geistes und der Kraft" (1777), in *Lessings Werke*, ed. J. Petersen and W. v. Olshausen, 23. Teil; *Theologische Schriften*, vol. 4, ed. L. Zscharnack (Hildesheim/New York: G. Olms Verlag, 1970), p. 49, l. 21.

language of faith, the need to establish the justification and limits of technical theological language in relation to these languages, and the need to attain criteria for the adequacy and productive power of the theological conceptual formation. The large field of tasks that this opens up can be cultivated with theological profit, certainly, only if one does not lose sight either of the relation to the subject matter of theology or of the fact that theological language is inseparable from the language of faith.

THE TRUTH OF THEOLOGY

The Certainty of Faith

If theology renders an account of Christian faith, then as a result of its subject matter an account of the certainty of faith is of central significance for theology. Therefore the peculiarity of this certainty must be made clear. For doing so, three aspects in particular must be considered. First, the certainty of Christian faith has the character neither of objective, demonstrable knowledge, or subjective arbitrariness, but of one being grounded outside oneself. Further, this certainty understands itself as a mode of being in the truth for which a constant asking about the truth does not present a contradiction but corresponds to the relationship of truth to life. Finally, this certainty always exists in temptation, that is, in a constant process of ascertaining and verifying this certainty. According to the self-understanding of faith this process, however, determines not the truth of what is believed but only whether the believer remains in the truth.

The Scholarly Character of Theology

All the lines belonging to the theme of fundamental theology converge in the problem of the scholarly character of theology. Thus the following principal problems crystallize.

First, theology cannot entrust or subject itself to an understanding of scholarship that is already given because there neither is nor can be an understanding of scholarship that stands beyond discussion and that is valid for everything. Nevertheless, that is not a passport for the absence of discipline and for dogmatism. Rather, fundamental theology must actively participate in the difficult discussion of scholarly theory in order to take the trouble to give an account of its own criteria without restraint. In doing so it will guard against overestimating the theory of scholarship as well as against carelessness, disguised as a strength of faith, in dealing with questions of the theory of scholarship.

Second, in contrast to the simple objection that theology thinks it already possesses the truth and therefore is not scholarship, there must be an investigation of the distinction between a truth that is to be probed in a scholarly manner and a truth that cannot be probed by scholarship as a difference that adheres to the essence of truth itself. Fundamental theology must create clarity about what it is for theology that can be probed by scholarship. Judged by the standards not only of theology but also of general scholarship, it would be absurd to hold that the question in relation to Christian faith itself could be scientifically decided in one way or another. However, by the standards not only of general scholarship but also of theology it would be absurd to hold that the way in which Christian faith is presented and developed is uncontrollable and without any criteria.

Finally, the methodology of theological verification has to work out the conditions of historical and systematic verification. In doing so, it has to pay attention to the connection between both. But it also has to keep in view the fact that one cannot talk about a verification of theological statements without simultaneously posing the question about the verification of the human person and reality as a whole.

The Call of the Theologian

As a doctrine of theology, fundamental theology also has to develop a doctrine of the call of the theologian. That this strikes a pastoral, edifying note can only be held as an objection if "pastoral" and "edifying" are caricatured as a way of speaking that is lacking in common sense and a sense of reality. Correctly understood, the subject matter of theology itself should save a person from the things that provide a justifiable basis for the suspicion about ideology. Protection from ideology is offered for the theologian by being prepared to place one's relationship to theology under two viewpoints, which only appear to contradict one another: the theologian is obligated to a theology and yet can never produce a theology that is self-sufficient. Both are connected with theology's relationship to life. Luther expressed it in a formula: "Sola experientia facit theologum" (Only experience makes a theologian).[2]

2. D. Martin Luthers Werke, Tischreden (Weimar, 1912–1921), vol. 1, p. 16, ll. 16, 13, No. 46 (1531). Cf. also ibid. 5, p. 384, ll. 5–6, no. 5864 (not precisely datable). D. Martin Luthers Werke, Kritische Gesamtausgabe (Weimar, 1883–   ), vol. 25, p. 106, l. 27 (Lectures on Isaiah, 1527/29).

Postscript

Luther Concerning the Study of Theology[1]

Moreover, I want to point out to you a correct way of studying theology, for I have had practice in that. If you keep to it, you will become so learned that you yourself could (if it were necessary) write books just as good as those of the fathers and councils, even as I (in God) dare to presume and boast, without arrogance and lying, that in the matter of writing books I do not stand much behind some of the fathers. Of my life I can by no means make the same boast. This is the way taught by holy King David (and doubtlessly used also by all the patriarchs and prophets) in the one hundred nineteenth Psalm. There you will find three rules, amply presented throughout the whole Psalm. They are *Oratio, Meditatio, Tentatio*.[2]

Firstly, you should know that the Holy Scriptures constitute a book which turns the wisdom of all other books into foolishness, because not one teaches about eternal life except this one alone. Therefore you should straightway despair of your reason and understanding. With them you will not attain eternal life, but, on the contrary, your presumptuousness will plunge you and others with you out of heaven (as happened to Lucifer) into the abyss of hell. But kneel down in your little room [Matt. 6:6] and pray to God with real humility and earnestness, that he through his dear Son may give you his Holy Spirit, who will enlighten you, lead you, and give you understanding.

Thus you see how David keeps praying in the above-mentioned Psalm, "Teach me, Lord, instruct me, lead me, show me," and many more words

1. From Martin Luther's "Preface to the Wittenberg Edition of Luther's German Writings" (1939), trans. Robert R. Heitner, in *Luther's Works*, vol. 34 (Philadelphia: Fortress Press, 1960), pp. 285–288; *D. Martin Luthers Werke*, Kritische Gesamtausgabe (Weimar, 1883–), vol. 50, pp. 658, l. 29–661, l. 8. Some of the translator's footnotes have been omitted.

2. Prayer, meditation, *Anfechtung*.

168 THE STUDY OF THEOLOGY

like these. Although he well knew and daily heard and read the text of
Moses and other books besides, still he wants to lay hold of the real
teacher of the Scriptures himself, so that he may not seize upon them
pell-mell with his reason and become his own teacher. For such practice
gives rise to factious spirits who allow themselves to nurture the delusion
that the Scriptures are subject to them and can be easily grasped with their
reason, as if they were *Markolf*[3] or Aesop's Fables, for which no Holy
Spirit and no prayers are needed.

Secondly, you should meditate, that is, not only in your heart, but
also externally, by actually repeating and comparing oral speech and
literal words of the book, reading and rereading them with diligent attention and reflection, so that you may see what the Holy Spirit means by
them. And take care that you do not grow weary or think that you have
done enough when you have read, heard, and spoken them once or twice,
and that you then have complete understanding. You will never be a
particularly good theologian if you do that, for you will be like untimely
fruit which falls to the ground before it is half ripe.

Thus you see in this same Psalm how David constantly boasts that he
will talk, meditate, speak, sing, hear, read, by day and night and always,
about nothing except God's Word and commandments. For God will not
give you his Spirit without the external Word; so take your cue from
that. His command to write, preach, read, hear, sing, speak, etc., out-
wardly was not given in vain.

Thirdly, there is *tentatio, Anfechtung*. This is the touchstone which
teaches you not only to know and understand, but also to experience how
right, how true, how sweet, how lovely, how mighty, how comforting
God's Word is, wisdom beyond all wisdom.

Thus you see how David, in the Psalm mentioned, complains so often
about all kinds of enemies, arrogant princes or tyrants, false spirits and
factions, whom he must tolerate because he meditates, that is, because he
is occupied with God's Word (as has been said) in all manner of ways.
For as soon as God's Word takes root and grows in you, the devil will
harry you, and will make a real doctor of you, and by his assaults[4] will
teach you to seek and love God's Word. I myself (if you will permit me,
mere mouse-dirt, to be mingled with pepper) am deeply indebted to my
papists that through the devil's raging they have beaten, oppressed, and

3. The very popular medieval legend of Solomon and Markolf was treated in a verse epic,
chapbooks, dialogues, and farces. The figure of Markolf, a sly and unprincipled rogue, was
known in Germany as early as the tenth century.

4. *Anfechtungen.*

distressed me so much. That is to say, they have made a fairly good theologian of me, which I would not have become otherwise. And I heartily grant them what they have won in return for making this of me, honor, victory, and triumph, for that's the way they wanted it.

There now, with that you have David's rules. If you study hard in accord with his example, then you will also sing and boast with him in the Psalm, "The law of thy mouth is better to me than thousands of gold and silver pieces" [Ps. 119:72]. Also, "Thy commandment makes me wiser than my enemies, for it is ever with me. I have more understanding than all my teachers, for thy testimonies are my meditation. I understand more than the aged, for I keep thy precepts," etc. [Ps. 119:98–100]. And it will be your experience that the books of the fathers will taste stale and putrid to you in comparison. You will not only despise the books written by adversaries, but the longer you write and teach the less you will be pleased with yourself. When you have reached this point, then do not be afraid to hope that you have begun to become a real theologian, who can teach not only the young and imperfect Christians, but also the maturing and perfect ones. For indeed, Christ's church has all kinds of Christians in it who are young, old, weak, sick, healthy, strong, energetic, lazy, simple, wise, etc.

If, however, you feel and are inclined to think you have made it, flattering yourself with your own little books, teaching, or writing, because you have done it beautifully and preached excellently; if you are highly pleased when someone praises you in the presence of others; if you perhaps look for praise, and would sulk or quit what you are doing if you did not get it—if you are of that stripe, dear friend, then take yourself by the ears, and if you do this in the right way you will find a beautiful pair of big, long, shaggy donkey ears. Then do not spare any expense! Decorate them with golden bells, so that people will be able to hear you wherever you go, point their fingers at you, and say, "See, See! There goes that clever beast, who can write such exquisite books and preach so remarkably well." That very moment you will be blessed and blessed beyond measure in the kingdom of heaven. Yes, in that heaven where hellfire is ready for the devil and his angels. To sum up: Let us be proud and seek honor in the places where we can. But in this book the honor is God's alone, as it is said, "God opposes the proud, but gives grace to the humble" [1 Pet. 5:5]; to whom be glory, world without end, Amen.

Bibliographic Appendix

PRELIMINARY REMARKS

The literature for each chapter is divided into two groups. Under *A* are mentioned publications of the author that can illuminate and supplement the brief presentations in this book and offer examples of his treatment of individual themes. Under *B* are mentioned books and essays that are recommended for further explorations of the problems involved in the discipline under discussion. Textbooks are not indicated. Section B is further divided into material available in English and in German. Subjectivity and accident cannot be excluded in selecting only a few titles. Nevertheless, the selections are not restricted to works that agree with what has been presented or to which indirect reference has been made. In both groups the sequence is chronological. Each bibliographic reference is indicated only once, although in some cases a reference may be important for the themes of various chapters.

ABBREVIATIONS TO A:

LuStud 1 *Lutherstudien*, vol. 1. Tübingen: J. C. B. Mohr (Paul Siebeck), 1971.
WF   *WG* 1 *Word and Faith.* Translated by James W. Leitch. Philadelphia: Fortress Press; London: SCM Press, 1963. German: *Wort und Glaube*, vol. 1. Tübingen: J. C. B. Mohr (Paul Siebeck), 1960; 3d ed., 1967.
WG 2 Wort und Glaube, vol. 2: *Beiträge zur Fundamentaltheologie und zur Lehre von Gott.* Tübingen: J. C. B. Mohr (Paul Siebeck), 1969.
WG 3 Wort und Glaube, vol. 3: *Beiträge zur Fundamentaltheologie, Soteriologie und Ekklesiologie.* Tübingen: J. C. B. Mohr (Paul Siebeck), 1975.
WGT The Word of God and Tradition: Historical Studies Interpreting the Divisions of Christianity. Translated by S. H. Hooke. Philadelphia: Fortress Press; London: Collins, 1968. German: *Wort Gottes und Tradition: Kirche und Konfession.* Göttingen: Vandenhoeck & Ruprecht, 1964; 6th ed., 1966.

1. THEOLOGY AS A WHOLE

A.

"Discussion Theses for a Course of Introductory Lectures on the Study of Theology" (1960), *WF*, pp. 424–33. German: "Diskussionsthesen für eine Vorlesung zur Einführung in das Studium der Theologie," *WG* 1: 447–57. "Memorandum zur Verständigung in Kirche und Theologie" (1969), *WG* 3: 484–514.

B. ENGLISH

Schleiermacher, Friedrich D. E., *A Brief Outline on the Study of Theology.* Translated by Terrence N. Tice. Richmond: John Knox Press, 1966. German: *Kurze Darstellung des theologischen Studiums zur Behuf einleitender Vorlesungen* (1811). 2d ed., 1830; critical ed. edited by Heinrich Scholz, 1910. Leipzig: A. Deichert, 1973.

Schaff, Philip. *Theological Propaedeutic: A General Introduction to the Study of Theology.* New York: Scribner's, end ed., 1894; 6th ed., 1904.

Rauschenbusch, Walter. *A Theology for the Social Gospel.* New York: Macmillan, 1917; reissued, Nashville: Abingdon Press, 1961.

Niebuhr, H. Richard. *The Purpose of the Church and Its Ministry: Reflections on the Aims of Theological Education.* New York: Harper, 1956.

Barth, Karl. *Evangelical Theology: An Introduction.* Translated by Grover Foley. London: Widenfeld & Nicolson, 1963; Garden City, N.Y.: Doubleday, 1965; London: Collins, 1965. German: *Einführung in die evangelische Theologie.* Zürich: EVZ-Verlag, 1962.

Healey, Francis G. *Preface to Christian Studies.* London: Lutterworth Press, 1971.

Sykes, Stephen W. *Christian Theology Today.* London/Oxford: Mowbrays, 1971; Richmond: John Knox Press, 1974.

Pannenberg, Wolfhart. *Theology and the Philosophy of Science.* Translated by Francis McDonagh. Philadelphia: Westminster Press, 1976. German: *Wissenschaftstheorie und Theologie.* Frankfurt am Main: Suhrkamp, 1973.

Kaufman, Gordon D. *An Essay on Theological Method.* Missoula: Scholars Press, 1975.

Tracy, David. *Blessed Rage for Order: The New Pluralism in Theology.* New York: Seabury Press, 1975.

Jennings, Theodore W. *Introduction to Theology: An Invitation to Reflection upon the Christian Mythos.* Philadelphia: Fortress Press, 1976.

Wiles, Maurice F. *What Is Theology?* London/New York: Oxford, 1976.

B. GERMAN

Bohren, Rudolf, ed. *Einführung in das Studium der evangelischen Theologie.* München: Chr. Kaiser, 1964.

Grass, Hans. "Der theologische Pluralismus und die Wahrheitsfrage," *Kirche in der Zeit* 20 (1965): 146–55; reprinted in idem, *Theologie und Kritik: Gesammelte Aufsätze und Vorträge.* Göttingen: Vandenhoeck & Ruprecht, 1969, pp. 71–92.

Neuhäussler, Engelbert, and Gössmann, Elisabeth, eds. *Was ist Theologie?* München: Huebner, 1966.

Amberg, E. H. "Die Frage nach der Einheit der evangelischen Theologie heute," *Theologische Literaturzeitung* 92 (1967): 81–88.

Jüngel, Eberhard. "Das Verhältnis der theologischen Disziplinen untereinander" (1968). In idem, *Unterwegs zur Sache: Theologische Bemerkungen.* München: Chr. Kaiser, 1972, pp. 34–59.

Schäfer, R., "Die Einheit der Theologie," *Zeitschrift für Theologie und Kirche* 66 (1969): 369–85.

Vorgrimler, Herbert, and van der Gucht, Robert, eds. *Bilanz der Theologie im 20. Jahrhundert: Perspektiven, Strömungen, Motive in der christlichen und nichtchristlichen Welt.* 3 vols. Freiburg/Basel/Wien: Herder, 1970.

Siemers, Helge, and Reuter, Hans-Richard, eds. *Theologie als Wissenschaft in der Gesellschaft: Ein Heidelberger Experiment.* Göttingen: Vandenhoeck & Ruprecht, 1970.

Mildenberger, Friedrich. *Theorie der Theologie: Enzyklopädie als Methodenlehre.* Stuttgart: Calwer, 1972.

Bayer, Oswald. *Was ist das: Theologie?* Stuttgart: Calwer, 1973.

2. THE STUDY OF THE NEW TESTAMENT

A.

"Geist und Buchstabe," in *Die Religion in Geschichte und Gegenwart*. 3d ed. Tübingen: J. C. B. Mohr (Paul Siebeck), 1957–62, vol. 2 (1958), pp. 1290–96.

"Was heisst Glauben?" (1958), *WG* 3: 225–35.

"Jesus and Faith" (1958), *WF*, pp. 201–46. German: "Jesus und Glaube," *WG* 1: 203–54.

The Nature of Faith. Translated by Ronald Gregor Smith. Philadelphia: Fortress Press; London: Collins, 1961, pp. 31–43. German: *Das Wesen des christlichen Glaubens*. Tübingen: J. C. B. Mohr (Paul Siebeck), 1959, pp. 31–47.

"The Question of the Historical Jesus and the Problem of Christology" (1959), *WF*, pp. 288–304. German: "Die Frage nach dem historischen Jesus und das Problem der Christologie," *WG* 1: 300–318.

"Der Grund christlicher Theologie" (1961), *WG* 2: 72–91.

"The New Testament and the Multiplicity of Confessions" (1962), *WGT*, pp. 148–59. German: "Das Neue Testament und die Vielzahl der Konfessionen," *WGT*, pp. 91–143.

"Tradition VII. Dogmatisch." *Die Religion in Geschichte und Gegenwart*. 3d ed. Tübingen: J. C. B. Mohr (Paul Siebeck), 1957–62, vol. 6 (1962), pp. 976–84.

" 'Sola Scriptura' and Tradition" (1963), *WGT*, pp. 102–47. German: " 'Sola scriptura' und das Problem der Tradition," *WGT*, pp. 91–143.

B. ENGLISH

Schweitzer, Albert. *The Quest of the Historical Jesus*. Translated by W. Montgomery with Preface by F. C. Burkitt. New York: Macmillan; London: A & C. Black, 1960. German: *Geschichte der Leben-Jesu-Forschung*. Tübingen: J. C. B. Mohr (Paul Siebeck), 1906; 8th ed., 1951.

Bultmann, Rudolf. "New Testament and Mythology: The Mythological Element in the Message of the New Testament and the Problem of Its Re-interpretation," in *Kerygma and Myth: A Theological Debate*, edited by Hans Werner Bartsch and translated by Reginald H. Fuller. New York: Harper, 1961, pp. 1–44. German: "Neues Testament und Mythologie: Das Problem der Entmythologisierung der neutestamentlichen Verkündigung," in idem, *Offenbarung und Heilsgeschehen*, Beiträge zur evangelischen Theologie 7 (1941), 27–69. Reprinted in *Kerygma und Mythos*, ed. Hans Werner Bartsch (Hamburg: Reich & Heidrich, 1948), pp. 15–53.

Käsemann, Ernst. "Does the New Testament Canon Establish the Unity of the Church?" (1951/52), *Essays on New Testament Themes*. Translated by W. J. Montague. London: SCM Press, 1964, pp. 95–107. German: Begründet der neutestamentliche Kanon die Einheit der Kirche?" in idem,

Exegetische Versuche und Besinnungen. Vol. 1. Göttingen: Vandenhoeck & Ruprecht, 1960, pp. 214–23.

Bultmann, Rudolf. *Theology of the New Testament.* Translated by Kendrick Grobel. 2 vols. New York: Scribner's; London: SCM Press, 1951, 1955. Vol. 2, pp. 237–51, 259–60. German: *Theologie des Neuen Testaments.* Tübingen: J. C. B. Mohr (Paul Siebeck), 1953; 6th ed., 1968, pp. 585–99, 619–20.

Kümmel, Werner Georg. *The New Testament: History of the Investigation of Its Problems.* Translated by S. McLean Gilmour and Howard Kee. Nashville: Abingdon Press; London: SCM Press, 1970. German: *Das Neue Testament: Geschichte der Erforschung seiner Probleme.* Orbis Academicus, vol. 3, part 3. Freiburg: K. Alber, 1958; 2d ed., 1970.

Braun, Herbert. "The Problem of a New Testament Theology," in *The Bultmann School of Biblical Interpretation: New Directions, Journal for Theology and Church* 1. Edited by Robert Funk and Gerhard Ebeling. New York: Harper, 1965, pp. 169–83. German: "Die Problematik einer Theologie des Neuen Testaments," Beiheft 2 to *Zeitschrift für Theologie und Kirche* (1961), pp. 3–18. Reprinted in *Gesammelte Studien zum Neuen Testament und seiner Umwelt* (Tübingen: J. C. B. Mohr [Paul Siebeck], 1962), pp. 325–41.

Von Campenhausen, Hans. *The Formation of the Christian Bible.* Translated by J. A. Baker. Philadelphia: Fortress Press; London: A. & C. Black, 1972. German: *Die Entstehung der christlischen Bibel*, Beiträge zur historischen Theologie 39. Tübingen: J. C. B. Mohr (Paul Siebeck), 1968.

B. GERMAN

Fuchs, Ernst. *Hermeneutik.* Bad Cannstatt: R. Müllerschön, 1954; 4th ed., 1970.

Stock, Alex. *Einheit des Neuen Testaments: Erörterung hermeneutischer Grundpositionen der heutigen Theologie.* Zürich: Einsiedeln, 1969.

Käsemann, Ernst, ed. *Das Neue Testament als Kanon: Dokumentation und kritische Analyse zur gegenwärtigen Diskussion.* Göttingen: Vandenhoeck & Ruprecht, 1970.

Conzelmann, Hans. "Die Frage der Einheit der Neutestamentlichen Schriften." In *Moderne Exegese und historische Wissenschaft*, edited by J. M. Hollenbach and H. Staudinger. Trier: Spee, 1972, pp. 67–76.

3. THE STUDY OF THE OLD TESTAMENT

A.

"Die Anfänge von Luthers Hermeneutik" (1951), *LuStud* 1: 1–68.
"The Meaning of 'Biblical Theology'" (1955), *WF*, pp. 79–97. German:
"Was heisst 'Biblische Theologie'?" *WG* 1: 69–89.
"Reflections on the Doctrine of the Law" (1958), *WF*, pp. 247–81. German:
"Erwägungen zur Lehre vom Gesetz," *WG* 1: 255–93.
"Zwei Glaubensweisen?" (1961), *WG* 3: 236–45.
"Luther und die Bibel" (1967), *LuStud* 1: 286–301.
Psalmenmeditationen. Tübingen: J. C. B. Mohr (Paul Siebeck), 1968.

B. ENGLISH

Hahn, Herbert. *The Old Testament in Modern Research.* Philadelphia: Muhlenberg Press, 1954.
Kraeling, Emil. *The Old Testament Since the Reformation.* New York: Harper, 1955.
Westermann, Claus, ed. *Essays on Old Testament Interpretation.* Translated by James Luther Mays. Richmond: John Knox Press, 1963. German: *Probleme alttestamentlicher Hermeneutik: Aufsätze zum Verstehen des Alten Testaments.* München: Chr. Kaiser, 1960.
Anderson, Bernhard W., ed. *The Old Testament and Christian Faith: A Theological Discussion.* New York: Harper, 1963.
Barr, James. *Old and New in Interpretation: A Study of the Two Testaments.* New York: Harper; London: SCM Press, 1966.
Lys, Daniel. *The Meaning of the Old Testament: Understanding and Appropriating Its Message in Today's Culture.* Nashville: Abingdon Press, 1967.
Childs, Brevard S. *Biblical Theology in Crisis.* Philadelphia: Westminster Press, 1970.
Bright, John. *The Authority of the Old Testament.* Grand Rapids, Mich.: Baker House, 1975.

B. GERMAN

Diestel, Ludwig. *Geschichte des Alten Testaments in der christlichen Kirche.* Jena: Mauke, 1869.
Bultmann, Rudolf. "Die Bedeutung des Alten Testaments für den christlichen Glauben," in *Glauben und Verstehen,* vol. 1. Tübingen: J. C. B. Mohr (Paul Siebeck), 1933; 7th ed., 1972, pp. 313–36.
Hirsch, Emmanuel. *Das Alte Testament und die Predigt des Evangeliums.* Tübingen: J. C. B. Mohr (Paul Siebeck), 1936.
Kraus, Hans-Joachim. *Geschichte der historisch-kritischen Erforschung des Alten Testaments von der Reformation bis zur Gegenwart.* Neukirchen: Neukirchen, 1956; 2d ed., 1969.

Gese, Hartmut. "Erwägungen zur Einheit der biblischen Theologie," *Zeitschrift für Theologie und Kirche* 67 (1970): 417–36. Reprinted in *Vom Sinai zum Zion: Alttestamentliche Beiträge zur biblischen Theologie*, Beiträge zur evangelischen Theologie 64. München: Chr. Kaiser, 1974), pp. 11–30.

Kraus, Hans-Joachim. *Die Biblische Theologie: Ihre Geschichte und Problematik*. Neukirchen-Vluyn: Neukirchen, 1970.

Schmend, Rudolf. *Die Mitte des Alten Testaments*, Theologische Studien 101. Zürich: EVZ-Verlag, 1970.

Wagner, S. "Zur Frage nach dem Gegenstand einer Theologie des Alten Testaments." In *Fides et communicatio: Festschrift für Martin Doerne*, edited by Dietrich Rössler. Göttingen: Vandenhoeck & Ruprecht, 1970, pp. 391–411.

Mauser, Ulrich W. *Gottesbild und Menschwerdung: Eine Untersuchung zur Einheit des Alten und Neuen Testaments*, Beiträge zur evangelischen Theologie 43. Tübingen: J. C. B. Mohr (Paul Siebeck), 1971.

Fohrer, Georg, et al. *Exegese des Alten Testaments: Einführung in die Methode*, UTB 267. Heidelberg: Quelle und Meyer, 1973.

Zimmerli, Walther, "Erwägungen zur Gestalt einer alttestamentlichen Theologie," *Theologische Literaturzeitung* 98 (1973), 81–98. Reprinted in *Studien zur alttestamentlichen Theologie und Prophetie: Gesammelte Aufsätze*, vol. 2 (München: Chr. Kaiser, 1974), pp. 27–54.

4. THE STUDY OF RELIGION

A.

"The 'Non-religious Interpretation of Biblical Concepts'" (1955), *WF*, pp. 98–161. German: "Die 'nicht-religiöse Interpretation biblischer Begriffe,'" *WG* 1: 90–160.
"Profanität und Geheimnis" (1968), *WG* 2: 184–208.

B. ENGLISH

Schleiermacher, Friedrich D. E. *On Religion: Speeches to Its Cultured Despisers.* Translated by John Oman with Introduction by Rudolf Otto. New York: Harper, 1958.
————. *On Religion: Addresses in Response to Its Cultured Critics.* Translated by Terrence N. Tice. Richmond: John Knox Press, 1969. German: *Über die Religion: Reden an die Gebildeten unter ihren Verächtern* (1799). Edited by H. J. Rothert, *Philosoph. Bibl.* 255. Hamburg: Meiner, 1958.
Hegel, G. W. F. *Lectures on the Philosophy of Religion* (1821/31). Translated by E. B. Speirs and J. B. Sanderson. 3 vols. New York: Scribner's; London: Paul, 1895. German: *Vorlesungen über die Philosophie der Religion.* In *Sämtliche Werke: Jubiläumsausgabe,* vol. 15/16. Stuttgart: F. Frommann, 1927–40); *Sämtliche Werke.* Edited by Georg Lasson, *Philosoph. Bibl.* 59/60/61/63. Leipzig: F. Meiner, 1928.
James, William. *The Varieties of Religious Experience: A Study in Human Nature* (1902). New York/London: Longmanns, 1911; reissued, 1952.
Troeltsch, Ernst. *The Absoluteness of Christianity and the History of Religions.* Translated by David Reid (Richmond: John Knox Press, London: SCM Press, 1972). German: *Die Absolutheit des Christentums und die Religionsgeschichte.* Tübingen: J. C. B. Mohr (Paul Siebeck), 1902; 3d ed., 1929. 1929.
Freud, Sigmund. "The Future of an Illusion" (1927). *The Standard Edition of the Complete Psychological Works of Sigmund Freud,* vol. 21. Edited by James Strachey with Anna Freud. London: Hogarth, 1961, pp. 5–56. German: "Die Zukunft einer Illusion." In idem, *Gesammelte Werke,* vol. 14. London: Imago, 1948, pp. 323–80.
Grensted, L. W. *The Psychology of Religion* (New York/London: Oxford, 1952).
Eliade, Mircea. *Sacred and Profane: The Nature of Religion.* Translated by Willard R. Trask. New York: Harper, 1961.
Wach, Joachim. *The Comparative Study of Religions.* Edited by Joseph M. Kitagawa. New York: Columbia; London: Oxford, 1958.
Eliade, Mircea, and Kitagawa, Joseph Mitsuo, eds. *The History of Religions: Essays in Methodology.* Chicago: University of Chicago, 1959.

Hick, John. *The Philosophy of Religion*. Englewood Cliffs, N.J./London: Prentice-Hall, 1963.

Luckmann, Thomas. *The Invisible Religion: The Problem of Religion in Modern Society*. New York: Macmillan; London: Collier-Macmillan, 1967. German: *Das Problem der Religion in der modernen Gesellschaft*. Freiburg im Breisgau: Rombach, 1963.

Anthropological Approaches to the Study of Religion, Conference on New Approaches in Social Anthropology. Edited by Michael Banton. New York: Praeger; London: Tavistock, 1966.

Berger, Peter L. *The Sacred Canopy: Elements of a Sociology of Religion*. Garden City, N.Y.: Doubleday, 1967. British ed., *The Social Reality of Religion* (London: Faber, 1969).

Cobb, John B., Jr. *The Structure of Christian Existence*. Philadelphia: Westminster Press, 1967.

Pannenberg, Wolfhart. "Toward a Theology of the History of Religions." In *Basic Questions in Theology Today*, vol. 2. Translated by George H. Kehm. Philadelphia: Fortress Press, 1971, pp. 65–118. German: "Erwägungen zu einer Theologie der Religionsgeschichte." In idem, *Grundfragen systematischer Theologie: Gesammelte Aufsätze*. Göttingen: Vandenhoeck & Ruprecht, 1967; 2d ed., 1971, pp. 252–95.

De Vries, Jan. *The Study of Religion: A Historical Approach*. New York: Harcourt, 1967.

Yinger, J. Milton. *The Scientific Study of Religion*. New York: Macmillan; London: Collier-Macmillan, 1970.

Glock, Charles Y., ed. *Religion in Sociological Perspective: Essays in the Empirical Study of Religion*. Belmont, Calif.: Wadsworth, 1973.

Oates, Wayne E. *The Psychology of Religion*. Waco: Word Books, 1973.

B. German

Wach, Joachim. *Religionswissenschaft: Prolegomena zu ihrer Wissenschaftstheoretischen Grundlegung*. Leipzig: Hinrichs, 1924.

Ratschow, C. H. "Die Religionen und das Christentum," *Neue Zeitschrift für Systematische Theologie* 9 (1967), 88–128.

Colpe, Carsten. "Die Funktion religionsgeschichtlicher Studien in der evangelischen Theologie," *Verkündigung und Forschung* 13 (1968), 1–12.

5. PHILOSOPHY

A.

"Verantworten des Glaubens in Begegnung mit dem Denken M. Heideggers: Thesen zum Verhältnis von Philosophie und Theologie" (1961), *WG* 2: 92–98.

"Theologie I. Begriffsgeschichtlich," in *Die Religion in Geschichte und Gegenwart*. 3d. ed. (Tübingen: J. C. B. Mohr [Paul Siebeck], 1957–62), vol. 6 (1962), 754–69.

"Theologie und Philosophie I. Problemstrukturen II. Historisch III. Dogmatisch," in *Die Religion in Geschichte und Gegenwart*. 3d ed. (Tübingen: J. C. B. Mohr [Paul Siebeck], 1957–62), vol. 6 (1962), 782–830.

Luther: An Introduction to His Thought. Translated by R. A. Wilson. Philadelphia: Fortress Press; London: Collins, 1970, pp. 76–92. German: *Luther: Einführung in sein Denken*. Tübingen: J. C. B. Mohr (Paul Siebeck), 1964; 2d ed., 1974, pp. 79–99.

B. ENGLISH

Frank, Erich. *Philosophical Understanding and Religious Truth*. Translated by Prof. & Mrs. Ludwig Edelstein. New York/London: Oxford, 1945; reissued, New York: Galaxy, 1966.

Hartshorne, Charles. *The Divine Relativity: A Social Conception of God*. New Haven: Yale University Press, 1948.

Hartshorne, Charles, and Reese, William L. eds. *Philosophers Speak of God*. Chicago: University of Chicago Press, 1953.

Heidegger, Martin. *What Is Philosophy?* Translated by William Kluback and Jean T. Wilde. New York: Twayne, 1958. German: *Was ist das—die Philosophie?* Pfüllingen: G. Neske, 1956.

The Hartshorne Festschrift: Process and Divinity: Philosophical Essays Presented to Charles Hartshorne. Edited by William L. Reese and Eugene Freeman. LaSalle: Open Court, 1964.

Piaget, Jean. *Insights and Illusions of Philosophy*. Translated by Wolfe Mays. London: Routledge & Kegan Paul, 1972. French: *Sagesse et illusions de la Philosophie*. Paris: Presses universitaires de France, 1965.

Pannenberg, Wolfhart. "Christian Theology and Philosophical Criticism" (1968). In *The Idea of God and Human Freedom*. Translated by R. A. Wilson. Philadelphia: Westminster Press, 1973, pp. 116–43. Br.: *Basic Questions in Theology Today*, vol. 3 [London: SCM Press, 1973], pp. 116–43. German: "Christliche Theologie und philosophische Kritik," in idem, *Gottesgedanke und menschliche Freiheit*. Göttingen: Vandenhoeck & Ruprecht, 1972, pp. 48–77.

Richmond, James. *Theology and Metaphysics*. London: SCM Press, 1970; New York: Schocken Books, 1971.

Gibson, A. Boyce. *Theism and Empiricism*. New York: Schocken Books; London: SCM Press, 1970.

B. GERMAN

Iwand, Hans Joachim. "Wie studiere ich Philosophie?" (1953). In idem, *Um den rechten Glauben: Gesammelte Aufsätze*. Edited by K. G. Steck, Theologische Bücherei 9. München: Chr. Kaiser, 1959, pp. 173–82.

Löwith, Karl. *Wissen, Glaube, Skepsis*. Kleine Vandenhoeck-Reihe, vol. 30. Göttingen: Vandenhoeck & Ruprecht, 1956.

Schulz, Walter. *Der Gott der neuzeitlichen Metaphysik*. Pfüllingen: G. Neske, 1957; 2d ed., 1959.

Gollwitzer, Helmut, and Weischedel, Wilhelm. *Denken und Glauben: Ein Streitgespräch*. Stuttgart: W. Kohlhammer, 1965.

Picht, Georg. *Der Gott der Philosophen und die Wissenschaft der Neuzeit*. Stuttgart: Klett, 1966.

Frey, Gerhard. *Philosophie und Wissenschaft: Eine Methodenlehre*. Urban-Taschenbücher, vol. 133. Stuttgart: W. Kohlhammer, 1970.

Heidegger, Martin. *Phänomenologie und Theologie*. Frankfurt am Main: Vittorio Klostermann, 1970.

Weischedel, Wilhelm. *Der Gott der Philosophen: Grundlegung einer philosophischen Theologie im Zeitalter des Nihilismus*. 2 vols. Darmstadt: Wissenschaftliche Buchgesellschaft, 1971–72.

"Das Studium der Philosophie in der Ausbildung der Theologen: Ein Brief der römischen Kongregation für das katholische Bildungswesen," *Herder-Korrespondenz* 26 (1972), 178–82.

Möller, J. "Der Glaube ruft nach dem Denken: Zur Rolle der Philosophie innerhalb des Theologiestudiums," *Herder Korrespondenz* 26 (1972), 239–43.

6. CHURCH HISTORY

A.

"Church History Is the History of the Exposition of Scripture" (1946), *WGT*, pp. 11–32. German: "Kirchengeschichte als Geschichte der Auslegung der Heiligen Schrift," *WGT*, pp. 9–27.

"The Problem of the Confessions" (1952), *WGT*, pp. 47–63. German: "Zur Geschichte des konfessionellen Problems," *WGT*, pp. 41–55.

"Confessional Study: Task and Method" (1952), *WGT*, pp. 32–46. German: "Über Aufgabe und Methode der Konfessionskunde," *WGT*, pp. 28–48.

The Problem of Historicity in the Church and Its Proclamation. Translated by Grover Foley. Philadelphia: Fortress Press, 1967. German: *Die Geschichtlichkeit der Kirche und ihrer Verkündigung als theologisches Problem.* Tübingen: J. C. B. Mohr (Paul Siebeck), 1954.

The Nature of Faith. Translated by Ronald Gregor Smith. Philadelphia: Fortress Press: London: Collins, 1961, pp. 19–30. German: *Das Wesen des christlichen Glaubens.* Tübingen: J. C. B. Mohr (Paul Siebeck), 1959, pp. 15–30.

"Verstehen und Verständigung in der Begegnung der Konfessionen" (1967), *WG* 3: 468–83.

"Luther und der Anbruch der Neuzeit" (1972), *WG* 3: 29–59.

B. ENGLISH

Baur, Ferdinand Christian. "The Epochs of Church Historiography." In *Ferdinand Christian Baur on the Writing of Church History.* Translated and edited by Peter C. Hodgson. New York: Oxford, 1968, pp. 41–257. German: *Die Epochen der kirchlichen Geschichtsschreibung.* Tübingen: Fens, 1852; new printing, Hildesheim: G. Olms, 1962.

Orr, James. *The Progress of Dogma.* London: Hodder & Stoughton, 1901; Grand Rapids, Mich.: Eerdmanns, 1952.

Thompson, James Westfall, and Holm, Bernard J. *A History of Historical Writing.* New York: Macmillan, 1942.

Collingwood, Robin George. *The Idea of History.* Oxford: Clarendon, 1946.

Niebuhr, Reinhold. *The Self and the Dramas of History.* New York: Scribner's, 1955.

Popper, Karl R. *The Poverty of Historicism.* Boston: Beacon Press; London: Routledge and K. Paul, 1957.

Jedin, Hubert. "General Introduction to Church History." In *Handbook of Church History,* vol. 1. Edited by Hubert Jedin and John Dolan. (New York/Freiburg: Herder & Herder; London: Burns & Oates, 1965), pp. 1–56. German: "Einleitung in die Kirchengeschichte." In *Handbuch der Kirchengeschichte,* vol. 1. Edited by H. Jedin. Freiburg: Herder & Herder, 1962, pp. 1–68.

Harvey, Van A. *The Historian and the Believer: The Morality of Historical Knowledge and Christian Faith.* New York: Macmillan, 1966; London: SCM Press, 1967.

Pelikan, Jaroslav. *Historical Theology: Continuity and Change in Christian Doctrine.* New York: Corpus; London: Hutchinson, 1971.

Ahlstrom, Sidney E. *A Religious History of the American People.* New Haven/ London: Yale University Press, 1972. Preface and pp. 1–13.

B. German

Overbeck, Franz. *Über die Anfänge der Kirchengeschichtsschreibung.* Basel, 1892.

Nigg, Walter. *Die Kirschengeschichtsschreibung: Grundzüge ihrer historischen Entwicklung.* München: C. H. Beck, 1934.

Rückert, Hans. "Personale Geschichtsbetrachtung: Einleitende Überlegungen zu einer Vorlesung über Kirchengeschichte der Neuzeit" (1948). In idem, *Vorträge und Aufsätze zur historischen Theologie.* Tübingen: J. C. B. Mohr (Paul Siebeck), 1972, pp. 1–11.

Karpp, H. "Kirchengeschichte als theologische Disziplin." In *Festschrift Rudolf Bultmann.* Stuttgart: W. Kohlhammer, 1949, pp. 149–67.

Wittram, Reinhard. *Das Interesse an der Geschichte.* Kleine Vandenhoeck-Reihe 59/60/61. Göttingen: Vandenhoeck & Ruprecht, 1958.

Benz, Ernst. *Kirchengeschichte in ökumenischer Sicht.* Leiden: E. J. Brill, 1961.

Wittram, Reinhard. *Zukunft in der Geschichte: Grenzfragen der Geschichtwissenschaft und Theologie.* Kleine Vandenhoeck-Reihe 235/236. Göttingen: Vandenhoeck & Ruprecht, 1966.

Meinhold, Peter. *Geschichte der kirchlichen Historiographie.* 2 vols. Orbis Academicus 3/5. Freiburg/München: Alber, 1967.

Wittram, Reinhard. *Anspruch und Fragwürdigkeit der Geschichte: Sechs Vorlesungen zur Methodik der Geschichtswissenschaft und zur Ortsbestimmung der Historie.* Kleine Vandenhoeck-Reihe 297/299. Göttingen: Vandenhoeck & Ruprecht, 1969.

Kottje, Raymund, ed. *Kirchengeschichte heute: Geschichtswissenschaft oder Theologie?* Trier: Paulinus, 1970.

7. NATURAL SCIENCES AND HUMANITIES

A.

"The World as History" (1960), *WF*, pp. 363–73. German: "Die Welt als Geschichte," *WG* 1: 381–92.

"Zeit und Wort" (1964), *WG* 2: 121–37.

"Das Problem des Natürlichen bei Luther" (1967), *LuStud* 1: 273–85.

"Überlegungen zur Theologie in der interdisziplinären Forschung" (1971), *WG* 3: 150–63.

"Zur Existenz Theologischer Fakultäten an staatlichen Universitäten" (1972), *WG* 3: 164–69.

Kritischer Rationalismus? Tübingen: J. C. B. Mohr (Paul Siebeck), 1973.

B. ENGLISH

Snow, Charles Percy. *The Two Cultures and the Scientific Revolutions.* New York/Cambridge: Cambridge, 1959.

Nagel, Ernest. *The Structure of Science: Problems in the Logic of Scientific Explanation.* New York: Harcourt, Brace and World; London: Routledge & K. Paul, 1961.

Danto, Arthur, and Morgenbesser, Sidney, eds. *Philosophy of Science* (New York: Meridian Books, 1960; Cleveland: World, 1962).

Prior, Moody Erasmus. *Science and the Humanities.* Evanston: Northwestern University Press, 1962.

Huxley, Aldous. *Literature and Science.* New York: Harper & Row; London: Chatto & Windus, 1963.

Rapport, Samuel B., and Wright, Helen, eds. *Science: Method and Meaning.* New York: Washington Square, 1964; New York: New York University, 1963.

Popper, Karl R. *Conjectures and Refutations.* New York: Basic Books, 1962; London: Routledge & K. Paul, 1963; 2d rev. ed., 1965.

Ramsey, Ian T. *Religion and Science: Conflict and Synthesis.* London: S.P.C.K., 1964.

Jones, William Thomas. *The Sciences and the Humanities: Conflict and Reconciliation.* Berkeley: University of California Press, 1965.

Crane, Ronald S. "The Idea of the Humanities" and "Shifting Definitions and Evaluations of the Humanities from the Renaissance to the Present." In *The Idea of the Humanities, and Other Essays Critical and Historical*, vol. 1. Chicago: University of Chicago Press, 1967, pp. 3–170.

Wartkofsky, Marx W. *Conceptual Foundations of Scientific Thought: An Introduction to the Philosophy of Science.* New York: Macmillan, 1968.

Kuhn, Thomas. *The Structure of Scientific Revolutions.* Chicago: University of Chicago Press, 1964; 2d rev. ed., 1970.

Gilkey, Langdon B. *Religion and the Scientific Future*. New York: Harper & Row, 1970.

Schilling, H. K. *The New Consciousness in Science and Religion*. Philadelphia: United Church Press; London: SCM, 1973.

Barbour, Ian. *Myths, Models and Paradigms*. New York: Harper & Row; London: SCM, 1974.

B. GERMAN

Kant, Immanuel. "Der Streit der Fakultäten" (1798). In idem, *Werke*, vol. 6. Edited by W. Weischedel. Wiesbaden: Insel, 1964, pp. 261–393.

Dilthey, Wilhelm. *Einleitung in die Geisteswissenschaften: Versuch einer Grundlegung für das Studium der Gesellschaft und der Geschichte* (1883). In idem, *Gesammelte Schriften*, vol. 1. 3d ed. Stuttgart: Teubner, 1963.

Rickert, Heinrich. *Die Grenzen der naturwissenschaftlichen Begriffsbildung* (1896–1902). Tübingen: J. C. B. Mohr, 1902; 5th ed., 1929.

Rothacker, Erich. *Logik und Systematik der Geisteswissenschaften*. München: R. Oldenbourg, 1926; new printing 1965 and 1970.

Anrich, Ernst. *Die Idee der deutschen Universität und die Reform der deutschen Universitäten*. Darmstadt: Wissenschaftliche Buchgesellschaft, 1960.

Blumenberg, Hans. *Die Legitimität der Neuzeit*. Frankfurt am Main: Suhrkamp, 1966; expanded and reworked new edition of the first and second parts under the title *Säkularisierung und Selbstbehauptung* (Suhrkamp Taschenbuch Wissenschaft 79). Frankfurt am Main: Suhrkamp, 1974.

Weidlich, W. "Fragen der Naturwissenschaft an den christlichen Glauben," *Zeitschrift für Theologie und Kirche* 64 (1967), 241–57.

Albert, Hans. *Traktat über kritische Vernunft*. Tübingen: J. C. B. Mohr (Paul Siebeck), 1968; 2d ed., 1969.

Müller, A. M. Klaus, and Pannenberg, Wolfhart, *Erwägungen zu einer Theologie der Natur* (Gütersloh: Gütersloh, 1970).

Laskowski, Wolfgang, ed. *Geisteswissenschaft und Naturwissenschaft: Ihre Bedeutung für den Menschen von heute* (Berlin: De Gruyter, 1970).

Von Weizsäcker, Carl Friedrich. *Die Einheit der Natur*. München: Hanser, 1971.

Weth, Rudolf; Gestrich, Christof; and Solte, Ernst-Lüder. *Theologie an staatlichen Universitäten?* Stuttgart: W. Kohlhammer, 1972.

Lord, Annan; Deveze, Michel; and Lübbe, Hermann. *Universität gestern und heute*. Salzburg/München: Pustet, 1973.

Oberman, Heiko A. *Contra vanam curiositatem: Ein Kapitel der Theologie zwischen Seelenwinkel und Weltall*, Theologische Studien, vol. 113. Zürich: Theologisches, 1974.

8. SOCIAL SCIENCES

A.

"Frei aus Glauben" (1968), *LuStud* 1: 308–29.
"Frömigkeit und Bildung" (1970), *WG* 3: 60–95.
Introduction to a Theological Theory of Language. Translated by R. A. Wilson.
Philadelphia: Fortress Press; London: Collins, 1973. German: *Einführung in theologische Sprachlehre.* Tübingen: J. C. B. Mohr (Paul Siebeck), 1971.
"Lebensangst und Glaubensanfechtung: Erwägungen zum Verhältnis von Psychotherapie und Theologie" (1973), *WG* 3: 362–87.
"Die Klage über das Erfahrungsdefizit in der Theologie als Frage nach ihrer Sache" (1974), *WG* 3: 3–28.

B. ENGLISH

Rogers, Carl R. *On Becoming a Person: A Therapeutic View of Psychotherapy.* Boston: Houghton Mifflin, 1961.
Oden, Thomas C. *Contemporary Theology and Psychotherapy.* Philadelphia: Westminster Press, 1967.
Lapsley, James N. *Salvation and Health: The Interlocking Processes of Life.* Philadelphia: Westminster Press, 1972.
Becker, Ernst. *The Denial of Death.* New York: Macmillan; London: Collier-Macmillan, 1973.
Menninger, Karl. *Whatever Became of Sin?* (New York: Hawthorn, 1973).
Frankl, Victor E. *The Unconscious God: Psychotherapy and Theology.* New York: Simon & Schuster, 1975. German: *Der unbewusste Gott: Psychotherapie und Religion.* Darmstadt: Wissenschaftliche Buchgesellschaft, 1966; München: Kösel, 1974.

B. GERMAN

Gehlen, Arnold. *Der Mensch: Seine Natur und seine Stellung in der Welt.* Berlin: Junker and Dünnhaupt, 1940; 8th ed., Frankfurt am Main; Athenäum, 1966.
Schoeck, Helmut. *Soziologie: Geschichte ihrer Probleme.* Freiburg: K. Alber, 1952.
Bitter, Wilhelm, ed. *Angst und Schuld in theologischer und psychotherapeutischer Sicht.* Stuttgart: Gemeinschaft Arzt und Seelsorger; im Kommissions-Verlag der Buchhandlung F. Stahl, 1953; 5th ed., 1972.
Sborowitz, Arië, ed., with Michel, Ernst. *Der leidende Mensch: Personale Psychotherapie in anthropologischer Sicht.* Düsseldorf: E. Diederichs, 1960.
Bally, Gustav. *Einführung in die Psychoanalyse Sigmund Freuds.* Rowohlts deutsche Enzyklopädie 131/132. Reinbek bei Hamburg: Rowohlt, 1961.

Condrau, Gion. *Angst und Schuld als Grundprobleme der Psychotherapie*. Bern: Huber, 1962.

Habermas, Jürgen. *Zur Logik der Sozialwissenschaften*. Edition Suhrkamp 481. Frankfurt am Main: Suhrkamp, 1970.

Hollweg, Arnd. *Theologie und Empirie: Ein Beitrag zum Gespräch zwischen Theologie und Sozialwissenschaften in den USA und in Deutschland*. Stuttgart: Evangelische Verlagswerk, 1971.

Piaget, Jean. *Epistémologie des sciences de l'homme*. Paris: Gallimard, 1972.

9. PRACTICAL THEOLOGY

A.

"Das Grund-Geschehen von Kirche" (1962), *WG* 3: 463–67.
"The Protestant View of the Sacraments" (1963), *WGT*, pp. 225–35. German: "Erwägungen zum evangelischen Sakramentsverständnis," *WGT*, pp. 217–26.
"Der Theologe und sein Amt in der Kirche" (1969), *WG* 3: 522–32.
"Die Notwendigkeit des christlichen Gottesdienstes" (1970), *WG* 3: 533–53.
"Das Gebet" (1973), *WG* 3: 405–27.
"Fundamentaltheologische Erwägungen zur Predigt" (1974), *WG* 3: 554–73.

B. ENGLISH

Hiltner, Seward. *Pastoral Counseling.* Nashville: Abingdon Press, 1949.
Niebuhr, H. Richard, and Williams, Daniel Day, eds. *The Ministry in Historical Perspectives.* New York: Harper, 1956.
Wingren, Gustav. *The Living Word: A Theological Study of Preaching and the Church.* Translated by Victor G. Pogue. Philadelphia: Fortress Press; London: SCM Press, 1960.
Nouwen, Henri J. *Creative Ministry.* Garden City, N.Y.: Doubleday, 1971.
Küng, Hans. *Why Priests?* Translated by Robert C. Collins. Garden City, N.Y.: Doubleday, 1972. German: *Wozu Priester? Eine Hilfe.* Zürich: Einsiedln; Köln: Benzinger, 1971.
Glasse, J. P., *Putting It Together in the Parish.* Nashville: Abingdon Press, 1972.
Nouwen, Henri J. *The Wounded Healer.* Garden City, N.Y.: Doubleday, 1972.
Schaller, Lyle E. *The Pastor and the People.* Nashville: Abingdon Press, 1972.
Cooke, Bernard J. *Ministry to Word and Sacraments.* Philadelphia: Fortress Press, 1976.
Cobb, John B., Jr. *Theology and Pastoral Care.* Creative Pastoral Care and Counseling Series. Philadelphia: Fortress Press, 1977.

B. GERMAN

Kant, Immanuel. "Über den Gemeinspruch: Das mag in der Theorie richtig sein, taugt aber nicht für die Praxis" (1793). In idem, *Werke*, ed. W. Weischedel, vol. 6. Wiesbaden: Insel, 1964, pp. 125–72.
Diem, Hermann. *Theologie als kirchliche Wissenschaft,* vol. 3: *Die Kirche und ihre Praxis.* München: Chr. Kaiser, 1963.
Metzger, M. "Praktische Theologie—Zugang zu ihrem Studium," *Theologia Practica* 1 (1966), 111–19.
Jetter, Werner. "Die Praktische Theologie," *Zeitschrift für Theologie und Kirche* 64 (1967), 451–73.

Krause, Gerhard. "Probleme der Praktischen Theologie im Rahmen der Studienreform," *Zeitschrift für Theologie und Kirche* 64 (1967): 474–95.

Rüssler, Dietrich. "Prolegomena zur Praktischen Theologie: Das Vermächtnis Christian Palmers," *Zeitschrift für Theologie und Kirche* 64 (1967): 357–71.

Jetter, Werner. *Was wird aus der Kirche? Beobachtungen, Fragen, Vorschläge.* Stuttgart/Berlin: Kreuz, 1968.

Jüngel, Eberhard; Rahner, Karl; and Seitz, Manfred. *Die Praktische Theologie zwischen Wissenchaft und Praxis.* München: Chr. Kaiser, 1967.

Dahm, Karl Wilhelm. *Beruf: Pfarer: Empirische Aspekte zur Funktion von Kirche und Religion in unserer Gesellschaft.* München: Claudius, 1971; 2d ed., 1972.

Krause, Gerhard, ed. *Praktische Theologie: Texte zum Werden und Selbstverständnis der praktischen Disziplin der evangelischen Theologie.* Wege der Forschung, vol. 264. Darmstadt: Wissenschaftliche Buchgesellschaft, 1972.

Picht, G. "Die Dialektik von Theorie und Praxis und der Glaube," *Zeitschrift für Theologie und Kirche* 70 (1973): 101–20.

Steck, Wolfgang. *Der Pfarrer zwischen Beruf und Wissenschaft: Plädoyer für eine Erneuerung der Pastoraltheologie.* Theologische Existenz heute, vol. 183, München: Chr. Kaiser, 1974.

10. DOGMATICS

A.

"The Significance of Doctrinal Differences for the Division of the Church" (1956), *WF*, pp. 162–90. German: "Die kirchentrennende Bedeutung von Lehrdifferenzen," *WG* 1: 161–91.

The Nature of Faith. Translated by Ronald Gregor Smith. Philadelphia: Fortress Press; London: Collins, 1961. German: *Das Wesen des christlichen Glaubens.* Tübingen: J. C. B. Mohr (Paul Siebeck), 1959.

"Worldly Talk of God" (1959), *WF*, pp. 354–62. German: "Weltliches Reden von Gott," *WG* 1: 372–80.

"Rudimentary Reflections on Speaking Responsibly of God" (1959), *WF*, pp. 333–53. German: "Elementare Besinnung auf verantwortliches Reden von Gott" *WG* 1: 349–71.

"The Word of God and Church Doctrine" (1961), *WGT*, pp. 160–80. German: "Wort Gottes und kirchliche Lehre," *WGT*, pp. 155–74.

Theology and Proclamation: A Conversation with Rudolf Bultmann. Translated by John Riches. Philadelphia: Fortress Press; London: Collins, 1966. German: *Theologie und Verkündigung: Ein Gespräch mit Rudolf Bultmann. Hermeneutische Untersuchungen zur Theologie,* 1. Tübingen: J. C. B. Mohr (Paul Siebeck), 1962; 2d ed., 1963.

"Die Botschaft von Gott an das Zeitalter des Atheismus" (1963), *WG* 2: 372–95.

"Der hermeneutische Ort der Gotteslehre bei Petrus Lombardus und Thomas von Aquin" (1964), *WG* 2: 209–56.

"Erwägungen zur Eschatologie" (1964), *WG* 3: 428–47.

"Existenz zwischen Gott und Gott: Ein Beitrag zur Frage nach der Existenz Gottes" (1965), *WG* 2: 257–86.

"Cognito Dei et hominus" (1966), *LuStud* 1: 221–72.

God and Word. Translated by James Leitch. Philadelphia: Fortress Press, 1967. German: "Gott und Wort" (1966), *WG* 2: 396–432.

" 'Was heisst ein Gott haben oder was ist Gott? ' Bemerkungen zu Luthers Ausletung des ersten Gebots im Grossen Katechismus" (1966/67), *WG* 2: 287–304.

"Zum Verständnis von R. Bultmanns Aufsatz: 'Welchen Sinn hat es, von Gott zu reden?' " (1966/67), *WG* 2: 343–71.

"Das Verständnis von Heil in säkularisierter Zeit" (1967), *WG* 3: 349–61.

"Gewissheit und Zweifel: Die Situation des Glaubens im Zeitalter nach Luther und Descartes" (1967), *WG* 2: 138–83.

"Thesen zur Frage der Auferstehung von den Toten" (1967), *WG* 3: 448–54.

"Schleiermachers Lehre von den göttlichen Eigenschaften" (1968), *WG* 2: 305–42.

"Was heisst: Ich glaube an Jesus Christus?" (1968), *WG* 3: 270–308.

"Der Aussagezusammenhang des Glaubens an Jesus Christus" (1969), *WG* 3: 246–69.

"Schlechhinniges Abhängigkeitsgefühl als Gottesbewusstsein" (1972), *WG* 3: 116–36.
"Luthers Ortsbestimmung der Lehre von heiligen Geist" (1974), *WG* 3: 316–48.

B. English

Diem, Hermann. *Dogmatics.* Translated by Harold Knight. Philadelphia: Westminster Press; Edinburgh: Oliver & Boyd, 1959. German: *Theologie als kirchliche Wissenschaft*, vol. 2: *Dogmatik: Der Weg zwischen Historismus und Existentialismus.* München: Chr. Kaiser, 1955; 4th ed., 1964.

Pannenberg, Wolfhart. "What Is a Dogmatic Statement?" (1962). In idem, *Basic Questions in Theology Today.* Translated by George H. Kehm. Philadelphia: Fortress Press; London: SCM Press, 1970. Vol. 1, pp. 182–211. German: "Was ist eine dogmatische Aussage?" In idem, *Grundfragen systematischer Theologie: Gesammelte Aufsätze.* Göttingen: Vandenhoeck & Ruprecht, 1967; 2d ed., 1971, pp. 159–200.

Wiles, Maurice F. *The Making of Christian Doctrine: A Study of the Principles of Early Doctrinal Development.* London: Cambridge, 1967.

Schillebeeckx, Edward C. F. A., ed. *Dogma and Pluralism*, Concilium, vol. 51. New York: Herder & Herder, 1970.

Dulles, Avery R. *The Survival of Dogma.* Garden City, N.Y.: Doubleday, 1971; New York: Image, 1973.

O'Collins, Gerald. *Has Dogma a Future?* London: Darton, 1975.

Hick, John, ed. *The Myth of God Incarnate.* London: SCM Press, 1977.

B. German

Troeltsch, Ernst. "Über historische und dogmatische Methode in der Theologie" (1898). In idem, *Gesammelte Schriften*, vol. 2. End ed. Tübingen: J. C. B. Mohr, 1922; new printing. Aalen: Scientia, 1962, pp. 729–53.

Kaftan, Julius. *Zur Dogmatik.* Tübingen: J. C. B. Mohr, 1904.

Ritschl, O. "Das Wort dogmaticus in der Geschichte des Sprachgebrauchs bis zum Aufkommen des Ausdrucks theologia dogmatica," in *Festgabe für d. dr. Julius Kaftan.* Tübingen: J. C. B. Mohr, 1920, pp. 260–72.

Rothacker, Erich. *Die dogmatische Denkform in den Geisteswissenschaften und das Problem des Historismus.* Abhandlungen der Bayerischen Akademie der Wissenschaften, vol. 6. Mainz, 1954.

Fritzsche, Hans-Georg. *Die Strukturtypen der Theologie: Eine kritische Einführung.* Göttingen: Vandenhoeck & Ruprecht, 1961.

Elze, Martin. "Der Begriff des Dogmas in der Alten Kirche," *Zeitschrift für Theologie und Kirche* 61 (1964): 421–38.

Grass, Hans. "Historisch-kritische Forschung und Dogmatik." In idem, *Theologie und Kritik: Gesammelte Aufsätze und Vorträge.* Göttingen: Vandenhoeck & Ruprecht, 1969, pp. 9–27.

Lehmann, H. "Die dogmatische Denkform als hermeneutisches Problem," *Evangelische Theologie* 30 (1970): 469–87.

Sauter, Gerhard. *Vor einem neuen Methodenstreit in der Theologie?* Theologische Existenz heute, vol. 164. München: Chr. Kaiser, 1970.

11. ETHICS

A.

"Die Evidenz des Ethischen und die Theologie" (1960), *WG* 2: 1–41.
"Die Krise des Ethischen und die Theologie" (1962), *WG* 2: 42–55.
"Die Beunruhigung der Theologie durch die Frage nach den Früchten des Geistes, (1969), *WG* 3: 388–404.
"Leitsätze zur Zweireichelehre" (1972), *WG* 3: 574–92.
"Kirche und Politik" (1973), *WG* 3: 593–610.
Die zehn Gebote in Predigten ausgelegt. Tübingen: J. C. B. Mohr (Paul Siebeck), 1973.
"Ein Briefwechsel zwischen Wolfhart Pannenberg und Gerhard Ebeling," *Zeitschrift für Theologie und Kirche* 70 (1973): 448–73.
"Theologie zwischen reformatorischem Sündenverständnis und heutiger Einstellung zum Bösen" (1973), *WG* 3: 173–204.
"Das Problem des Bösen als Prüfstein der Anthropologie" (1973), WG 3: 205–24.
"Kriterien kirchlicher Stellungnahme zu politischen Problemen" (1974), *WG* 3: 611–34.

B. ENGLISH

Niebuhr, Reinhold. *Moral Man and Immoral Society: A Study in Ethics and Politics.* New York: Scribner's, 1932; 1960.
Forell, George. *Faith Active in Love: An Investigation of the Principles Underlying Luther's Social Ethics.* Minneapolis: Augsburg, 1954.
Niebuhr, H. Richard. *Christ and Culture.* New York: Harper, 1956.
―――. *The Responsible Self: An Essay on Christian Moral Philosophy.* New York: Harper, 1963.
Fletcher, Joseph. *Situation Ethics: The New Morality.* London: SCM Press, 1966.
Forell, George, ed. *Christian Social Teachings: A Reader in Christian Social Ethics from the Bible to the Present.* Garden City, N.Y.: Anchor, 1966.
Ransey, Ian T., ed. *Christian Ethics and Contemporary Philosophy.* New York: Macmillan; London: SCM Press, 1966.
Furnish, Victor. *Theology and Ethics in Paul.* Nashville: Abingdon Press, 1968.
Ramsey, Paul, and Outka, Gene H., eds. *Norm and Context of Christian Ethics.* New York: Scribner's; London: SCM Press, 1968.
Gustafson, James M. *Theology and Christian Ethics.* Philadelphia: Pilgrim, 1974.
―――. *Can Ethics Be Christian?* Chicago: University of Chicago Press, 1975.

B. GERMAN

Pannenberg, Wolfhart. "Die Krise des Ethischen und die Theologie," *Theologische Literaturzeitung* 87 (1962): 7–16.

Jüngel, Eberhard. "Erwägungen zur Grundlegung evangelischer Ethik im Anschluss an die Theologie des Paulus," *Zeitschrift für Theologie und Kirche* 63 (1966): 379–90.

Gadamer, Hans-Georg. "Über die Möglichkeit einer philosophischen Ethik," in idem, *Kleine Schriften*, vol. 1: *Philosophie, Hermeneutik*. Tübingen: J. C. B. Mohr (Paul Siebeck), 1967, pp. 179–91.

Honecker, Martin. *Konzept einer sozialethischen Theorie: Grundfragen evangelischer Sozialethik*. Tübingen: J. C. B. Mohr (Paul Siebeck), 1971.

Patzig, Günther. *Ethik ohne Metaphysik*. Kleine Vandenhoeck-Reihe 326 S. Göttingen: Vandenhoeck & Ruprecht, 1971.

Rich, A. "Was macht das Handeln der Kirche zum christlichen Handeln?" in H. Schulze and H. Schwarz, eds., *Christsein in einer pluralistischen Gesellschaft*. Hamburg: Wittig, 1971. Pp. 276–88.

Ringeling, H. "Ethik als Integrationswissenschaft," *Gesellschaft und Entwicklung* 3 (1974): 84–94.

12. FUNDAMENTAL THEOLOGY

"The Significance of the Historical Critical Method for Church and Theology in Protestantism" (1950), *WF*, pp. 17–61. German: "Die Bedeutung der historischkritischen Methode für die protestantische Theologie und Kirche," *WG* 1: 1–49.

"Theology and Reality" (1956), *WF*, pp. 191–200. German: "Theologie und Wirklichkeit," *WG* 1: 192–202.

"Hermeneutik," in *Die Religion in Geschichte und Gegenwart*. 3d ed. Tübingen: J. C. B. Mohr (Paul Siebeck), vol. 3 (1959), pp. 242–62.

"Word of God and Hermeneutics" (1959), *WF*, pp. 305–32. German: "Wort Gottes und Hermeneutik," *WG* 1: 319–48.

"Faith and Unbelief in Conflict about Reality" (1960), *WF*, pp. 374–85. German: "Glaube und Unglaube im Streit um die Wirklichkeit," *WG* 1: 393–406.

"The Necessity of the Doctrine of the Two Kingdoms" (1960), *WF*, pp. 386–406. German: "Die Notwendigkeit der Lehre von den zwei Reichen," *WG* 1: 407–28.

"Theological Reflections on Conscience" (1960), *WF*, pp. 407–23. German "Theologische Erwägungen über das Gewissen," *WG* 1: 429–46.

"Hermeneutische Theologie?" (1965), *WG* 2: 99–120.

"Erwägungen zu einer evangelischen Fundamentaltheologie," *Zeitschrift für Theologie und Kirche* 67 (1970): 479–524.

"Leitsätze zur Frage der Wissenschaftlichkeit der Theologie" (1971), *WG* 3: 137–49.

"Beobachtungen zu Schleiermachers Wirklichkeitsverständnis" (1973), *WG* 3: 96–115.

B. ENGLISH

Chenu, Marie Dominique. *Is Theology a Science?* Translated by A. H. N. Green-Armytage. New York: Hawthorn; London: Burns and Oates, 1959. French: *La théologie est-elle une science?* Paris: Librairie A. Fayard, 1957.

Gadamer, Hans-Georg. *Truth and Method.* Translated by Garrett Barden and John Cumming. New York: Seabury Press; London: Sheed & Ward, 1975. German: *Wahrheit und Methode.* Tübingen: J. C. B. Mohr (Paul Siebeck), 1960; 3d ed., 1972.

Ferré, Frederick. *Language, Logic and God.* New York: Harper; London: Eyre & Spottiswood, 1961.

Nygren, Anders. *Meaning and Method: Prolegomena to a Scientific Philosophy of Religion and a Scientific Theology.* Translated by Philip S. Watson. Philadelphia: Fortress Press, 1962.

Van Buren, Paul. *The Secular Meaning of the Gospel.* New York: Macmillan; London: SCM Press, 1963.

Ramsey, Ian T. *Models and Mystery.* New York/London: Oxford, 1964.

Metz, Johannes Baptist, ed. *The Development of Fundamental Theology.* Concilium, vol. 46. New York: Paulist Press, 1969.

Gilkey, Langdon B. *Naming the Whirlwind: The Renewal of God Language.* Indianapolis: Bobbs-Merrill, 1969.

Lonergan, Bernard J. F. *Method in Theology.* New York: Herder & Herder, 1972.

Farley, Edward. *Ecclesial Man: A Social Phenomenology of Faith and Reality.* Philadelphia: Fortress Press, 1972.

Hick, John. *God and the Universe of Faiths.* London: Macmillan, 1973; London: Collins, 1977.

B. German

Fuchs, Ernst. *Was ist Theologie?* Sammlung gemeinverständlicher Vorträge und Schriften auf dem Gebiet der Theologie und Religionsgeschichte, 203/204. Tübingen: J. C. B. Mohr (Paul Siebeck), 1953.

Fuchs, Ernst. "Über die Aufgabe einer christlichen Theologie," *Zeitschrift für Theologie und Kirche* 58 (1961): 245–267.

Jüngel, Eberhard. *Die Freiheit der Theologie.* Theologische Studien, vol. 88, Zürich: EVZ-Verlag, 1967.

Diemer, Alwin, ed. *Der Wissenschaftsbegriff: Historische und systematische Untersuchungen.* Studien zur Wissenschaftstheorie, vol. 4. Meisenheim a. Glan: Hain, 1970.

Sauter, Gerhard, ed. *Theologie als Wissenschaft: Aufsätze und Thesen. Theologische Bücherei,* vol. 43. München: Chr. Kaiser, 1971.

Metz, Johannes Baptist, and Rendtorff, Trutz, eds. *Die Theologie in der interdisziplinären Forschung.* Interdisziplinäre Studien, vol. 2. Düsseldorf: Bertelsmann, 1971.

Rendtorff, Trutz. *Theorie des Christentums: Historisch-theologische Studien zu seiner neuzeitlichen Verfassung.* Gütersloh: Gütersloh, 1972.

Sauter, Gerhard, et al. *Wissenschaftstheoretische Kritik der Theologie: Die Theologie und die neuere wissenschaftstheoretische Diskussion: Materialien, Analysen, Entwürfe.* München: Chr. Kaiser, 1973.

Pannenberg, Wolfhart, et al. *Grundfragen der Theologie—Ein Diskurs.* Urban Taschenbücher 603. Stuttgart/Berlin/Köln/Mainz: Kohlhammer, 1974.